Take Your Cookies
When They're Passed

by Jean Galt Coblentz and
Kathleen Coblentz Miana

Jean Coblentz Cap and Gown Scholarship Fund

Gifts to the Jean Coblentz Cap and Gown Scholarship Fund may be made online or by check made payable to Stanford University and mailed to Development Services, P.O. Box 20466, Stanford, CA. 94309-0466 Please add a note for both checks and online donations regarding your desire to direct your gift to The Jean Coblentz Cap and Gown Scholarship Fund.

Take Your Cookies When They're Passed
©2020 Jean Galt Coblentz and Kathleen Coblentz Miana
The Creating Calm Network Publishing Group
Kimberly Burnham, Publisher
Michael S. Wright, Photo Editor
ISBN: 9798656474825

Take Your Cookies When They're Passed

Why Take Your Cookies When They're Passed? 7

The Cookie Legacy 9

    Meeting Jean 11

Biography of Mabel Moore Galt 15

    Mabel's Birth to Leaving Home 20

    College 21

    Our Honeymoon 25

    Porto Rico 27

    The Trip to China 28

    Life in Yunnan 38

    Leper Colony 46

    The Tai People 48

    Farewell Yunnan 63

Recognizing Cookies In Jean's Life 67

Ancestry: A Brief History 70

China 79

    Leaving China on Furlough, 1928 94

    Cornelia's Birth 111

One Journey's End 131

This Clan is Your Clan 134

Life Continues After China 142

    Visiting Grandma Moore for a Year 142

    Manteca 150

Beginning at Stanford.. *157*

Stanford Univeristy Presidents............................ 163

Job Opportunity: The Cookie Casa Ventura............... 165

Fond Memories of Jean from Former Classmates..... 169

Cap and Gown Senior Year 171

Meeting Harry *177*

The Ring 180

Marriage and Cookies 186

Jean's Mother Post Father................................ 199

Each Family Member Unique *207*

Kathleen.. 208

Janis (1951-2010).. 213

Marty... 224

Scott.. 238

Harry 241

Family Celebrations.. *253*

Married Life *261*

Christmas Cards... 263

For Jean G. Coblentz at 88 275

50th Wedding Anniversary Jun 12, 1998............. 280

Work and Volunteer Experience *284*

Avenidas... 287

Volunteer Work for Stanford University............... 289

Paid Employment *299*

Overview of Professional Experience 304

Dick Bennett and How I Got to Stanford............... 310

Farewell Party.. 325

A Fundraising Story 326

Jean's Tenure on the Parents' Advisory Board 331

Philosophy 335

Thoughts on Growing Older 337

Getting Older 342

Regrets vs. *Cookies* 347

Greatest Contribution to Volunteer Work 348

Notes from Jean's Allied Arts Friends 349

Birthday Celebrations 355

Birthday Wishes 356

Friends 363

Accepting Aging 370

A Last Tribute 372

Appendix 398

Appendix 1: A Few Original Notes from Jean 399

Appendix 2: Jean's Notes from 2000 403

Appendix 3: Baby Book 407

Appendix 4: Jean's Baby Book 408

Appendix 5: Jean's Birth in China 423

Appendix 6: Book Clippings About Curtis Galt 425

Reviews 429

Jean Galt Coblentz
December 27, 1925 – December 5, 2017

Why Take Your *Cookies* When They're Passed?

At age ninety, Jean started writing a book entitled, <u>Take Your Cookies When They Are Passed</u>. Cookies, or opportunities, come unexpectedly, not necessarily when you are looking for, or yearning for them. She encourages us all to "keep our minds open and prepare ourselves for taking advantage of an opportunity that helps our focus to keep on track with our goals. Study your surroundings and you will create positive change that will help you attain current and long-term plans for the things that you feel are important for your own talents and those of others."

The same is possible for anyone reading her words and seeing their potential. As you read this story from the wisdom of Jean herself, we welcome you into the Coblentz family where each unique spirit is encouraged to follow their dreams, look for cookies along the way, and never forget how much they are loved.

Her dream for writing this book stems from her desire to inspire future generations to see their worth, give to others and take as many cookies as possible.

Jean started writing this book several years ago while taking a memoir writing class at Avenidas in Palo Alto, California. She has known for many years; it would be an undertaking to write her memoir once she retired.

It is the story of Jean's life as well as an inspiring message about seizing opportunities to better yourself. Jean exemplifies the importance of giving back to community.

She states that "life is more than a college degree. When something sounds interesting, follow that curious spirit. Just put up your hand! Be your best self and always live by the Golden Rule. You never know who is watching. I have never in my life applied for any job and have had a lifetime of meaningful work to celebrate."

"Here I tell my story of the cookies I have taken, choices I have made that became something special, out of the ordinary, taking me places I'd never been before. Almost as though, any one cookie given and taken way back then has had a journey, weaving itself into almost all that has made a difference in my life."

When asked what advice she would give herself at age 20, Jean shared her wisdom: "Take time to analyze yourself. What will fulfill you? Are you the kind of person who needs a four-year degree and then another four years of study before you feel that you have something especially important to give? By your actions, create for your children a portrait of giving back, so the treasures, education, and contact given to you, can be refreshed."

—Susan Knight, Personal Historian.

"Take your Cookies When They're Passed: This phrase was passed around a lot, especially during my employment years at Stanford (1977-2000)."

—A Favorite Saying.

The Cookie Legacy

As a tribute to Jean, submissions from friends and people across her lifetime, have been collected and recorded to demonstrate that her legacy lives on in the lives of all those she inspired. As she seized the day and took cookies as they were passed, Jean also distributed an immeasurable number of cookies that continue to impact those who were fortunate to know her. She may never know just how sweet her recipe for life truly was. She was our "Queen Jean."

While processing all the incredible tributes for this book, I was blown away by the expansive reach that her cookies had. She said Yes! to cookies throughout her lifetime, using the experience and wisdom she gained to pass along to others. There are now three generations of recipients of that wisdom who are out in the world living her legacy. Just as life events, jobs, and opportunities serve as cookies to take, so do chance meetings with people.

Jean's "Seasons Greetings" rolodex rivals that of many Manhattan socialites, and that is not because of her philanthropy or stunning wardrobe. Her extensive list of friends is because she looks people in the eye, sees who they are, and extends her hand and heart to make a connection. The process of creating this book, for those of us involved, has proven time and time again what an impact Jean has had on the lives of countless people.

As I read the beautiful submissions, for which we are so grateful, I am even more in awe of her. Respecting Jean's wishes, tributes for Jean from friends and family members are interspersed in each section or at the end of the section for more depth and appreciation of Jean's spirit.

This book is roughly organized into eight sections. What follows is Mabel Galt's biography. Curtis Galt, who was a medical missionary in China and Jean's father wrote a biography of his wife and family's life. Jean, who was born in China writes the next section about life in China, lessons learned, and her subsequent return to the United States.

The third section is entitled, This Clan, about Jean's larger family and events where they gathered to share love and comradery. This is followed by Jean's life after her family returned from China. Section five is all about family and meeting her husband, "Handsome Harry."

Next Jean writes about her life's work and volunteer experiences including many years of service at Stanford University followed by a Wit and Wisdom section. The book concludes with a final tribute to Jean from her many, many friends and family members.

—Kelly Crittenden, Granddaughter

**I JUST DID IT
WISHED YOU
HAPPY HOLIDAYS
CHEERS. JEAN**

Meeting Jean

Jean has a twinkle in her eye when she smiles and a laugh that gives a glimpse of who she is and why she took up all those cookies along the way. She once said of her father, Curtis Martin Galt, "If he ever had a faraway look in his eyes, there was always a twinkle." I say that the apple didn't fall far from the tree. Her quiet and wry sense of humor often catches me off guard – until I see those smiling eyes.

She is very coy and unassuming about her many volunteer and work activities. She never wants anyone to think she became involved because she is better than anybody else, just perhaps more curious, and able to jump right in.

Jean and I talked about the trust factor that needed to be in existence throughout an oral history interview process. I respected and honored that trust.

Jean's history is an amazing story of how a person's life became shaped by taking opportunities (cookies) as they were presented to her. The opportunities were usually not sought after by her. It was more like they came along, and she just naturally accepted them as they were passed to her. Little did she know how one might lead to the next.

Most of us know that we must go after what we want in life. For Jean, it was not that everything came easy for her, but rather that she had the insight to recognize and the determination to seize an opportunity. That is the point! She never gave up! Her burning desire from an early age was to be like her parents. They exemplified living life by seizing those cookies that came along. She fulfilled that desire – and aren't we glad she did?

Jean attributes much of her ability to be successful, to taking those cookies, from the examples set by her parents that began in 1923, two years before Jean's birth, when they became medical missionaries in China. There seemed to be a mantra of "Just Do It." Handed down through generations, this mantra is still being echoed today in the Galt-Coblentz family.

Jean and her daughter Kathy turned over to me various documents, along with Jean's handwritten notes regarding memoir writing. This material included articles on the art of writing a life story and many pages in her beautiful script listing the topics she might someday write about. All this proved to me, that for a very long time, Jean had been thinking about telling her life story. I thank both her and Kath for the opportunity to collaborate.

In the appendix are some of Jean's notes about what she considered central to the telling of her life story. Her handwriting is not how many of you remember it, because by 2015, at almost 90 years of age, her eyesight had worsened, and she was declared "legally blind" by her ophthalmologist. Her determination, nevertheless, guided her hand to map out the path her story should tell, and we respectfully have adhered to her storyline.

It has been a great honor to meet, work with and get to know Jean Galt Coblentz. This very grand lady and her daughter passed me a cookie, and I am very glad, I took it! Thank you, Jean, Kath, Marty, Scott, Milena, and Kelly, for the honor and opportunity to work with you.

—Susan Knight, Personal Historian
April 18, 2016

What Makes Me Laugh

"Almost anything. I love it when people laugh with me and at me. I always find the fun in life and happenings. Mostly it is a game of thoughts and words, and I have a head that makes fun of a lot of things. Some things I think are just ludicrous. My children make me both laugh and cry, mostly laugh a lot now.

'Did you ever wonder if the reason you stood upright to walk was so the coins wouldn't fall out of your pockets?'

I made you laugh, didn't I? To think I just made that up!"

—Jean Galt Coblentz

Grandma Galt's Biography

Jean decided to write her memoir as a continuation of the biography of her mother, Mabel Florence Moore Galt, which was written by her father, Curtis Martin Galt, MD in 1945 as a loving tribute to his wife for their 25th wedding anniversary. Jean talks about this event in her story and was adamant about having her mother's biography precede hers in this book. Jean shared Mabel's biography with many, many friends and they encouraged her to continue forward with her own story where her mother's biography ends. So, respecting Jean's wishes, please also enjoy the story of her parents and family and begin to get a glimpse of how Jean's exceptional character was shaped during her early childhood years in China.

—Kathy Coblentz Miana

BIOGRAPHY OF
MABEL MOORE GALT

by:

Her most ardent admirer,

C.M.G.

Mabel and Curtis Galt

Forward to The Original Text

In 1945 my father, Curtis M. Galt, M.D., returned alone to China for UNRRA (the United Nations Relief and Rehabilitation Administration) and during the voyage across the ocean wrote this biography of mother, Mabel Moore Galt. He sent the document to me at Stanford for typing, in sections as he completed them, and on June 4, 1946, their 25th wedding anniversary, we four children presented it to mother. To have been a part of this loving tribute was a thrilling honor and privilege.

Jean's Additions

My father, Curtis M. Galt, MD, returned to China without the family to reestablish hospitals for UNRRA, the United Nations Relief and Rehabilitation Administration. Daddy, as I affectionately called him, had not been able to go into any of the armed services during the war, which bothered him. He felt he had not done enough for his country. Since he was already familiar with the local language and had medical expertise, returning to China was his opportunity to continue something really worthwhile – to help rebuild the local infrastructure after the war was over.

He would be away for three years and realized he would miss his 25th wedding anniversary. Hence, in his hotel room in New York, the night before his voyage, he made up his mind about what he was going to do. He would pay tribute to his wife of 25 years and tell their story, encapsulated from his perspective, including the China memories and experiences of their thirteen years in China together. He sent me a chapter at a time in his own handwriting. He wrote to me, "You know, it is going to be our 25th wedding anniversary and I can't be there because I am in China."

As I received his handwritten chapters, I typed them on my Royal Typewriter. I still have the original manuscript. This biography was his gift and is included in its entirety with my story.

On June 4, 1946, their 25th wedding anniversary, I drove from Stanford to pick up my brother Alan in Livermore where he was stationed in the Navy. We met up with our two younger sisters and surprised Mother at our home in Manteca.

We had saved our money and bought them a pair of silver candlesticks to give her, along with the biography from Daddy. Her response was typical of mother. She had invited the doctor who took over Daddy's medical practice while he was away and his wife to lunch that day as a way of introducing them to the town. Hulling strawberries at the sink when we walked in, she asked what we were doing there. We four said "Happy Anniversary" and gave her the presents. She said, "How nice, thank you," and went right on hulling strawberries. I think that was the secret of her success, BALANCE IN ALL THINGS and never complaining. Her reaction was cool, calm, and collected – so like my mother. If that had happened to me, there would have been at least tears and possibly some hysterics.

To be involved in this gift of love from my Father to my Mother, was a most touching experience, especially at the age I was. An age, I might add, where I thought I knew everything and felt so sophisticated! From this event, through a different lens, I saw what my parents were really like as people, as opposed to just being my parents. How fortunate I was, for at that relatively young age of twenty-one, rarely does one have an opportunity to realize how exceptional parents can be. Early on, it meant a great deal to me to have that kind of relationship with my parents. To be part of this loving tribute was an honor and privilege. It gave me insight into their deep love and an ensuing appreciation for my family.

I have also included Daddy's biography of Mother as an introduction to my early life. Between my Father's words and my recollections, we hopefully give the reader a clear picture of what life was like for our family while living in China.

—Jean Galt Coblentz, 2015

Dedication

To Sarah Grimm Moore without whose collaboration on February 12, 1898, this epochal work would not have been attempted.

Dr. Curtis Galt in Tengchung (1946-1947)

Preface

To write a biography of a wife presents two real difficulties.

First: Though one may try to be objective and impartial, one is prone to look back over the years.

Second: When two lives have been so constantly intertwined for 25 years, and when the biographer is a mere male, whose family has never been noted for self-effacement, something is apt to creep in regarding her husband. But greater biographers than the present writer have gone far afield and introduced many and varied characters to enrich the tale, so we may be pardoned for slight offenses.

In speaking or writing, both the content and style should be adapted to the people who are supposed to benefit most from the effort. This humble offering is made primarily for my children, and, I hope for their children. Its purpose is to acquaint them, in a rather superficial fashion and with no attempt at literary elegance, with their mother as she was before they remember her, and to trace her steps from birth to the present. And as they read, it is hoped that their own childhood will become more real to them.

This was written entirely from memory, without letters, diary, or consultation. On many occasions I found myself turning to ask about a date or circum-stance, only to find that she was not there and then telling myself that it would not be proper to consult her on this work anyhow. But perhaps writing in isolation (New York to Shanghai on a small freighter) has two compensations.

First: It is easier to detach oneself from the characters and to treat them more objectively.

Second: Depending on memory alone, much of the detail which crowds most biographies, is necessarily omitted.

Since the children have already formed their opinions of their mother, no attempt is made to "sell" her to them. If, by reading this, they gain a better appreciation of her character and her contribution to their development, the effort will have been justified.

—Curtis M. Galt, M.D.

Mabel's Birth to Leaving Home

Mabel's early years are not memorable—at least I do not remember them.

History states that she was born near Alexandria, Nebraska on February 12, 1898; that her parents were honest, thrifty farmer folk—Grimms on the mother's side and Moores on the father's. Her first four years were spent on the home farm, and then the family moved to Alexandria.

Here we may assume that she attended grammar school and later high school; during which period she was just about like other girls of that period: growing (a little), developing, hoping, fearing, dreaming, planning her future, and taking active part in home, school, church, and social activities. She had some reputation as a singer; the community recognized and profited by her talent.

In 1915 our heroine graduated from Alexandria High School (A.H.S.) with honors, setting a precedent that she was proud to see her eldest daughter continue many years later. The following year was spent in Alexandria, dividing her time between home, her father's bank, and post graduate courses in High School. It was during this period that Father Moore died suddenly with heart trouble, leaving the mother with the responsibility of guiding the six girls to maturity. Mabel, being number three, was advised and admonished by her seniors, Nellie, and Hazel; and nagged, heckled, and teased by her juniors, Maude, Blanche and Edna. Molded by these sisterly influences and the faithful teaching of her mother,

1919 or 1920 photo of House in Alexandria from Northwest corner.

Mabel developed character, disposition, and personality which were to bring her a host of friends and to see her through many difficulties with a poise and sense of humor which were an inspiration to all who knew her.

College

September 1916! After months of planning, sewing fitting, corresponding, room assignment, of advice what to do and not to do, came the day of departure for Hastings, about 60 miles from home. It wasn't the distance, nor the difficulty of getting there and back; the train took one there and the same train could be depended upon to bring one back. But this was the first time one of the Moore girls had left home to go away to school. And in any life, there is probably no other day that equals this one in importance. One is looking forward. (True, one looks a little backward the first few days.) But Life looms ahead. In those four years, the mind expands, personality develops, new friendships are formed, some of them to endure throughout life. For many, Life's two most important questions are answered during the College Years.

1. What do I want to do with my Life?

2. Whom shall I marry?

And our heroine found the answers to both of these questions before her course was half finished. But I anticipate.

The Freshman year began with the usual settling down in the dormitory, lining up classes, sizing up the instructors and trying not to be homesick. Then, just when you have learned the names of your immediate associates, you are invited to the New Student's Reception. Here you write your name hundreds of times and try to remember a few of the hundreds who write in your book. After that evening you have been officially introduced and may cultivate anybody who appeals to you. And our little Mabel was not slow in making friends, or better stated, in attracting friends. I make this distinction because I knew several girls in college who deliberately tried to become popular, with rather lamentable results.

Strict honesty compels me to state that I do not remember just how and when our friendship began. Being a junior, I looked over the freshman field with a practical eye and, early in the year, marked Miss Moore as one of several possibilities. But one does not immediately forsake the old for the new and it was not until Christmas vacation that we really became acquainted. We were to take the same train, my stop coming a few miles before hers. But at the station we learned that the train was late, so we went to a movie. Since she needed glasses, I read the titles to her. Later, on the train, in making conversation, I asked about her family and learned the ages of the Moore girls. I suggested that I might take Hazel, and that, since we should have her in our family, she should wait for Cle, my younger brother who would be in college the following year. But it did not come to pass. From that time on, I found Miss Moore a remarkably interesting person and we became good friends.

How can one explain or describe attraction? This is about how she looked to me when she was 18 years old: A small, pleasingly plump young lady, about 5'2" tall and about 110 pounds in weight. Rather round face with a ready smile, and plenty of it. Her eyes were indescribable; that is, they were no particular color. It seemed that the blue of the Moore and the brown of the Grimm must have been scrambled together to produce such a result. Her Hair! Ah, that made you look twice. Beautiful brown, neatly braided, two strands encircling the head. Her clothes? I remember only the green suit; one saw that often enough to make an impression. Like everyone else, she wore high top shoes and black stockings. Whatever she wore was always neat and becoming.

After the Christmas vacation, Mabel joined the Alpha Phi Literary Society and later became its Poet Laureate. She also "made" the Glee Club and for the next two months the practices and the Annual Trip took a great deal of time. There was something about those trips. About 30 girls and boys with accompanist and director took to the road, traveling from town to town by train, mostly scrubby locals. Once we rode a freight train, the overflow from the caboose riding in the freight car. The usual routine: walk to town, sometimes many blocks, carrying suitcases; gather at church or "opera house" where the concert was to be held; practice awhile, get assignments to private homes and locate the house; then, if not already done, locate the house of your date, so you could find it in the dark. Then evening concert, date, and back to your own room. On this particular trip (she went on three trips) Mabel permitted Luther Stein and me to carry her suitcase about equally. One evening we had a long, long walk. The concert was canceled because of the tragic death of one of the local High School girls, so we had the evening to spend.

Still Getting Acquainted

These trips usually lasted about ten days and were climaxed by the Home Concert in which we always did our best.

There seems little to record of Mabel's life until about Christmas of the Sophomore year. That may be due to the fact that I did not know that this biography was to fall to me. But a little incident occurred the day after Cle and I returned to school. My incredibly good friend, Paul Chandler, and I met in the hall of the dormitory, clothed in "nighties" and had one of those long, serious talks which are as significant as they are rare. In the course of our talk, Paul said he was tired of scattering his affection, and that he was getting nowhere. He said he had decided to concentrate on Miss Moore. I believe that we both had exchanged letters with her during the vacation. His statement came as a sort of shock to me because her many charms were doing something to me, too. I believe that we "shared the wealth" and that there was no great rivalry, for we were the best of friends.

Not long after that, in a spell of very cold weather, the college heating plant broke down and school was dismissed for a few days. Some of the students could not easily get home so Cle and I took our roommate, C. Swinban, Mabel, and two other girls about her size, to our home in Franklin. It requires little imagination to picture the fun that a sextette of that age would have under those circumstances.

At that time the Student Volunteers, a group of prospective missionaries, were quite active at Hastings College, holding weekly meetings for mutual inspiration. In looking about for good material for the cause, someone mentioned Mabel Moore, and all agreed that she should be invited to consider becoming a missionary. It would be sacrilege to try to find out what conflicting thoughts, ambitions and emotions struggled in her mind those few weeks. She made her own decision and was welcomed as a Volunteer.

One day a very minor incident occurred. (Perhaps there are no minor incidents in Life). Between classes, we two were sitting on the steps of McCormick Hall, just enjoying each other. It was a beautiful, balmy spring morning and we were oblivious of the passage of time. Someone called "Mabel, you have a voice lesson with M. Fuhr", but it was then quite late, so we just sat it out.

To show how broadminded Mabel was, I will relate an incident in the late spring of 1918. The Home Economics girls were required to plan, cook, and serve a series of meals and were allowed to "invite" their own guest. For one of her dinners, Mabel invited me and a former Hastings College student, who at the time was studying medicine in Omaha. There was some gossip current that I was engaged to another girl, but Mabel must have noticed that I enjoyed being with her, so it seemed fine that she should have invited us. And I must add that we really enjoyed the dinner.

We now reach June 30, 1918. I reached Alexandria by train about 10:30 A.M. and was met by Mabel and Maude. We went to church and afterward I sat down, quite defenseless, with the seven Moore women. The afternoon passed quietly, then we attended evening service, where Rev. Butter preached on the text, "Watch". It is well he did not say "Watch Out"; the destiny of two lives might have been different. After service Mabel took me for a ride in her Buick, and we came home.

And now we must draw the curtain, for we tread on Holy Ground. By midnight we were engaged and agreed that ours would be the perfect marriage. And, speaking for myself, it has been. And thus, began a three-year correspondence, a scheming to see each other and an increasing mutual dependence.

During the Junior and Senior years, Mabel roomed with Lois Whitlock. There is an interesting parallel between the two families. Wallace Whitlock and I were in college together in 1915, Lois and Mabel 1916-20, Clarice and Maude 1918-1922, and Horace and Edna 1924-26. To continue the parallel, Horace and I were each two years ahead of our wives in college, each went to the University of Nebraska Medical College, wives each taught Home Economics one year, each couple married after Junior year in medicine, and each went to China as missionaries, and each served two terms.

On November 11, 1918, Mabel sent me off to war from Alexandria, but in two days I was back in Omaha.

During Christmas vacation we both attended the National Conference of Student Volunteers at Des Moines and met many interesting people.

I believe that our engagement was never formally announced but by constantly wearing one of my football sweaters, Mabel aroused suspicion at college which was later confirmed by a ring on the telltale finger. During the senior year, she lived the first semester in the Domestic Science Cottage, which I helped to build in the summer of 1916.

The second semester, she, Lois, and four other girls made an experiment in community living in a house off campus and it seemed to work out very well. It was from this house that we dated for the activities of Commencement Week. On a fine June morning 1920, Mabel proudly received her diploma and, at the same time, her teaching credentials. She was hired very soon to teach at Schuyler, Nebraska. Most of that summer was spent at home, but for a week she was at Edgar during threshing season. Since I had some wheat, and was staying with Maurice and Stella, we thought it fair for Mabel to come and share the housework. We both worked hard all day and ran around in the evening.

One night we saddled a couple of horses and rode about 10 miles. Though unaccustomed to riding, my girlfriend took all speeds without difficulty and seemed to enjoy it. A good omen for later riding in China. We are happy to give public thanks to Stella and Maurice for the very many kindnesses extended to us during the three years 1918-1921.

During the Schuyler year we saw each other at infrequent intervals. She came to Omaha two or three times and I went to see her once. The red-letter experience was when Mabel and Mac, her roommate, came to Omaha where Horace Campbell and I met them in a borrowed Ford. After a ride in the country and dinner, we attended the Caruso Concert. Hearing the greatest tenor of all time was, indeed, a great experience.

Our Honeymoon

Near the close of the school year, Mabel was asked to teach another year, but she had decided to choose marriage rather than career, so on June 4, 1921, we were married.

It was a quiet home wedding with only our immediate families and a few close friends present. Ceremony was at 12 noon, followed by one of the excellent Moore dinners. There were many nice wedding presents, many of which we still have.

Most impressive to me personally was a hundred-dollar check from my father, because the trip's finances were not very well assured up to that moment. The Goodenbergers had been married on Thursday and then came for our wedding on Saturday.

Dinner over, we changed to our traveling clothes and were soon on the road in Maurice's Ford. Some of our friends had painted the appropriate information all over the car and had maladjusted the carburetor, so our leaving town was no secret. We spent that night at Maurice's, and after changing his tires for ours, we were on our way to Estes Park, Colorado. Mabel wore a classy outfit including trousers (rather bold at that time) and a nice pair of hiking boots, which she later wore during most of our trip in China. In those days a long trip in a Model T Ford was a real undertaking. There were no surfaced roads; the tires punctured and blew out with monotonous regularity; there were no detachable rims nor wheels. Rain could wet the ignition, there was no self-starter, no easily closed windows and no trunk. But nothing stopped us long. Goody and I took the tires off; the girls patched them. Many of our meals were cooked over a gasoline blow torch - loaned by John Glaum - along the roadside and eaten where we stood. For rest and recreation, we pitched horseshoes, and our theme song was, "Ain't We Got Fun"·

The third day found us following the Big Thompson River up toward Estes Park. It was a long steep grade and we had to use low gear most of the way. This meant pushing one's foot down to the floorboard without rest. It also made the radiator boil and every few minutes we had to stop and refill from the River. But we made it and reached our cabin in the afternoon. This cabin was offered to us rent free by one of my medical school professors. This man had no reason to befriend me, for I did not shine in his course and it really required a lot of nerve on my part to ask. We intended to pay rent, but I believe Mrs. Willard took pity on us. We made several small improvements about the place and were happy there in those beautiful mountain surroundings. While there, we four decided to ask the Presbyterian Mission Board to send us to the same place and eventually it worked out that way, but at the time they gave us no encouragement. But we had all been in college together and knew we could get along, each supplementing the others. The ten days passed all too soon, and we went home via Scottsbluff where we left Goodies and hurried home to harvest our wheat.

Summer over, we went to Omaha to finish Medical School. Immediately on arrival Mabel was taken to Omaha University by one of my classmates, and after an interview with the President, was offered the Department of Home Economics.

But the position called for teaching some subject that she felt unprepared for, and while considering it, the former teacher decided to return, so she declined the offer. After some house hunting, we moved in with an old lady, and spent the year there. We had two upstairs rooms and shared parlor, kitchen, and dining room with our hostess. We both worked a little here and there, sold our old T Ford coupe, and with the usual help from my father and some dowry from Mabel's teaching of the previous year, we finished school without debt. All during the year we attended Lowe Ave. Presbyterian Church, where we taught Sunday School classes and sang in the choir. We made many friends there, and they were truly kind to us in many ways through the years.

Porto Rico

Immediately after I graduated, we went to New York and took ship for Porto Rico [1] (Puerto Rico), where Mabel was commissioned a missionary under the Women's Board of Home Missions, with the title, Dietician in the Presbyterian Hospital, salary fifty dollars per month. My position, noncommissioned was intern—salary, ten dollars monthly. We spent a remarkably interesting year there. We had a nice, three-room apartment in the hospital, overlooking the patio; board and laundry furnished, plenty of work, regular time off, interesting people, new foods and fruits and no worries. The hospital overlooked the sea, and we could hear the waves lapping on the shore. We were at liberty every Friday afternoon and usually we took the streetcar to San Juan. There was always something new to see, shops to visit, streets to investigate, and curios to buy.

From the very first day we became close friends of Dr. Alice and Dr. Garry Burke, and we spent nearly every Sunday evening at their house near the hospital. We prepared and ate supper and then just talked. Our conversation roamed far afield, but as is the custom with doctors, always came back to cases. This was the year that Mabel learned Laboratory and Clinical Medicine. The parlor in our apartment was the common meeting place during the day, and here we discussed cases, operations, funny things from the Outpatient Department; ate Nell's unfailing supply of chocolates and wrote in the diary which we all kept as the spirit moved us. This was a valuable experience for Mabel for she learned a great deal and so became an able consultant for our work in China. If she did not know the answer, she had an uncanny talent for finding it in the books.

In addition to our Sunday and weekday contacts with the Burkes, we took a number of short trips with them to various places in that interesting little island. They had a T Ford and we got around nicely. One dark evening we came to a place where the road was flooded, and not knowing the channel, hired a man with cart and oxen to pilot us across. When we were at a most critical moment; water deep, no sign of road, perhaps in danger of falling into the ditch, Mabel said to the driver "Now don't trot 'em." We roared. Dr. Burke never forgot that timely remark.

On another occasion we four decided to climb El Junca, Porto Rico's highest peak. Burke's maid, Natividad, became famous for

---

[1] The editors have chosen to leave the spelling from Dr. Galt's day with the current spelling in parenthesis on first mention.

asking "Para verlo nada mas?" (Just to see it?) We drove to the foot of the mountain and spent the night in someone's cabin where we had much trouble with the cots folding up or falling to pieces. Next day we reached the top and had a wonderful view of the whole island. But the trip was more difficult than we had anticipated; there was little or no trail; there were many roots, rocks, and branches. We were all very tired when we reached home.

Spanish is spoken almost exclusively in Porto Rico, but the nurses spoke fairly good English, so Mabel learned some Spanish from the girls who assisted her in the diet kitchen. As always, she was friendly, and the girls liked the assignment of working with her.

Early in June 1923, our year was up, and we bade farewell to our American and Porto Rican friends and another chapter closed. Five days on a boat and we were in New York, ready for the next experience.

The Trip to China

We were now to go to China as Foreign Missionaries. Under the Presbyterian Board. Together with the Goodenbergers and about 125 other young people, were called to New York City for a two-week training period.

This included physical examinations, many lectures and introduction to language study. We were busy most of the time, buying supplies of all kinds when not in classes, but did manage to see something of the city. The conference closed with a big banquet, attended, and addressed by several big men in the church.

Our next stop was Washington, D.C., where we were met by some friends of the Burke's: Mr. and Mrs. Cook. This was a treat, for they drove us around to all the points of interest and entertained us in their home. Goodies were with us, and while we had written that they were coming, our hosts were a little skeptical about them. All they knew was that they were from Chicago, Illinois and, since Cooks had a simple country home in Maryland, they were afraid it was too lowly for the City Slickers. This gave us all a lot of fun and we all had a good time together. Mabel and I went home to Alexandria through St. Louis and to that point it was a trying trip. It was late June, hot; the car was poorly ventilated, very smoky, and dusty. This was one of the very few times I ever saw her "down".

The next six weeks we spent planning, sewing, packing, and being entertained by friends and relatives. This parting was quite a memorable event in Alexandria; one of the unrugged hometown girls leaving the comforts and security of home to plunge into the unknown dangers of sea and jungle; unknown language and customs of foreign peoples with a comparatively strange and untried husband. But she comes of good stock, and they not only did not oppose, but helped us in many ways. Since it has not been mentioned elsewhere, I want to state that I have never had any but the finest treatment by every one of the Moores and Grimms. For this I am devoutly thankful.

Westward then to Hughson, California, where we had two or three weeks with my parents and Cle and Marguerite. Two trips were taken. Mother sponsored a Reo trip to Los Angeles and Pasadena which included, besides herself, Cle, Ellis, Mabel, and me. The roads and cars in 1923 were not as now, so we stopped at Bakersfield for the night. Since we could find no other accommodations, we rented a tent for the ladies and we boys slept on the ground. Mabel spent part of the night trying to keep us covered. After a few days in the South, we returned. Next, Dad took the Goodies, who had just arrived, Ann Bracken and us two, to Yosemite.

What a trip! Dirt and rock roads, one-way controlled traffic, steep grades, sharp turns, and deepening twilight made the trip, in all, quite an adventure. Living in a cabin, we spent a few days enjoying the waterfalls, mountains, lakes, and other beauties of nature. Our last night coincided with the season's closing of Camp Curry. After the spectacular Fire Falling ceremony, a lady sang "Goodbye Summer." Very appropriate for us. For we were to leave San Francisco on September 6, and it was soon "Goodbye" as we left the California Galts.

Our sailing on the President Taft was delayed a few hours in order to load more wheat for the stricken Japanese, whose homes had just been destroyed by the great earthquake on September 1, 1923.

We were now on the Pacific, on a large passenger boat, and we really enjoyed the trip. We had a good cabin, good food, deck games and sports, and interesting fellow passengers, including several of our own coworkers. We had a whole day in Honolulu, where we visited the Pali, Punchbowl, pineapple plantations, aquarium, and Waikiki. We enjoyed the beach but were not clever enough for the surfboards. The first Sunday service on Board was led by a fine missionary to China who talked on the text, "Ye must be cast upon a certain island." It was a happy choice; we often looked back and felt that it was intended especially for us. For there appeared many islands.

We stopped outside Yokohama, but the harbor and most of the city were destroyed and we were not permitted to go ashore. But we had a day at Kobe, and after seeing something of the city, Goodenbergers and Galts took the train for Kyoto and Nara where we visited some famous temples. It was a holiday and a gay sight. Thousands of people clomping along the streets on their raised, wooden shoes, laughing and chatting; their kimonos and lacquered hair making a memorable picture. It as improper to enter the temple with shoes on and there many hundreds of pairs left on the steps outside. We had no difficulty finding ours, but theirs looked all alike to us. We had a stroll in the park where the sacred spotted deer met and escorted us about. They were so cute.

This map is neither exact nor to scale but will give you reference points.

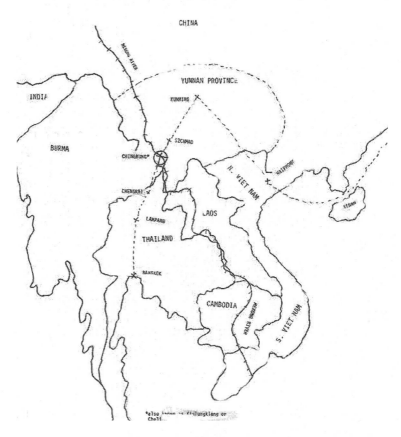

The train back to Kobe arrived there about 11 P.M. and we took a rickshaw to the ship. When we arrived there, we gave the pullers all the Japanese money we had left, certainly more than the usual fare, but they were not satisfied.

There was no meeting of minds, no common language, except signs and no way of breaking the deadlock. They seemed intent on holding us, by force, if necessary, so the girls went up the gangplank and fortunately found someone who could speak Japanese. He gave them another coin and bade them be gone or they would be reported.

That was the first of several little incidents that have occurred to make it difficult for us to love the Japanese as we do the Chinese.

Three more days and we were in Shanghai. Most of our party were housed in a missionary home, but Mabel and I were sent to a French Hotel. It was an ancient affair, odd beds, odd plumbing, and odd meals.

Our destination was one of the two stations in Yunnan Province. Shanghai was our first island. The China Council was in session and Mr. Beebe, of the Yunnan Mission was expected to attend the meeting. Since we had plenty of time, the missionaries suggested and arranged a trip to Soochow and Nanking for the four of us. This was our introduction to interior China, and we were royally entertained by missionaries in both cities.

Back in Shanghai, it was decided that we four should proceed to Hongkong (Hong Kong) and Canton (Guangzhou) and await Mr. Beebe there. One of the problems confronting the Yunnan stations was purchase and transportation of supplies. We were to investigate the situation in Hongkong and later in Haiphong. So, three weeks after arrival in Shanghai, we started South on another President liner and in three days were in Hongkong. The earliest available passage for Haiphong—and that for only two people, was some ten days later, so after our business in Hongkong was finished, we took a night boat upriver to Canton.

We spent nearly a week there, with Alice Carpenter, a college friend who had gone out the year before to help in a school for blind girls. I am sure she was as glad to see us as we were to see her, for she was housed with a couple of elderly saints whose ideas were far from modern and Alice must have been lonesome. We really "did" Canton. We visited churches, schools, hospitals, temples, and pagodas.

We walked, rode rickshaws, motorboats, and canal boats. There are many canals in Canton; thousands of people live in boats and spend their entire lives in them. One afternoon, we five were being rowed along a canal, and in a carefree mood were singing an old Hastings College song, when splash! we were doused by a stream of water thrown from an upper story window. This dampened our clothes but not our spirits.

Back in Hongkong, it was decided that, since Mabel had studied French, we should proceed to Haiphong, the others to follow as soon as possible. We had done some shopping in Hongkong, including a bedspring and mattress and wicker chairs.

But the one most memorable purchase was a fine doeskin covered pith hat which was Mabel's constant outdoor companion for many years. The three-day trip to Haiphong was dull. We were on a small French boat, quite rolling, quite smelly and not too clean. The gorgeous sunsets were the bright spots of that trip.

Haiphong! Another island! And a large and rocky one! Everything French, and fussy. They do everything possible to annoy the traveler. The next five weeks proved to be an interesting nightmare. We stayed at a French Hotel and were extremely comfortable. But there was little to do; we found only two people in the place who spoke English: a banker and a missionary. It was on one of those days, while in our room, that Mabel began crying. She didn't know why, probably homesick. I mention it only because it was repeated just once, some years later. Another quality for which I give thanks.

Since we would not be stopping in Hanoi, we went up on the train and got a room in a hotel. What a room! It was big enough for a dozen people, and bathroom and bed were in proportion. We were thoroughly enjoying the place when a missionary came to call. He could not imagine missionaries living in such luxury, so he insisted on taking us to his home. He and his wife were really a pair; she read Latin for recreation and he was all wrapped up in his printing presses.

They believed that distribution of tracts and scripture portions was the best way to evangelize a people. We liked neither the food nor the accommodations, so we returned to Haiphong.

Finally, Goodies came and a few days later, Mr. Beebe, and we began in earnest to get our goods through customs. The years have not dimmed nor softened our memories of the French Customs. But we finally wore them down and after five weeks, were on our way to Yunnanfu, now Kunming. This railway, built by the French, was justly famous. Most of the way it ran through beautiful mountains, seventy-five tunnels making the road possible. The train was supposed to run only during the day because they were afraid of bandits. But one day we had engine trouble and did not reach the hotel until 2 A.M.

We reached Yunnanfu the third afternoon and were met by Mr. Mylne who was to be our host. He was an ex-missionary Scotsman, at that time running a boarding house, purchasing and transportation agency for several missionary groups. Besides our group there was a party of eight, getting ready to go up toward Thibet (Tibet). They were to go fifty-five days by caravan and among their supplies were several muleloads of candles. The board at Mylnes was not remarkable except the bread. We had been enjoying the French bread and were not prepared for the dark, heavy offerings of Mrs. Mylne. Our host must have noticed our oversight, for he urged us to eat more. "Much better than that French bread. Nothing but air—nothing but air."

We spent a busy week there. Up to this time we had packed with no thought of size, shape, or weight. But now everything must be packed for one-half mule load, about sixty to seventy pounds. Things too bulky for pack animals were packed to weigh 150 pounds for two men, 225 for three, or 300 for four. For one man, there had to be two half loads of equal weight. These loads were made up of cots, chairs, bedding rolls, food and cooking utensils, and other things needed for making camp each night.

While we were packing, Mr. Mylne and Mr. Beebe were hiring the muleteers and carriers. In China, this takes time. First a request is made and an offer my probably about half that figure, is countered. As the days pass, each side compromises a little until each feels that the limit is reached. If they are together, the deal is made, and one worries no more about it. The Chinese are hard bargainers, but a contract once agreed to, they are honest and cooperative.

Just one week in Yunnanfu and we slipped off another island. Literally, this time, for we took an old side wheeler to cross the lake just south of the city. Now we were embarked on the last stage of our journey, looking forward to twenty-four days across the Switzerland of China. But looking backward, it was not so simple. Reaching the opposite shore of the lake, we learned that a riding pony, supposed to have been taken there had not arrived. After some delay, it was decided that Mr. Beebe should wait for the horse and we four should go on ahead, accompanied by two Tai (Thai) boys. So, we started, Mabel, Goody and I mounted, and Hilda in a sedan chair, borne of four. There was something special about Mabel's pony, a Chinese carrier suddenly blew a mouthful of water into the eye, and Mabel was nearly unseated. The man's motive was the cure of the eye, but the treatment failed.

It was about four o'clock when we started, the time when it was customary to stop for the night. We soon learned that to keep up with chair bearers, we had to trot our horses part of the time. Those men have a gait that is just between a walk and a trot, but they shift into two lower gears for climbing. They go about an hour and then stop for a short rest, tea, and smoke. That evening they made one stage and stopped at a Chinese inn. There we found no mules and no carriers. Then we discovered that our boys were not with us. No bedding, no food, no friend, no language. Then a couple of soldiers came with a letter. That didn't help any, for we did not know whether we were being arrested or protected. Darkness settled and the kindly inn keeper brought blankets and showed us where to sleep—bare board beds. That, in December, was not a pleasant prospect. About that time our boy-escorts arrived and soon we had a supper of hard-boiled eggs and peanuts. And so, to bed.

The next morning, more peanuts and eggs—more soldiers—no Beebe. The chairmen wanted to start but we refused to budge. About ten, Mr. Beebe came along, but still no horses. We pushed along as fast as possible that day but did not overtake any carriers. That night we were in a better inn, better food, and better mental attitude, for we had our guide and had learned the function of the soldiers. They were sent from town to town to protect us. Sometimes we had the same ones for three or four days, sometimes only one day. They were really quite useless. Sometimes they were an hour ahead and sometimes they loitered behind in some inn. Once we saw them shoot at something, perhaps to thrill us.

The third day we overtook our carriers and from then on, we had our own food and bedding. But, even so, three of us were not in exceedingly high spirits. After two days riding and two night's poor sleep we were too stiff to walk and too sore to sit on the saddle. That day was livened by a little adventure of Mabel and her horse. Goody and I had just crossed a foot-wide stone bridge when we heard a splash and there was Mabel's horse struggling to get out of the little stream. He had slipped on the stone and fell into water deep enough to immerse a couple of sweaters tied on behind the saddle. His mistress' feet were wet, but no other damage was done. That night reached a new low, perhaps an all-time low, in our traveling experiences: while the nights were cold, the sun was hot during the day and we had made insufficient preparation for the drinking water.

When we reached the inn, we were all tired, thirsty, and probably a little cross. This inn was really indescribable. Dark and filthy below, it was little better on the second story. We four shared a room in which there were two bare board beds. There was just room to walk between the beds, and just room for two cots on each bed. We had difficulty finding a way to suspend our nets. Supper over, the pots and pans were put into our room, and since it seemed like a tough place, we slid the bolt and tried to sleep. But the loud talking; constant coughing and spitting; and the sickening stench of smoke from dozens of opium pipes below, were poor hypnotics. Finally, weariness won, and we slept. At 2:45 there was knock at the door. It was our guide-escort asking for the frying pan for the boys to cook the eggs for breakfast. Maybe he couldn't sleep either. About 4:30 we had breakfast and then waited a long time for the carriers to get ready to leave. After that night, nothing mattered; we had seen the worst.

On the morning of the seventh day, Mr. Beebe left us. He had been gone a long time, was concerned about his family, and felt he could make the remaining two stages in one day. The day passed uneventfully, and we reached the inn rather late. We were in the mountains and this stop was quite high.

The next morning, we looked upon a world unknown! The sun was shining brightly over a vast sea of white; a scene that remains as vivid today as the morning we saw it. We were above the clouds. As we descended, we passed through the mist and then saw the clouds from below. Our path was a long steep descent, on a stone road which illustrated the Chinese saying, *"Chinese roads are good for ten years and bad for ten thousand."*

The ten years must have been up. There is no comfort for horse or rider on such a descent, so we always walked. Mabel never seemed to tire, but I must confess that my legs were quite shaky when we reached the river.

Here we were to ferry, and after a short delay during which the sun shining on the rocks nearly cooked us, we were across the river and up to the Mission Compound at Mosha. We looked in vain for a town. Mosha is the name of a region, and only on market day (every five days) can one see more than a few people. The mission compound consisted of a small level area, dotted by small school and church buildings and three small residences.

From this spot rising in three directions, almost as far as the eye could see, were the terraces of the rice fields. Some say that is the most extensive series of terraces in all China. It was a sight. Imagine the infinite labor involved in leveling and banking up each small plot. Consider the engineering, without modern tools, and labor in leading water in ditches at various levels, tens of miles from the mountain streams.

Truly by the sweat of their brow do they eat. At first, one sees only the fields, but hidden here and there in clumps of trees are the villages where the Tai Ya live. It was a hot, lonesome place for a mission station, but there had been prospects of a mass movement there, and that site was chosen.

The personnel consisted of Mrs. Dodd, an elderly widow, who, with her husband had pioneered the place; Dr. Mason, whose family was in America, Mr. and Mrs. Perry and Mr. and Mrs. Beebe.

The Galts lived in the second story of the schoolhouse and ate with the Perrys. Goodies stayed with the Beebes. While on this island, we had mission meetings and decided on division of forces. Dr. Mason, Goodies and Galts were to go to Chiengrung, sixteen days south, the rest were to carry on at Mosha. This suited us for it was the final answer to our scheme in Estes Park. After spending Christmas there, and attending to various matters, we decided to move on. When we left Yunnanfu, some of our goods and several muleloads of Yunnanese silver half dollars were supposed to follow us. But there were delays, mails were slow and uncertain, and we did not know when to leave. But since Mosha is several miles from the main road, it was thought best to move down to the road and be ready to go when the caravan came.

We took boats from Mosha to Yuankiang and what a thrilling trip. There were dozens of rapids and it was fun to speculate whether the boatmen would miss the rocks and whether the current would smash us against the bank. But we always missed, often by inches, and we developed great confidence in our boatmen.

At several places it was necessary to get out and jump from rock to rock while the boatmen eased the boat down with ropes. We stopped for the night and camped on a sandy beach. The moon shone through our nets, the air was cold, and this night under the stars gave just the right touch to our little adventure.

The next afternoon found us in a Christian village about two miles from Yuankiang, a small city on the main road. They gave us a hearty welcome, and though we could not talk to each other, we could smile in the same language. Our arrival coincided with Chinese New Year and it was the custom of these people to put up a supply of meat at this time. Each family butchered a hog, and we ate at a different home for twenty-one consecutive meals. In addition to pork, we ate rice and some vegetables. That is a lot of pork, but it was really delicious.

Our living quarters there were on the second floor of one of the larger houses and again our cots were like peas in a pod.

Time hung rather heavy on our heads; every day some of us went to get the mail and see if the caravan had arrived. The village was built on a long sand bar in the bend of the river and the wind blew the sand all through our clothes and bedding. There was little to do; we shot a few wild chickens in the fields and some ducks from a boat. The villagers even organized a wild boar hunt for us; we saw one at a distance, but he escaped.

But all things end, and finally we learned that the caravan had arrived. We hastily packed and joined it for the last lap of our journey. From there on, the regular inns gave way to caravan series, a hollow

36

square, surrounded by roofed stalls for animals and the center, open to the sky for goods and packs.

We liked this much better, there was abundance of air and the animal odors were much preferable to those filthy inns. And the road became a regular series of mountains and plains, one day from one plain to the next. We were hardened travelers now, and enjoyed the scenery, the people, various types of bridges, hog back trails, narrow mountain-side paths, from which one looked both straight up and straight down, and the changing flora and fauna. One afternoon, Mabel and I were riding ahead as we often did, and, just as we rounded a curve in the trail, a mule slipped and rolled down the slope. After a few revolutions, the pack slipped off and both rolled out of sight. What was in the pack? After a deal of effort, the muleteer led the animal with his pack up an easier grade and we discovered that one side of the load was our portable Victrola. It was not injured.

The question of Sunday travel was one that often came up for discussion. There were no rules but generally, when the carriers or horsemen were mostly Christian, Sunday was observed. Usually, with Chinese men, we traveled. But one Sunday, it was agreed that we would stop, let the men rest and attend to a few of our own chores. Before we arose, there were quite a number of people, near the cots, anxious to see the "Foreign Devils." The crowd increased to the point that we could scarcely move about, so we tied ropes from one post to another, to make the arena larger.

We know there were many, especially children, who spent the entire day there. It was at this place that Goody and I started out with bath towels, and not knowing the town, by sign language asked a boy where the bathing facilities were. He would show us. The parade gathered people as we passed through town and when we reached a pool in the river, we had over a hundred escorts, and they were an interested audience. Both Chinese and Tai (Thai) were amazed at the whiteness of the unexposed areas of our skins.

About ten days from Yuankiang, we reached Szemao, the last town before our destination. There was a French doctor and his wife there; they invited us to put up at their place. They were acting Consuls for the French Government and knew a great deal about the region. We enjoyed them and their food, but not their wine. From Szemao, it was only six days, and at 2 P.M. March 10, 1924, we looked down upon the Mekong River and across to the opposite bank where we were to make our home for the next thirteen years. Six months and four days from San Francisco.

Life in Yunnan

The Mission Compound was a level area about 400 yards long and 100 yards wide. The main caravan road formed the west boundary while the east overlooked the river. About a quarter mile to the south were the Chinese temple, Yamen (home of Chinese officials and seat of Government) and the small market town. This place had three names: Kiulungkiang (nine dragon river) commonly used by the Chinese, Cheli, official post office name, and Chingrung, the Tai name. On the compound at that time there were three buildings, the oldest was a long, stone walled, thatched roof structure which housed the hospital and church.

The Hospital

The next was a large two-story house, quite a mansion from the outside but quite primitive within. The first story walls were built of rock, the second story of brick, and the gables of stones. The roof was of thatch and bamboo. The other building was a partly built house, not ready for occupancy. At a meeting held immediately after our arrival, it was decided that Dr. Mason would live in one of the hospital rooms and that the Goodenbergs and Galts would share the residence. After we got settled, with bamboo mats overhead to keep out the dirt and dust from borers eating the bamboo rafters, and similar mats on the floor to cover up the unevenness and odd widths and colors of the flooring, we were quite comfortable. We always lived upstairs, there was no privacy at all below. People wandered at will all through the rooms downstairs and many did not hesitate to go upstairs unannounced, though it was against their own custom to do so.

Upstairs there were three large rooms and one small one. Goodies took one, we, one, and we divided the small one by a curtain and used it for a washroom and closet. They used the downstairs dining room, and we ate in our living-dining-bed room. We had our own servants; a cook, boy, and man-of-all-work. In addition, a woman came to do the laundry once or twice a week.

And so, we settled down to mission life. Our first task of course, was language study. We spent all of each morning in group study, Dr. Mason outlining the work and then turning us over to Nan Chai Tate, a meek young man who had recently left the Buddhist Priesthood and had become a Christian. He knew his stuff alright, but who was he to correct the foreigners when they made mistakes?

Galt House

In the afternoons, we pursued our several ways; helping with buildings, hospital, home or pursuing individual language study.
We were introduced to all station affairs, and gradually learned its history and the life stories of its founders.

Chingrung was started as an out station of the Siam Mission and we later came to know most of the members of that mission. As soon as we were sized up by Dr. Mason, our senior, the work was divided up and officers elected. Hilda was to take over the school, Goody the church and building work, Mabel was Chairman Secretary and I treasurer-medical officer.

The climate at Chiengrung was subtropical, about 21 degrees latitude, and one season merged into the next without very much contrast. Roughly speaking there were three seasons.

1. The rainy season, from late June to early October, was hot and humid. Traveling was difficult because roads were muddy, streams were swollen and bridges were out, and it was difficult to keep man or goods dry. This was the season of mold. Books, saddles, shoes, and other leather goods grew thick green coats of mold and were often ruined.

2. Following the rains, the nights grew cooler and winter was there. The temperature did not fall below 40 degrees, but a dense fog with a most penetrating chill settled down about 3 A.M. and usually lasted until about 10 A.M. It was always hot in the sun.

3. As February gave way to March the hot season took over. There was no moisture, the grass dried up, the mountain sides lost most of their greenery and the sun glared down upon the world. This was the season for preparing non-irrigated rice fields, and as the jungle was cleared, it was burned. The popping of burning bamboo could be heard for miles and the fires on the mountain sides were beautiful at night.

Our arrival, then, was in the hot season. Since Mabel had a bountiful supply of beautiful brown hair, she found it quite a burden in the heat. After some discussion she decided to sacrifice most of it and we cut it off. From then on, we barbered each other, she in constant terror (not without reason) that I would snip her ear lobes, and I was not always happy about occasional "pulling".

The red-letter day of that year was the birth of John L. Goodenberger. He made his appearance about 2 P.M. one fine June day and from that moment on, life was not the same.

Caring for the baby, nursing the mother, and watching the young man develop, engaged the attention of all of us. I would not say that we had anything to do with John's upbringing, but certainly we missed nothing of his first two years. For the most part, he was a good boy, but seemed to have an allergy to afternoon naps.

In October, Goody and I planned a little trip. Dr. Mason was to leave soon, and it was felt that we should get to know the region a little before he left. Mabel and I had not been separated since our wedding day, so this was a new experience, the first of many. Dr. Mason's going left us four new missionaries in charge of the work. Had it not been for two splendid young men from Siam, both of whom spoke English, we would have felt very inadequate. Both had been in the station for some years, Kru Muang, with his Siamese wife and Kru Luang, who had married a local girl. We were all about the same age and worked well together in church, hospital, building, school, and travel.

In March 1925, Mr. and Mrs. Beebe and Mary Lou were coming down from Mosha to help us. Since Ted was momentarily expected, it was decided that I should meet them half-way. Since there was no way of communicating, and they were delayed in starting, I went several days past half-way, and the farther I went the more I feared we had missed each other. But finally, we met. This, of course, kept me away a week longer than planned and those at home were quite concerned about us. So much can happen on those mountain trails. Ted came along early one April morning and there was another baby to care for.

During our stay there, eight babies were born. The problem of which neighbor would bathe and tend the new baby seems to have been solved but I do not remember the system.

Speaking of babies, we come to one of the most trying, but in the end, for us, most joyful times of our career. On December 22, Mabel seemed to be taking cold. A few aches and pains, slight fever, nothing severe. The next day temperature was a little higher, not too interesting. On the 24th I examined her blood and found more malaria parasites than I have ever found in anyone. She had lived there nearly two years without having malaria and this attack did not fit the usual picture.

Treatment was begun immediately but her temperature mounted. On the morning of December 25, it was 105°. On that morning, Mrs. Beebe required an emergency operation with general anesthetic. All helped, Mr. Beebe was errand boy, Goody gave the anesthetic (his first) and Mrs. Goodenberger was the nurse. I was scrubbed, gloved and gowned so could only direct the others by word of mouth.

Gradually the patient went under the chloroform but not without reciting some semi-intelligible things that did not tend to help any of us. My nurse fainted and collapsed on the floor, and I, myself, was not too calm, but patient under, we finished the operation without incident.

When everything was in order, I hurried home and found my other patient's temperature nearly 106°. That seemed a bit high, so we thought to reduce it a little by sponging. Poor girl! What an ordeal! A less forgiving soul would still resent our nursing. About the time we finished, a native child was brought in, in convulsions. Merry Christmas!

The following day, temperature again nearly reached 106° and, in the evening, she began labor. At 6:30 A.M., December 27, Jean was born without too much difficulty, but for some reason, refused to breathe. We spent a bad ten minutes, but efforts to establish respiration were successful and from then on everything was fine. If this were my biography, much would be made of changing diapers, heating water for water bottles and changing her clothes and bedding two or three times daily. All these things were soon dimmed by the thrill of having our first child. Parents!

Another bond between us. Sometime in 1926 Goodies moved to their new house and in October Alton was born there. In December after three false starts, Betty Beebe arrived and the foreign community numbered twelve.

Missionary Kids

Then on May 4, 1927 our Alan was born about 4:30 A.M. A Boy! Now we had everything! When he was four days old, a very unusual rainstorm suddenly came up. The thatch was blown up so that the rain began pouring down on mother and babe. Fortunately, I was at home and moved them before too much damage was done. We now had a child on each side of our bed. And since myriads of insects, especially mosquitoes, found their way into our room, each bed had to have a net. And every time one got in or out, or did something for the children, there was danger of mosquitoes getting inside the net. They were a nuisance. But by rolling together one side of the big net with the adjacent side of the small net to form an arch and with a pin here and a tuck there, Mabel devised a clever system. We could service the children without leaving bed or untucking the nets.

This of course worked better for her than me because she was much more agile in small quarters than I.

Trip to Dentist

It was inevitable, that in the course of years, some dental problems would arise, and in the Fall of 1927, Mrs. Goodenberger, Mabel and I were given permission to go to Bangkok to have our teeth cared for. John, age three, Alton, one, Jean, two, and Alan, five-months-old, completed the party.

Caravan

None of us had yet traveled with children. Had we known the score in advance, we might have neglected our teeth. Since the children were all small, we constructed strong, but light weight rectangular play pens, and roofed them with oilcloth tacked to a frame. This was hinged to permit easy access to the inside. Wicker chairs were placed in the front of each for John and Jean, leaving the space behind long enough for Alton and Alan to lie down. Since there is no English word for these, they will be referred to as Haam, the Tai word. A long bamboo pole was roped along each side, a cross bar joined the ends, and it was carried by two men, one in front, one behind, the cross bar being shifted from one shoulder to the other as they became tired. The children were quite comfortable in them, but John and Jean were always begging to ride the horses with the adults. On level roads this was freely permitted, and I enjoyed Jean's prattle

43

as we conversed in combined Tai and English.   The trip south, by caravan, took fifteen days, two from home to the Burma border, ten across Burma, and three in Siam, to Chiengrai. This was accomplished with only the usual vicissitudes of that kind of travel, with one exception. Early in the trip Mabel's horse elected to roll with the saddle on and her regular glasses, carried in a bag on the saddle horn, were broken. She then had to wear dark glassed all the time, even in Bangkok until the others were repaired.

From Chiengrung we traveled entirely in Tai country. There are no inns nor caravansaries. Each village has a Buddhist temple, and, while women were not supposed to sleep in the temple, exception had been made in the case of foreign women, and missionaries always stopped there.

Truck in Chiengrai

These temples varied from small, dirt-floored, thatched-roofed, split-bamboo-sided sheds with a two-foot-tall image of Pra Kautama, one head priest and four or five novices, to large imposing structures having tile roof, concrete floor, many tall pillars, fifteen-foot image of Buddha and forty or fifty priests.

We were always present to enjoy the sunset prayers, chanted by all the priests; the leader sitting nearest the burning taper in front of the image, the rest sitting in circles behind him. There never seemed to be the least reverence about the ceremony, but we always insisted that our party be quiet during its rehearsal.

Temple courtyard (local "motel")

Life is made of contrasts. The home of Dr. and Mrs. Beach in Chiengrai (Chiang Rai), North Siam, would have been a credit to any city. To us, after weeks on the trail, it was an oasis, nearly a heaven. House and hospitality made us welcome. This was the first of several occasions when we put off the jungle and put-on civilization in their home. The motor road to the south began at Chiengrai and Beaches had a nice car.

Luckily for us, they were going to a meeting in Bangkok and took us with them to Lampang. This was an eight-hour drive on a gravel road, passing through farming country and many miles of teak wood forest.

From Lampang we took the train and in twenty-four hours were in Bangkok. Here we separated, Mrs. Goodenberger being entertained in one home and we in another. While this was primarily a trip to the dentist, there was time for a series of teas, dinners, theater parties and shopping.

Three things impressed us in Bangkok.

1. The hospitality of the missionaries.

2. The mosquitoes. They are the largest, hungriest, and most vicious in the world. So annoying are they, at dinners each guest is furnished a large bag, into which feet and legs are put and the top tucked to prevent any entrance of the pests.

3. The hours they keep. Dinners start at 8 or 9 P.M. and theaters 9:30 to 10:00 One evening we were taken to the Royal Theater to see the King's Dancers. It was a beautiful place, and Mabel greatly enjoyed the performance, but either the dancing was too slow or the hour too late, and I missed the last several numbers.

Leper Colony

Came the end of our city interlude and we started north again. We were toying with the idea of starting a leper colony and wished to discuss it with Dr. McKean. So, we kept on the train to the end of the line, Chiengmai, and spent three pleasant and profitable days with Dr. and Mrs. McKean. They had founded and built up one of the world's finest leper colonies and were happy to show us everything they had.

They not only encouraged us to start work for lepers, introduced us to the American Mission to Lepers, and gave us a cash donation too, its results were a valuable byproduct.

Back in Chiengrai, we prepared for the road again. Misfortune struck the first afternoon. The pack horse carrying our cots, table and chairs scared at something and took to the jungle. After a long search, he was found but the pack was never recovered. So, for the next fourteen nights we slept on temple floors with truly little padding under us. One night we were awakened by streams of ants. Following their lines, we discovered that they were after the oil with which Mabel had anointed Alan's scalp.

Two days from home we heard rumors of political trouble, so hurried along as fast as possible. The second night at home, the people of the Christian village across the road, poured into our houses, bringing their worldly possessions with them. They were afraid of being looted. The Government did change hands, but the Tai were not molested. Late the next Spring there was a counter revolution, and we were caught between the opposing forces. One day we learned that the "Ins" had brought all the boats to our side of the river.

We knew there would be trouble. We prepared and at sight of the first soldiers on the mountain opposite, we mounted horses and went to the newly established leper colony some three miles from home. Alan, just a year old, rode with me, and Jean with her mother. A large, new house had just been built for Noi Yawt and his wife, the leaders of the colony and they did everything possible to make everybody comfortable, and since everything was new, it was not too bad. Goody and I felt that we should stay on the compound, in order to prevent, if possible, any destruction of property. We were almost directly between the "ins" and "outs". The "battle" consisted of occasional shots by high powered rifles which we could hear singing through the trees.

One evening Goodie came to my house for a visit and, on the way home, turned his flashlight on for a moment. Immediately we heard a bullet whizzing by above where he was.

Lepers at the colony

And the next day I dug a bullet out of the plaster of the inside wall of the house where I was staying. This "war" lasted three or four days. When the "ins" knew they were outnumbered, they stole away in the night. The "outs" unknown to us, had gotten some boats and were crossing the river, while we were preparing to take some supplies to our families. We started out, leading our horses.

Just past the compound, at a curve in the road where bushes obstructed the view, we met the vanguard of the oncoming soldiers. The leader, an evil looking chap, on the alert and with bayonet fixed, was not twenty feet away when we first saw him. We were surprised and I freely admit, frightened. It seemed there was nothing to do, so Goodie pulled to the right and I to the left and the soldiers passed between us.

Apparently the first group were looking for more worthy foes, but soon we were stopped and asked where we were going. We explained our mission and asked permission to proceed. But they said we must see the Captain. We waited at home until the shooting was over at the Yamen and then called on the officer in charge. He did not look very friendly. His first question was "What nationality are you?" When we said, "American" his smile was worth our lives. Had we been French or English, there would have been no smile. Since that day our American heritage has been even more precious.

From the "War" until Furlough time in October, life flowed smoothly along. But before going home we should detail some things that were either continuous or had no chronological significance.

The Tai People

It has always been difficult for our friends at home to get the distinction between Chinese and Tai. Politically and geographically, we lived in China. The officials and perhaps five percent of the population were Chinese. But all church and schoolwork and some sixty per cent of the medical work was for the Tai people. All the missionaries spoke Tai; in addition, I used some medical and business Chinese. The Tai have been called the Elder Brothers of the Chinese, and originally lived in North Yunnan and Szechwan Provinces, gradually migrating south, the bulk of them becoming Siamese. But during the migration, small groups were left here and there along the way and these became the Tai Sai, Tai Ya, Tai Baw, Tai Lu and Tai Yuan, and some others. Basically, their language and customs are the same, but the women's clothes and the language tones and idiom vary from tribe to tribe. Those who became Buddhist are partly literate, the rest are not. All are animists, for the Buddhist Tai have the literature, temples, and images of that religion but fear of evil spirits colors their whole life.

Our people were the Tai Lu; perhaps 100,000 people living in some ten plains with mountains between. They are small of stature, the men averaging about Mabel's height, 5'2". They have light brown skins, brown eyes, and black hair. They are a friendly folk, easy going, not capable of very great mental attainment and are quite childlike in many ways. They live in houses on stilts, built of poles, bamboo, and thatch. The people live above, and the buffalo, horse, cow, pig, and chicken are on the ground below. They are an agricultural people, living in villages and working their irrigated rice fields in the surrounding plain.

Beside rice, they eat pork, chicken, vegetables, fruits, and some soybeans. They buy cotton, spin and weave and dye the cloth and make their clothes. The men wear simple jacket and trousers.

Church and Tai Lu members

The women, in common with their sisters the world over, wear brighter colors and more elaborate garments. The children wear nothing most of the year.

All go barefoot, except on market days and other special occasions. Their principal diseases are malaria, dysentery, worms, and leprosy, all caused, they think, by evil spirits. Each village has a Buddhist temple, and this building and grounds are the center of the village life. Most of the men can read a little. Their only education is obtained when, as a boy of ten, they are given to the temple and put-on yellow robes. They may stay a year or the rest of their lives, the rest of the village feeds them. A mayor and several assistants handle the village affairs and collect levies and taxes for those above. Most of these "Head Men" are glib talkers. I have timed them when they came to confer about some little matter, the essentials of which should require a few minutes: fifteen or twenty minutes without pausing for breath was not unusual.

A Tai Lu Family

Work and Recreation in China

We often said that we had no work, it was all interruptions. Which really means that we were overseeing work of various kinds and trying to do some ourselves. The ladies kept up their homes, cared for their children, taught the cooks and boys, entertained countless visitors, supervised, and taught Tai school and later their own children, and taught classes of women in singing and reading. The men were preachers, teachers, doctors, translators' bankers, carpenters, masons, and plumbers. No talent, however, small though it might be, went undiscovered.

Our first physical recreation, was, in some ways, our best. Very soon after arrival we found that Dr. Mason and Goodie vs. the Galts made a very even match in tennis. What the game lacked in skill was compensated for in determination to win. Many an evening we played until darkness hid the ball trying to break a 14-13 set. After Dr. Mason left, our tennis was in and out through the years but never as keen as at first.

At one time we took up cow pasture golf with homemade equipment. It was fun for a while but did not grip us very hard. Croquet was a good dependable game but that too, was rather spasmodic. At times we played partners, three against three and had some exciting times. Occasionally we swam in the Mekong, but it was always icy cold, and the bottom was covered with stones, so it wasn't much fun. Swimming was, and is, the only sport that Mabel would have nothing to do with. She just could not be persuaded.

Our indoor sports were few. Occasionally we played Rook and when we did, we enjoyed the game and the gossip that went with it. It seems strange that, isolated as we were, we did not spend more evenings together. But each had so much to keep up in his own work, we did not get very lonesome. Besides, we saw each other about every day and so kept up on the news. We did have many dinners together. Every holiday, and every birthday was occasion for a dinner. And when there were sixteen of us, they were not too far apart. Our private recreation consisted of reading and music. We read to ourselves, to each other, and to the children. We had a Victrola and a good supply of records, to which we continually added. What a large contribution music made to our happiness and contentment! I am sure that it was, at times, valuable in keeping us sane. At one time, we had a very rollicking record, and we would each snatch up a child and dance around the room.

Time and Seasons

Since we had no connection with the outside world, we took liberties with times and season. About once a week, usually at Prayer Meeting, we decided what time it was and set our watches accordingly. There were times when most of the time pieces were out of order, but a bell was rung several times a day for workmen, and that gave us the time. We did pretty well, keeping clocks repaired but watches were too fine for us. The calendar came in for revision too. We always kept Sunday, but Easter, Christmas and Thanksgiving were sometimes changed to suit local conditions.

Yunnan Goats

No chronicle of our Yunnan life would be complete without some goat stories. Dr. Mason had built up a large flock of milk goats and when he left, we four bought them. Soon after the Beebes came, we sold the goats to them and began milking cows. Goats are an interesting nuisance. They are too familiar, too destructive, and too smelly. One day a nanny was licking salt under our kitchen stove when someone came in. She jerked up her head and thrust her horn through the bottom of the reservoir.

One Sunday, on returning from church we saw a vicious Chinese caravan dog trying to catch a baby goat and the mother was having a difficult time protecting it. Goodie quickly got his shotgun, and intending to scare the dog with fine shot, fired. Either the distance was too short or the shot too large, for the animal dropped in his tracks. The owner of the dog protested the murder to the local magistrate, and he wrote his version of the affair to the Governor of Yunnan Province. He in turn consulted the American Consul and in due course we heard from the Consul. Since Beebe owned the goats and Goodie used the gun, it fell to me to handle the correspondence. We gave our version of the affair, which was relayed to the Governor and in turn to the local magistrate. All this covered about three months' time, and the final sentence was for us to scare the dogs more carefully.

Purchasing Supplies

The "stores" in our little market village furnished only a few items such as matches, candles, horseshoe nails, needles, and a few Chinese medicines. On market days the streets were crowded.

This was every fifth day, and local people brought for sale, rice, meat, vegetables and fruit, sugar cane, bolts of cloth, cloth shoes and other little things. Merchants, both Tai and Chinese, brought goods imported from Burma, Siam, or North China. These included small crude hardware, money belts and pouches, brightly colored cloth and ribbons, blankets, hats, and a variety of things which appealed to the Tai but were of little use to us. For that reason, we bought many things elsewhere. Most of our household goods, cloth, some clothes, shoes, saddles and accessories, hardware and notions came from Montgomery Ward & Co. Food, such as flour, sugar, and canned goods, including butter were ordered from New York, and most of the drugs and hospital supplies came from London.

Kerosene and gasoline came from Siam. And by no means least, many things were ordered through the Moores. Most of these were annual orders, though a few little things came in during the year, by mail.

There was a right time to order, as we learned from an early experience. In November 1924, Dr. Mason ordered supplies for the hospital and they arrived in February 1926. They reached Chiengrai too late for the last caravan in the spring of 1925 and so were brought up on the first trip in 1926. So, we studied the catalogues in May, ordered in June, and received the goods some- time after Christmas. For emergencies we could send runners to Siam and get things back in three or four weeks. What excitement when those caravans came! It was a great occasion. It was, of course, not easy to anticipate all ones needs, nor was everything satisfactory when it came. The children often had outgrown their shoes before they arrived. In that line especially we did some exchanging. Shoes too small for John might fit Jean and so on.

Annual ordering had other drawbacks. Oatmeal and graham flour never kept, and white flour usually "came alive" before it was used up. But for the most part the system worked well.

Letters from Home

There was a daily mail service between Yunnanfu and Szemao. From there to home, it was uncertain. In the dry season, it usually came every five days, in the rains, from seven to ten. Magazines and packages were brought by carrier only if his first-class load was too light. They accumulated in Szemao until there was a horse load and it was sent by caravan. This might be once a month or much longer, so we took no daily papers. Once we received a package in June marked "Open December twenty five".

Since we did not know which Christmas was meant, we opened it then. Mabel and her mother carried on a very faithful correspondence and Nell wrote many long, newsy letters. Several other people, especially Cle and Marguerite, wrote quite often and all mail helped to maintain our morale.

In October we started home on our furlough. Jean and Alan each had a haam and two carriers. The rains had not stopped, the roads were very muddy in places and the streams hard to ford. It rained the first day and the going was difficult because the carriers were easing down a bad place when one of them slipped and fell. The children were always strapped in, so no harm was done. But the whole thing was too much for Jean and she begged to ride with me. My horse wasn't doing too well, either, but we let her come.

Usually, the stopping places were well spaced, but we had to cross one high mountain. With pack horses and carriers, it was extremely difficult to go from plain to plain in one day, so we usually spent the night near the top. There was no shelter, firewood was scarce, there was no chance to buy food for man or beast and it was cold. We had a small tent, and since there was room for only two cots, we tried to sleep double. In our cot, I am sure Alan slept more than I did. The next morning there was ice in the wash pan and breakfast was no picnic.

In due time we reached Chiengrai, and after freshening at Beach's home, took the truck to Lampang. Those trucks carry everything; freight, baggage and people are crowded in together. They make many stops, and the trip takes from ten to twelve hours.

After a night in the Government Rest House, and a twenty-four-hour train ride, we were in Bangkok. From there we had a small freighter to Hongkong. The deck space was narrow and the rail spaces wide, so we had to keep Alan harnessed and on leash all the time. He was a highly active lad and got into everything. From Hongkong we went via Shanghai and Japan, to Seattle. Somewhere near the Aleutian Islands, we ran into a severe storm, with extremely high waves and much rolling of the ship. The children were tossed and rolled from one side of the cabin to the other and were quite disgusted. During the night, we heard pots and pans and dishes racing across the galley floor. We stayed in Seattle with friends for a few days and then reached Hughson, California in time for Thanksgiving. After three weeks visiting the folks there, we took train for Alexandria and were there for Christmas. There we bought an old Chevrolet and about February first, moved to Omaha, where Mabel, Jean and Alan kept house while I did post graduate work in medicine. Jean started to Sunday School and surprised her teacher by what she could learn at three years of age.

In April we four and Grandma Moore took a trip in the family Buick to Ohio, where we visited the churches that were contributing through the Mission Board to our support. While there we had an opportunity to meet and address the people of the two churches. One of the goals of the trip was a visit with a very fine, mission minded couple, Dr. and Mrs. Stewart. We spent several days in their lovely home and they enjoyed our children. Mrs. Stewart named Alan "Perpetual Motion."

Horace Whitlock and Edna Moore were married at home in Alexandria, early in June, and Mabel and I had the honor of taking them to Omaha the same day. The children were left at home and the separation must have been difficult for Mabel for she wakened me at four the next morning and proposed that we start home.

After spending most of the summer in Omaha, we were ready to start back to China in October. Sometime during that year, the Burkes had moved from Porto Rico to Alameda, California and we were happy to renew our contacts with them as well with the California Galts before sailing.

Home Again to Yunnan

This time our course from Hongkong was different. We went to Manila, where our friendliness toward a lonesome young Filipino on board ship, paid quick dividends. He took us for a long ride, all over the city, in his own car. This was a very pleasant experience for us. From Manila we went to Singapore and there bade farewell to the President Monroe, after a forty-two-day trip. Failing to get boat passage, after a few days in Singapore, we took the train up through the Malay Peninsula, stopping overnight at Penang. The trip from Bangkok to Chiengrung was rather routine and, by pushing a little, we arrived home on Christmas Eve.

The beginning of this term was quite different from the first. We had the language, knew the people, and could go right to work. And there was plenty to do, but it would not make exciting reading.

The low spot in 1930 was the episode of Mabel's tooth. A wisdom tooth began to decay and give trouble, and since there was nothing above it, we decided to extract it. I succeeded only in breaking it off, and it became necessary to dig out the root. "Doc" gave the chloroform, intermittently and I chiseled and pried until we had it all out. It was a terrible ordeal for all of us. The only notable complication was inability to fully open the mouth; but by using wedges and some force, full motion was re- stored. Brave patient!

On August 4, 1931, 11 A.M. Alice was born in the same house as the other children, but each had a different delivery room.

When Jean and Alan were called home to see the new baby, they were quite excited. After one good look Alan said, "Gee, it's an American baby!" When Alice was about six months old, we started giving her cow's milk. She reacted very badly, and we soon discovered that she was allergic to all milk; cow, goat, buffalo, powdered, malted, evaporated, and condensed. But by starting with one drop each meal she was desensitized and had no further trouble.

In the meantime, she was fed soybean milk and ripe bananas. Later that year, Ruth Goodenberger was born and she and Alice "took the air" together in their carts until they could walk and then they could walk and then they played together all the time.

Time marched on for Jean and it was time for her to start school. We ordered the Calvert Course and school began. Mother and daughter now became teacher and pupil between 9 and 11:30 or 12 A.M. Alan started a year or so later and he and Alton Goodenberger had some classes together. Mabel was a good teacher. The lessons needed no planning; it was a splendid course, but to get those children to get it done and not give in when they begged to omit part of it, required a real teacher. I am sorry to say there were some tears on the part of the pupils. The course covered a wide variety of subjects and they delighted to highbrow their dad at the lunch table with stories and myths and even some science that were lacking in his education.

Goodenberger Family

The saddest event in our Yunnan years was the death of little Ruth Goodenberger. She was a beautiful little girl, plump, and jolly. One evening, when she was about three years old, she had some trouble with croup. The next day she seemed perfectly all right, playing around as usual. But in the evening, she began to choke up and by midnight, was gone. It was so sudden and so unexplainable, that we were all dazed by the shock. We helped with the preparations, including the coffin, and then it fell to the me to conduct the service. Beebes had gone home and there were just the two families. There was a service at the church attended by all the Christians and grave side committal attended by a few close friends. Great as the sorrow was, it seemed to be lightened a little by having the Tai share it with us.

About this time, we had one of several changes in the local magistrate's office. The new magistrate, Mr. Shi, was a friendly man whose family consisted of his wife, his twelve-year-old boy, and a twenty-year-old nephew. We saw them quite frequently and exchanged dinners several times. Each group enjoyed the meals and method of serving of the other and they were jolly occasions.

The nephew was an amateur magician and was glad to entertain the Goodenberger and Galt children with his tricks. There was one thing wrong with the Chinese meals. We all used chopsticks, could eat, and enjoy everything, but no drinking water was served. Although it really was impolite, our children took their own canteens of water and used them freely at the table, and though this amused, I am sure it did not offend, the hosts.

During this period Mrs. Shi's mother died and she had to observe the mourning customs. For a long time, she could eat no animal products and for a longer time she could wear only simple cotton clothes. For that reason, and because she liked Mabel, Mrs. Shi gave her a fine heavy silk dress. She was also helpful in getting Jean a coat-trousers Chinese suit. Then when Cornelia was born, they presented her with a complete baby outfit including the spirit repelling cap.

One's children grow up and pass-through various stages and one loses track of which did what, but one cannot forget Alice's "Goose Book". Someone sent her an unabridged "Mother Goose", and before long, it had to be read to her before she could sleep. Luckily, I skipped many pages when we started for after a short time there was no skipping. She would spot the omissions and had to have the entire book each evening. She had the same fixation for "Nicodemus and the Little Black Pig", sometime later.

She was the best child I have ever known for taking afternoon naps. Up to the time we left, age four and half, she would go to bed right after lunch, without a word from anyone, and take her nap.

End of An Era

In February 1935, while on a short trip, Goodie came down with the flu. He came home and complications followed which kept him in bed for a long time. March and April brought little improvement, so it was decided that he should go home. On May 1, the Goodenberger family, Alan and I started for Siam. This left Mabel, Jean (age nine) and Alice (age three) at home alone. Their nearest white neighbors were eight days away, in Burma.

Galt Family 1935

They were lonesome but were surrounded by Tai friends and had nothing to fear. The patient was carried on a long litter by four men and in some of the mountain paths it was exceedingly difficult to make the short turns. Dr. Beach was to meet us somewhere on the way and we kept sharp watch for him! One evening, after getting settled for the night, in a place where we had hoped to meet him, John, Alan and I rode on to the next village to look for him.

There we were told that he had reached there the day before, had been told we were not coming, and had gone back. I could have cried!

That meant at least a week longer away from home. There being nothing else to do, we went on. Our mission accomplished,

Alan and I went home as fast as possible. One evening, about forty miles from home, I asked Alan if he thought we could make it the next day. He was just eight years old and I was not sure about the wisdom of trying it. Never loquacious, he said "I guess so". At 5 P.M. the next day we rode in, he probably less tried than I. Ah! Home Sweet Home.

This, then, was the end of an era for us. For more than ten years, Hilda, Goodie, Mabel and I had traveled together; planned, hoped, worked, and prayed together. We had rejoiced at birth and sorrowed at death. Our children had been brought up together and were as one family. As Hilda said, "We were closer than brothers and sisters", and now they had gone.

And our work was not to be in the same place again. For Chiengrung Station, too, it was the end of an era, for we, too, were soon to leave.

From May until the following January, we had supervision of all the work of the station, including the leper colony and an outstation down the river. We had some very faithful Tai associates and they carried on well. The first vacancy to be filled was that of church organist. Hilda and Mrs. Beebe had both served, but no Tai had learned to play. Hilda had been teaching Jean for a year or more and Mabel had been checking her practicing. The latter was important, for while she does not play very much, she has an ear for mistakes in notes and time, and she called them too. Thanks to the two ladies and to her native ability, Jean made good progress, and when the emergency came, she arose to the occasion. And let me tell you it was not an easy assignment. We all had folding organs and the bellows had to be pumped by foot all the time. The one at the church had the best tone but was hard to pump. The numbers of the songs were given to her for advance practice, but we shall not soon forget the courage displayed by our nine-year-old daughter as she faced the church, both foot work and hand work just a little too much for her but doing her best. But it became easier and she did very well the rest of the time.

Summer and fall passed, Jean, Alan, and their mother busy with schoolwork during the forenoons. In the afternoons, the ladies took up whatever tasks came to hand, and Alan roamed far afield. He had a group of Tai companions, all older than he, but since he was a foreigner and owned most of the playthings, including Hunky, the mule, his place among them was secure. One day while they were throwing stones at a rock pile, one skipped and struck him on the tooth, breaking off a large corner.

December came, and with it, at 6 A.M. came Cornelia. She chose Alice's delivery room, and with Doc and Saang Nang assisting, everything went smoothly. This time there was no question who would bathe the baby. On the eighth day, Mabel said she was going to get up and watch me. I said she might get up, but no one was going to watch my baby-technique. She took over on the tenth. We missed only one day of school. I helped a little, but Mabel ran the show from her bed. She was letting her hair grow at this time and none of us enjoyed its appearance.

About Christmas time Mr. and Mrs. Callender and Mrs. Park came and gradually assumed all the station responsibility. Our furlough was due and there was much to be done before leaving. Since there was no school nearer than Shanghai or India, each about five weeks travel, we had asked the Board to accept our resignation, which they did. We sold sewing machine, Victrola, rifle, saddles, mules, cows, some clothes, and many little things. This money was turned over to Mrs. Callender, the new Treasurer, to be used in supporting the leper colony. There were then about two hundred fifty patients and it required considerable money to keep them eating. We spent some time planning what to leave and what to take and packing it. Breaking up a home and leaving a house with so many associations is a rather difficult emotional experience. But before we leave, we want you to meet some of our friends.

People in Our Lives

When we first reached Kiulungkiang, we hired a Chinese boy to cook and he learned quickly, both cooking and English. But in a few months, he contracted black water fever and in two days was dead. We felt this keenly for we had become quite attached to him.

Our next cook Ai Sai was a man of indefinite age and varied qualities. He was illiterate and could not learn to read. He was odd in looks, in dress and in speech. He was loyal to the point that he followed a goat-chasing dog into its master's house to give it a beating. This loyalty cost us some embarrassment and a little cash. He enjoyed watching the children grow and was good to them when they were little. As they grew up, it seems they got in his way at times. During our second year, a family of five came to live in the Christian village. The father had been a head priest in a Buddhist temple before his marriage. The mother was a little deaf and little queer, and it was said that their move was at the request of their own village, because of the oddities and sharp tongue of this woman. They said she had an evil spirit.

The children were a boy and two girls. They were above the average; one girl later became a schoolteacher and married one of our leading young men. At that time the boy, Kateya was about seventeen, short, stocky, pleasant, intelligent, and hard working. He seemed so promising that we decided to see what could be made of him. We asked him if he would like to go to school in the morning and work for us in the afternoon. He was glad to do this and in due course, we transferred him from the school to the hospital, where he learned English, medicine, and surgery. We called him "Doc" and were immensely proud of his progress.

Another boy, Ai Kaan, who began as our table boy, while attending school, grew and developed to the point that we sent him to Chiengrai to school. Later, he studied in the hospital in Chiengmai. He became a capable, and dependable worker and was given much responsibility. His success meant much to all of us for both we and our children looked upon him as one of the family.

There was one Tai woman who stood high on our list of friends.

A young widow, she came to the village with her little boy and very soon began to do our laundry. In many ways, she was above the average. She was quite nice looking, neat, friendly, and faithful. She studied hard, attended every service and in a few years became an ordained elder in the church. She must have had some influence on our children, for it was she who went with us to Bangkok to care for Jean and Alan while we attended to our dental and other chores. So far as we could learn, she was the only Tai Lu woman ever to reach that city. I am sure that Jean learned a great deal of Tai language and customs and gossip from Saang Nang as they washed and ironed clothes, side by side, in the back porch. It was she who usually stayed with the children in the evening when we attended meetings at the neighbor's house. And to her I handed Cornelia when she was born. Saang Nang was a real friend and I am sure the grief at parting was mutual.

E La, Alice's amah, so to speak, was a good looking, pleasant girl about fifteen years old when she began work. She took her charge out in a little cart for an hour or two each morning and evening. She taught her to speak Tai and was enormously proud of all her accomplishments. One day she gave Alice a pencil and was so pleased when she held it correctly, without being taught that we photographed her. Before we left E La had a baby of her own and our girls made much ado over her.

Visitors

During our first term of five years there were no visitors. But during the second term, we had more than one per year. First to come were Mr. and Mrs. Ken Wells and Mr. Holliday from our mission station in Chiengmai, Siam. They were a most welcome trio and we thoroughly enjoyed their visit. We were glad to have Mr. Wells back again four years later.

One time, a White Russian, alone, with no food, no money, and no extra clothes, stopped at our compound for a few days. He spoke little English, so we did not learn much about him. We fed him, attended to his wardrobe, and sent him on his way.

Another time a man came down from the North who claimed to be a Roumanian (Romanian) Consul, just returning from a term of service in the Chinese capitol. He stated that his last carriers had made off with his goods. He honored us with his presence for ten days and tried to teach us how to prevent malaria. One day Jean had fever and at the table I gave her quinine. Our guest was shocked; he said all one needed to do was to eat plenty of garlic and throw away the quinine. We learned later that when he reached Muang Hai, two days west, he was quite sick, and our Chinese friends gave him the best of care. A little improved, he insisted on going on and died the next day. Perhaps not enough garlic.

Our next visitor was our boss, Mr. Ralph Wells, head of the China Council in Shanghai. We did not have a real guest room, but with a little arranging, one was made ready. On the way up from the river Jean told him that we had spent most of the week getting his room ready. He was a jolly fellow and told the children many stories and showed them some magic and tricks. He was there in tangerine season and during recess between meetings, we consumed many of those big, sweet, juicy, easy-to-peel Mandarin oranges.

Our bravest and most welcome guest was Dr. Esther Morse. Brave because she came alone from Hainan and made the overland trip with no company except Ai Kaan and a few other Tai. Knowing neither language nor road, and unaccustomed to riding, she made the trip up and back with no trouble. Welcome, because we were all in college together and had not seen her for years. She was the only doctor who visited us in Yunnan, and we were especially pleased to have her present when we dedicated our new hospital.

Mr. R. Schuller, German druggist, and Mr. Bantli, a Swiss professor, both of Bangkok, accepted our offer to send down horses and men, and we enjoyed their three day visit very much, Mr. B delighted the children with his butterfly hunts, and Mr. S. became locally famous by swimming the Mekong River twice within an hour. The natives said only one man had ever swam it before and he was partly intoxicated. After these men finished their tour through Yunnan and Indo China, they wrote us saying it was their opinion that few places are as far from any water, motor, or rail transportation as Chiengrung.

Our last visitor was Mr. Wissman, a German professor of Geography in Nanking University. He was with a Chinese surveying party and, when he reached our place, was in dire need of good homecooked food. He seemed to be quite lonesome with the Chinese group, so we took him in. He made our house his headquarters for about six weeks, but he was out on trips much of the time. Mabel mended his clothes, and I polished his shoes and saddle. He was grateful and wanted us to visit his mother in Germany if we went home that way.

Farewell Yunnan

On April 6, 1936 we left "home" and started "home. Most of the village escorted us to the Nam Ha River, about two miles out. And there it was farewell to the life and the people we had known so long. The ties had become too strong to be easily broken. We forded the river and waved back as long as we could see the folks; then we were on our way. Alice and Cornelia were in haarns, the rest of us riding. We had a good trip; Cornelia was a perfect traveler. The sun was hot, but the roads were good and the streams shallow. On the mountain we slept under the stars and found it good.

But misadventure awaited us. One day at eleven o'clock, we stopped to rest beside a little stream. The saddle horses were grazing and drinking, and everybody was relaxed. Then we saw two women coming toward us with firewood on their shoulders, slapping and brushing with their hands and jackets. Someone called "Bees" and the Tai men started to run. We were a few feet from the road, and we hoped, by keeping still, we might be unmolested.

The horses bolted and soon we were in the thick of it. The children started dashing off through the trees; we wrapped Cornelia as best we could with a little blanket and my bandana and were soon following. What a flight! Yelling, slapping, brushing, we went about a quarter of a mile before we came to a blacksmith shop where there was a good smudge. We stayed there about a half hour, and then went over to a house where a kindly woman gave us some food and we inspected our wounds. First prize went to Jean with eighteen, second to Mabel with twelve, Alice, Alan, and I "also ran" with six or eight, and Cornelia got the booby prize for just one on her little fat hand. After an hour or so we cautiously returned to the stream mounted the horses and started out again. About a hundred yards down the road, we met a few bees, but we fought them off and were soon out of danger.

Since then, the word "Bees" means only one thing to our family. That night our company was a sight. There were closed eyes, swollen lips, lumpy ears, and hundreds of itches. Mabel developed quite a fever and spent a bad night.

Leaving Yunnan, 1936

Then we reached Muang Len, where we expected to hire a truck for the rest of the journey. This place was on the newly built Siam-Burma Road and several trucks passed through daily. We paid off our men and they started home early the next morning. We soon learned that a heavy rain from above had taken away part of the local bridge, so we could not cross. That night a terrible wind and rainstorm struck the house where we were staying, and when we heard a nearby house crash, we were quite concerned, but nothing happened. We then heard that a bridge to the south was out too. Thinking we might be stuck there for some time I started out south looking for oxen and carts to move us. After walking for miles and meeting no luck, I saw a truck approaching and hailed it. The driver said the bridge that way was repaired.

Returning to our stopping place, the driver stored his load there, and started back. What a ride! It was dusk as we covered a slippery hilly road with many sharp turns and dark as we splashed and skidded the last hour of road. Then, once more, Chiengrai and the Beach's home!

Journey's End

We had crossed our last mountain, ferried, and forded our last stream, waded our last mud hole. We had dismounted and unsaddled for the last time. We had taken down the mosquito net, folded the cots, rolled up the bedding and packed the food and pan basket for the last time. Farewell to pith hats, to burning sun, to lukewarm, smoky tasting, boiled water, meager meals, candles, and lanterns, to horses and haams.

All these were now behind us. Altogether I have watched Mabel travel the caravan trails of China, Burma, and Siam for more than one hundred days. To her, burning sun, frosty nights, mountain rocks, and jungle mud were all part of the game. She has slept on bare board beds in Chinese inns, on concrete Buddhist temple floors, and on cots in stables, in tents and under the stars.

She has put up and taken down beds late at night and early in the morning. She has eaten lunches standing or sitting on a rock, and suppers surrounded by dozens of curious people. She has retired and arisen with the same eager audiences. She has nursed and changed babies by the roadside and washed their clothes in the streams. She has been hot, hungry, thirsty, dirty, and tired.

There were no toilets but the woods, no baths but the streams. Sun burn, wind burn, saddle sores, bee stings; she has known them all, yet I can truthfully say that never once have I heard her complain.

Fellow Traveler: I salute my Superior!

Mabel Galt

Recognizing Cookies In Jean's Life

My favorite saying: *"Take Your Cookies When They're Passed."*

Sometimes I wasn't even aware a *cookie* had come to me until time had passed and I said, 'Aha, that was a *cookie*.' You would be amazed at how many people I've encountered and gotten to know as I have journeyed through life taking up those *cookies* as they were passed. For privacy reasons, I have often not included full names. Just know that not one person was one bit more important than the other, aside, perhaps, from my parents who started it all.

Curtis and Mabel Galt in Nebraska

It is often not until much later when you realize that the most difficult part is what you said or did or didn't say and do that made a difference in somebody else's life. Best not to be aware of that happening, lest one becomes nervous. But I think we can do some fun things with *cookies* at the moment when they are passed.

I was first introduced to the saying, Take Your *Cookies* When They're Passed, when living in Menlo Park and reading the society pages in the Chronicle, a San Francisco daily newspaper. A woman being honored for an event she had taken charge of said, "You know, it worked out really well, because I took my *cookies* when they were passed." I thought, 'I like that! I like that a lot! It's like "*Carpe Diem – Seize The Day*." It tickled me and has been my favorite saying ever since.

During the early 70s while my youngest children were in high school, I worked in PR/Development for the Meals on Wheels Program of Santa Clara County. Meals on Wheels is a service available for persons sixty years of age or over, regardless of income, who are homebound because of illness, disability or have any difficulty obtaining food or meals for themselves. A weekly delivery of fourteen nutritionally balanced and delicious meals is provided, each of which then included milk, fresh fruit, bread, fruit juice and other grocery items.

The program was part of Santa Clara County Social Services and the United Way. Along with the delivery of meals, social workers visited people to inquire about their eating habits. For the volunteers, a list was made up each day of the people to be visited and their addresses.

I have a framed plaque in my kitchen saying, "*Take Your Cookies When They Are Passed.*" People were associating me with that phrase. One of my co-workers made the plaque as a farewell gift for me when I left the Meals on Wheels program in 1977 to go to work at Stanford, and on the back of that saying is one of those lists showing where the volunteer or social worker was to visit that day.

I have always loved *cookies*, especially these kinds of *cookies*. The giving goes on and on.

A *cookie* for me was an opportunity, perhaps a situation I found myself in where a decision was needed about whether to be part of something or not. At the time of the experience, I didn't necessarily think in terms of *cookies*. Having to make a decision is what it boiled down to. If the project or activity interested me and my help was needed, I gave it a go. I rarely said, 'Ohoooooo, I can't do that.'

The whole point is how each *cookie* made a big difference in my life. It didn't matter whether the difference was apparent immediately or later down the line. This story is largely about the *cookies* of my life.

Ancestry: A Brief History

Information about my mother's side of the family is taken from, *Biography of Mabel Moore Galt,* written by my Father, "Her most ardent admirer, C.M.G."

My mother, Mabel Moore Galt was born February 12, 1898, (the third of six girls). She died in Pasadena while at Alice's on June 29, 1982 at age 83.

Mabel was born in a small town near Alexandria, Nebraska.

Mabel's Mother: Sarah Grimm

Her parents were honest and thrifty farm folk. Her mother's maiden name was Sarah Grimm and her father, Charles Moore was a banker.

My father, Curtis Martin Galt, was also born in Nebraska on November 28, 1896, the third of five brothers. He died March 10, 1966 in Manteca, CA.

Curtis' father, Amos Alan Galt was a hardware store owner and banker. Curtis' mother was Anna Cameron. I always just said, 'Hi Grandma!' The Galt family later lived in Houghson, California.

Amos Alan Galt
(Curtis' father)

Mabel's Father: Charles
Moore, died in 1916

CHARLES ISAAC MOORE
the late President of the
STATE BANK OF ALEXANDRIA
Presented by
L. H. THORNBURGH, a stock holder

Grandmother Sarah Moore

As said before, Mother was the middle child of six girls: Her elder sisters, Nellie, and Hazel, advised and admonished Mabel. Her younger sisters, Maude, Blanche, and Edna, nagged, heckled, and teased Mabel.

▲ Amos Alan Galt and Anna Cameron Galt's five sons:
Maurice, Stuart, Curtis, Clarence, and Ellis

▼ Curtis' Parents: Amos and Anna

Sarah Grimm Moore (center bottom) and her six daughters: (from top left) Mabel, Maude, Blanche, Nell (from bottom left) Edna, Sarah, and Hazel.

Sarah Moore's daughter Edna and Horace Whitlock

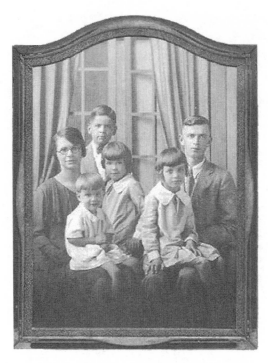

Sarah Moore's daughter Blanche and her family

Mabel spent her first four years on the home farm in Nebraska. Then the family moved to Alexandria, Nebraska, where she attended grammar school and high school. Mother took an active part in home and school, church, and social activities. She had some reputation as a singer, with the community recognizing and enjoying her talent.

The family did not know they were poor but worked extremely hard.

Mother divided her time between her father's bank, home, and high school. During this time, her father died suddenly from heart problems, leaving her mother with six girls to raise on her own.

In my eyes, Mother was the outstanding one! All through school she was the brightest and funniest, wrote poetry and all around was an exceptionally good student. She was the smallest of the six girls, and her mother used to say to her, "That's alright, you'll grow." But she never did.

In 1915 Mother graduated from high school with honors, setting a precedent that she was proud to see her eldest daughter Jean continue many years later. At age sixteen, daughter Jean was valedictorian of her 1942 high school graduating class.

Molded by her five sisters and the faithful teachings of her mother, Mother developed character, disposition and personality that brought her a host of friends and saw her through many difficulties with poise and a sense of humor. She was an inspiration to all who knew her.

In September 1916, after months of planning, sewing, and gaining advice on what to do and what not to do, she entered Hastings College, a denominational Presbyterian School about sixty miles from home. Although she did not like to cook, she majored in home economics!

In his biography about Mother, my father stated, "In those four years, the mind expands, personality develops, new friendships are formed, some of which endured throughout her life. For many, life's two most important questions are answered during the college years:

1. What do I want to do with my life?
2. Whom shall I marry?"

After her freshman year at the New Student's reception, Mother wasn't slow in making or attracting friends. She and my dad became acquainted during

Christmas vacation. He found her an interesting person, and they became very good friends. Mother was not a beauty, but she sparkled. Daddy was very handsome and athletic: "all state" in football, a four-year track man and a basketball player.

Father described Mother at eighteen as, "small, about 5'2" tall, 110 pounds with a rather round face, a ready smile and plenty of it. Her eyes were indescribable; that is, they were no particular color. It seemed that the blue of the Moore and the brown of the Grimm must have been scrambled together to produce such a result. Her hair! Ah, that made you look twice. Beautiful brown, neatly braided." Daddy remembered the green suit she wore and, like everyone else, the high-top shoes and black stockings. "Whatever she wore, she was always neat and becoming."

In college, Mother joined Alpha Phi Literary Society and later became its Poet Laureate. She made the Glee Club and toured with about thirty others by train to towns, where they were to find their assigned homes, carrying suitcases back and forth. Another fella, Luther Stein, and my dad were permitted by Mother to carry her suitcase. Daddy too was in the glee club and had a wonderful voice. Many of the songs I remember most fondly are ones he sang to us in China. Music was always a big part of our family life.

During 1917, their Sophomore year, my father's very good friend Paul Chandler and he, met in the hall of the dormitory, clothed in nighties, to have one of those long and serious talks that are as significant as they are rare. Paul mentioned how he was tiring of scattering affections and getting nowhere, and that he had decided to concentrate his attention on my mother, Miss Moore, of whom he was especially fond. My dad was shocked because her many charms were also doing something to him. He said to himself, "Hmmmmm Mabel, I like her. I like dating her. She is wonderful." He knew he didn't want anyone else to have her. Dad won out in the end, and Paul Chandler went on to become a very fine eye surgeon in New York.

During those college years, both Mother and Father were involved in church youth groups. Many of the young folks in those days, if they had any feelings about the world and their relationship to it, became missionaries. At the time, it was like young adults now think of the Peace Corps or other worthwhile causes and organizations.

The #1 *cookie* in my life turned out to be when my mother and father met, and Curtis chose Mabel. Their relationship began to truly grow following my father's talk with Paul Chandler.

So, Daddy concentrated on Mabel Moore and on June 30, 1918, they became engaged, agreeing theirs would be the perfect marriage. Their engagement was never formally announced.

In November 1918, Mother sent my father off to war from Alexandria; but in two days' time, he was back in Omaha. As the story goes, he had flat feet; but the war ended just a week later anyway.

Christmastime, 1918, they both attended the National Conference of Student Volunteers in Des Moines, Iowa.

In June 1920, Mother graduated and accepted a teaching job in Schuyler, Nebraska.

Dad wrote, "During the summer, she visited me on the farm where I was threshing wheat. One night we saddled a couple of horses and rode about ten miles. Though unaccustomed to riding, my girlfriend took all speeds without difficulty and seemed to enjoy it. (A good omen for later riding in China!) One highlight that year was while she was at Schuyler, we attended a Caruso concert together." Daddy loved Caruso and brought his records to China to play on the Victrola.

On June 4, 1921, they married quietly at home with only a few friends and immediate families present. The ceremony at twelve noon was followed by an excellent Moore dinner. They honeymooned at Estes Park, Colorado, with the Goodenbergers, good friends who were married two days before them and who also planned to travel to China as Presbyterian Missionaries. Daddy felt he needed to give back, do something with his medical education.

The next stop was Omaha, Nebraska, where Daddy finished medical school at the university. Then off they went to New York to catch the ship for Puerto Rico to do an internship.

Mother was commissioned a missionary under the Women's Board of Home Missions with the title: Dietician in the Presbyterian Hospital with a salary of $50.00/month. She learned Laboratory and Clinical Medicine. If she did not know the answers, she had an uncanny talent for finding them in books. My dad was positioned as a non-commissioned medical intern with a salary of $10.00/month.

China

The next *cookie* was when my parents moved to China in 1923. They went under the auspices of the Presbyterian Mission, which meant they went where they were sent. Headquarters in New York where they signed in, chose mission sites. Their final posting was to a small Presbyterian mission of three families in Kiulungkiang, Yunnan Province in the Southernmost part of China. The three men to be stationed at that site were a minister, a linguist, and a doctor. At that time, China was a vastly different world. The three missionary families housed in the compound were: The Beebe's, the linguist; the Goodenberger's, the minister; and the Galt's, the doctor, all with wives in attendance.

The trip to China for my parents was long and arduous, harrowing, and amazing. During the treacherous ride over the mountains, guides helped them. Mother and Dad brought their Victrola that was fortunately retrieved after it fell off the mule that fell down a cliff, losing his pack. A mule load could be up to 150 pounds, but a mule usually carried a smaller load of fifty-sixty pounds. Not before too long, the mule was led back up the hill with the pack. All was well, and the Victrola came to play an important role in our family life out in remote China.

The journey took six months and four days from San Francisco, CA to Chingrung. They went by ship and horseback and ended in Yunnan Province – about sixty miles from the Burmese border on the bank of the Mekong River. My parents did not speak the language and told many tales of getting there from the North. As they traveled further South, the language changed. The language of the south is Tai, more like Laotian and Vietnamese. But they traveled through areas that spoke Cantonese or a dialect of that language. They were at the mercy of a people's culture of which they had truly little knowledge and who spoke an unfamiliar language, using a money system they still had to learn. As they traveled South, occasionally, a band of soldiers came up to their caravan. Never knowing what they might do, they were surprised to find out they were their escorts through the bandit territory. All those arrangements somehow had been made through the Presbyterian mission offices in Shanghai. However, the further they got away from headquarters; communication became less available. You never knew where your caravan would end each evening.

It took twenty-four days across the South of China with the gait (horseback and mule) between a walk and a trot, slower for climbing. When the caravan stopped to rest, Mother and Dad were given tea while the locals smoked. There were soldiers nearby for protection. The caravan drivers stayed in opium dens along the way. The guest areas were above the opium dens but within hearing range of all the hacking, coughing, and spitting that went on in the dens. When they stayed in inns at sundown, too stiff to walk and too sore to sit, they were given two bare board beds with netting for their night's rest.

Along the way, in the Mosha region, there were terraces of rice fields. On their last lap, there were no inns, only stalls for the animals; they slept in an open area under starry skies. Everything for the caravan stopped on Sundays. Villagers followed the "foreign devils" (the name for missionaries) down to the river to watch them bathe. Dad wrote about their early travels before the children were born.

"Back in Hong Kong, it was decided that since Mabel had studied French, we should proceed to Haiphong, the others to follow as soon as possible. We had done some shopping in Hong Kong including bedsprings and mattress and wicker chairs. But the most memorable purchase was a fine doeskin covered pith hat – Mabel's constant companion for many years."

I do remember my mother wearing it all the time but have no recollection as to where it ended up. Each of us had a pith hat as part of our uniform to help fight the sun.

Jean, age 4

Jean age 7½ in her pith helmet

The Layout of the Compound

The station where we lived was relatively small. There were three houses, one for the doctor, one for the minister and one for the linguist. A hedge bordered the station.

The grounds of the compound led right down to the Mekong River. Our home was built of stones from the Mekong River, a home previously ordered by the Presbyterian Mission under the guidance of the female doctor who preceded my father in caring for the locals. Another doctor lived there for a year prior and began the rudiments of a hospital. The last structure to be built was a church.

Jean's sister Alice with her Pith Helmet.

Our home was a two-story dwelling. On the first floor were the kitchen, dining room and a covered laundry room outdoors. A woman did our laundry in washtubs with a washboard, using coal from the wood-burning stove in the kitchen to heat the iron. Each house had its own well for water, which was carried into the house by hand. The dining room housed a huge table with chairs and a hutch with lots of dishes. Up the stairs off the kitchen was our sleeping porch where each of us had our own chamber pot for nighttime usage. A banana tree outside a corner of our sleeping porch made beautiful music when the rain hit its leaves. Our parents' bedroom was adjacent to the sleeping porch. Also, upstairs was the schoolroom, library and music room that housed the Victrola. Above that was an attic for storage where a year's supply of potatoes was kept, delivered once a year by caravan from North China.

Curtis with baby Jean.

We lived upstairs since we were like a sideshow for the local people who wandered through the downstairs with their animals. We made do. We had a generator from Bangkok that worked most of the time. When it didn't, we used kerosene lanterns. We had our own barn for horses and mules and a separate area for the chickens at night.

My father wrote, "We settled down to mission life. Everything was transferred from the mules into the house before being introduced to all station activities. As mentioned before, that particular station was opened three years before our family arrived by a woman doctor. "As soon as we were sized up by Dr. Mason, our senior, the work was divided up and officers elected." The church was also built during that time, and the leper colony was first started.

Hired Help with the children

We had servants because mother spent a great deal of time not only with us children, but also in language study. She later became our schoolteacher. We had an

"Uma" who came to be with us in the afternoon so mother could have rest time. Most of the servants were illiterate. We had a cook, a houseboy, a woman who did the laundry, a babysitter (uma) and people who took care of the horses and mules. Hiring people from the community was a given when families moved into the area.

Mother stayed home and interacted with the hired help, who were like family to us and never treated like servants. We were a self-contained unit.

The cook, referred to by us as "cook," was mischievous and teased us children who, in turn, would scream. My parents allowed such shenanigans, knowing that it was all just done in fun. "Cook" loved teaching us bad things like swear words. His favorite trick was showing us how to kill a lizard. He lit his pipe that gave off a Godawful smell and held the little critter over that horrible smelling smoke. Before long, the critter was dead! We watched with fascination, and although he may have been playing doctor, we knew at the end, the lizard would play no more.

The Tai Lu People

Our people were the Tai Lu, simple and friendly folk who lived in the plains. The women dressed in bright colors, the men in trousers and jacket and the children mostly wore nothing. The women's clothing differed for each tribe. They wore skirts and depending upon the width of the stripes and configuration of colors, you could tell which tribe they belonged to. They wore a petticoat with glistening on it when dressing up. When in mourning, they wore white. They were short, little people, the average man about 5'2". I never saw a fat Tai

Lu. All went barefoot except on market days and other special occasions.

Many of the nearby villagers were considered outcasts from other villages for a number of reasons, and all the local folk were fearful of evil spirits. The people were either Buddhists or Animists and felt that everything had a spirit. If somebody's spirit was upset, then maybe it was the evil eye being put on him or her. If they could convince the headman that someone was putting the evil eye on them, then that accused person would be thrown out of the village. Most of the people who became Christians, were outcasts from other villages. I'm sure that a great deal of their Christian zeal was due to the fact that in the village, they felt safe. Beyond the compound, the nearby village was composed primarily of people who had been thrown out of their own villages, accused for one reason or another of having an evil eye. This village near the mission station was their safe haven.

The people around us were more Vietnamese. So, when you read ethnic information about the Vietnamese/Laotian culture, that is the kind of people who lived around us. There were actually five Thai tribes – each tribe occupied a valley. Their language was similar but dissimilar so that you knew when you were with another tribe. It is very different from what one expects. The Vietnamese language is a tonal language. I considered the bravery of those two preachers trying to learn this language and teach something like religion to the people, a concept very foreign to them. It must have been extremely difficult because, for example, being a tonal language, the word for "a congregation" is very similar to the word for "a group of pigs." There is not very much difference to our ears and Mr. Beebe used to call his congregation "a group of pigs" all the time!

Everyone had pierced ears. When first pierced, a string was put through the hole. After one or two weeks, the string was replaced with a small sliver of bamboo. The bamboo piece size increased until it could take an earring made out of pith, which was light as a feather.

Ladies wore their hair in a stylized kind of knot on top of their heads.

Children's clothing was like their parents or none.

There were no surnames given at birth. A child was given a first name, and the parents' names were changed to: "Mother/Father of (child's name)"

Jean carrying her "Uma's" baby on her back

They made Chinese Prayer leaves out of an Agapanthus-type leaf and wrote prayers on the leaf with a very fine stylus. When the leaf was dry, the prayer was then permanent. Many years later, I remember showing the prayer leaves to a children's group at the Junior Friends of the Library meeting in Menlo

Park. Upon seeing my leaves, one little boy exclaimed, "Good Heavens, Buddhist Prayer Leaves. I haven't seen any of those for years." I laughed and laughed since he was only about nine years old. Those leaves were also, apparently, a part of his history.

Jean dressed like the villagers.
Alice carrying water

This starts to describe the kind of lives surrounding us. Everybody kept their own names when they married so that you were somebody's daughter, or father, or mother of somebody. My dad was called, "Fauling Gaught" since "Gaught" was the best they could do with GALT.

The native people lived in houses with permanent poles that were treated so the white ant would not eat them. The rest was bamboo and thatch. Bamboo used for walls and floors, and roofs were made of thatch. Their houses were built on stilts so that rain and other water would run right under them. When finished with a meal, they would part the bamboo thatch floor and dump the garbage down below where chickens and other animals would eat.

When it came time for spring housecleaning, or if the house got too dirty or awful, they just tore it down and burned it! Out to the jungle they then went to cut down more of what they needed to rebuild.

They dried their clothes by sticking them through hanging bamboo poles.

Most people tilled their own little vegetable plots. A five-day market traveled from village to village where they could buy the basic commodities indigenous to that area. A smooth spot was selected where merchants and locals displayed their wares. There was also intervillage training for dyeing handmade cotton material, making mats out of elephant grass and other trades.

Market Day

When the five-day market came to town, it was a big deal. All our goods and necessary items were bought from there. No just running down to the nearest supermarket every time you ran out of something. Some of our supplies came less often and were packed in by horses and mules. Imports like kerosene and gas from Burma and Siam took six months to reach us.

Industry, Education and Language

Home industries, farming of rice, vegetables, and fruits, Betel nut.

Betel nut was a nut used fresh, dried, or cured by boiling, baking or roasting. The Betel nut can be used in a manner similar to the western use of tobacco or caffeine.

There were no Tai schools. The Chinese were rebuilding schools, mostly elementary. Girls were not educated. School was not compulsory.

The language had forty-six characters, eight different tonal sounds. When we spoke, the people were polite and never corrected us.

Dr. and Mrs. Galt with Chinese magistrate
and his wife

All the missionaries spoke Tai. My father also spoke some Chinese for medical and business purposes.

Government

Our area was close to Thailand, Laos, and Burma, leaving the local people more influenced by those tribal ways and customs. The Chinese government people were there to be Governors and spoke different languages. Since it was not their language, when sent to govern somebody, they did not speak Tai.

The government where we lived was three pronged.

One: At the edge of town, a compound housed the central government people. The Chungpai, the Governor (magistrate) for that compound area, was sent from the North (Shanghai) down to our area. He was Chinese, married and spoke his Chinese language, not Tai, the language we learned to speak. This magistrate from the North had his own school for his wife, his concubines, and his children. We were invited often to their Chinese feasts and theatre presentations. The Chungpai's Chinese wife became interested in the sewing ability of my mother. She and my mother interacted occasionally. She loved and was fascinated by mother's sewing machine. Mother taught her how to sew and gifted her with the sewing machine before we left. The wife shed many, many tears of gratitude for that lovely gift

Then there was the ethnic Tai Lu, a tribe with whom we lived. The Chou-Pha was the hereditary priest of heaven, the liaison between the local people and the government. He collected the taxes and turned them over to the Magistrate, the ruler from the North. We got to know them quite well because the Yamen lived about a quarter of a mile from the station.

Third: Each village also had a headman, Yamen, responsible for the procedure of the local inhabitants in the village under his control.

The headman was an elected representative of Central Government, a fluent person who collected taxes and took care of any civil problems, the governor of rice fields and villages. The money was silver coins with no paper money. Barter system was also used.

Family, Religious Life, and Health

Marriage: Strings of dry beetle worn around wrists was the traditional gift. The headman of the village performed the marriage ceremony.

Divorce: There were few divorces, most just left. Crime: Mostly petty. Criminals were executed. Playtime: Thai liked boat races, fireworks, and games.

Religious Traditions: Our Christian traditions, Easter and Christmas and holidays like Thanksgiving, were celebrations that were changed to suit local customs. Priests blessed rice fields. Animists and Buddhists coexisted. Animists believe that nature is alive, that all things have a spirit or soul. This includes animals, plants, rivers, mountains, stars, the moon, etc. Buddhists do not believe that the Buddha is a god, but that he is a human being who has woken up and can see the true way the world works. They believe this knowledge totally changes the person. Some say this puts them beyond birth, death, and rebirth. Every village had a temple where boys who were schooled lived. They had prayers two times a day. Temple had a two-foot wall and no seats.

Worshippers were mostly women who brought rice and fruit as offerings: people were neurotic about evil spirits.

Food: Each family had its own rice field and vegetable patch and ate pigs, chickens, ducks (no beef as cows were sacred), eggs, beans, Kai (moss), mangoes, apples, bananas, tangerines, oranges, and potatoes. Caravans from the south carried salt, cotton, tea, deer horns. Two or three carriers (people) brought these goods. Dogs were plump, well treated and well fed. They were part of the families and ran about freely.

Houses were made up of bamboo trees used for posts (permanent) and elephant grass. All helped with the building of a house. A ladder was used for stairs to the front room and sleeping rooms where they slept under dark blue moss netting.

We were home schooled in China and did not need much supervision. We had the entire outdoors for our play area in the missionary compound. Each of us had our own pony or horse. We went down to the river and made non-collapsible caves in the sand, climbed trees and threw rocks without the fear of any breaking windows. We played with the native children and spoke Tai like natives. So, years later, I reflected that one of the most difficult adjustments when Harry and I were raising our own children was sending them to an established elementary school and living in a "tightly populated" area, Suburban Park in Menlo Park, CA.

There were eight babies born to the three families during that tour of duty. I was among the oldest born there and left China when almost twelve. My parents were there almost fourteen years with only one furlough back to America during that time.

Jean (3 ½) and Allan (2) Galt in
Alexandria Nebraska during the furlough
year 1928-1929

Leaving China on Furlough, 1928

Our family of four at that time, Alice and Corny not yet
born, started for America in October 1928. We went for
dental work, visits to my parent's families, and for Dad to
further his education. This was our first trip back to
America. I was almost three years old, and my brother
was two years younger. We each were carried out in a
Haam. The rains were heavy, and the going was rough.
One of our carriers slipped and fell – but being strapped
in, no harm was done to me. I did beg to ride with my
father, whose horse also was not doing well. He let me.

(My dad wrote quite thoroughly about the furlough in the Mabel Galt biography (earlier in this book.)

I remember Mother had some dental work done in Bangkok. On a small freight, we made it up to Hong Kong. From Hong Kong, we went via Shanghai and Japan to Seattle. From Seattle, WA, we came down the west coast into California to Hughson, CA, a city in Stanislaus County and part of the Modesto Metropolitan Statistical Area. We came to spend Thanksgiving with the Galt family there.

City of Hughson.1F1FMotto: A Small Community with a Big Heart

China Memories

As you can imagine, my early childhood was vastly different from what most Americans have experienced. I was born in China, December 27, 1925, and lived there almost twelve years before we left the village and came back to America. I grew up in a three-family, Presbyterian mission compound where each of the three families had their own home and where the children were raised and schooled by their own parents. My youngest sister Corney was only four months old when we left China. If my parents disciplined us in any way, they didn't make a scene of it. The disciplinarian was the person who, at the time, felt the need to discipline. The discipline was usually very benign, like being banned from playtime with friends and forced to stay inside. We were never spanked or hit even though I'm sure there were circumstances where it might have been the appropriate thing to do. I remember us a tight-knit family unit with parents who loved each other in a wonderful way, leaving me no time to not feel loved, protected, and safe in this strange world. The protection I felt as a child carried on after we left China. As a family, we were totally blessed!

A runner delivered our mail. The nearest Post Office was six days away. Mail from the states took three months to reach us. First class mail came regularly. When a pack full of mail was gathered, they would bring it to us. When it arrived, it was like Christmas in July!

Caravans Coming Through

Hearing the gongs begin way far away in the distance, followed by dogs yelping, were signals of caravans coming through. They brought salt, potatoes, money (silver coins), anything from the North. Every once in a while, you saw one man come by with an incredible load on his back. Always in his load were slippers – shoes made out of some kind of grass. He had fifty-seven pairs of slippers. Wherever he went, he'd find a discarded shoe. He often reached back for another pair to put on before continuing on to where he was going. Those were the people from the North. Most of our people went barefoot. We children always went barefoot, and our feet became tough as leather.

One day, I was looking through one of our magazines and read, "Try our Lux Soap. It is ...," a description was given. I thought, 'Oh man, that sounds really good.' Asking for mother's help, I wrote down my name and address and told what I liked about Lux soap, sent it off and waited for a little box of soap flakes to arrive. The box arrived, and I still have that almost 100-year-old box that contained the soap flakes. The box now holds the silver belt we brought home from China.

Silver Belt

I still have the belt (at least eighty years old) made in China by the husband of our washerwoman. All the pieces are detachable so you can build the size you need. It fluctuates as you do.

I also have a cloisonné necklace given to me by Dr. Esther Morse who was stationed in Northern China. She came down by herself on mule to visit my parents. My parents and Dr. Morse had been in school together. Because the necklace is very tarnished and fragile, I have yet to find a jeweler who will clean it.

My mother's sister, Aunt Nel, used to send the funny papers third class along with all kinds of marvelous stuff. She understood what "far away" meant. And here you were worrying about these poor children growing up in the wilds without any kind of culture.

A church in Evanston, IL adopted our mission and sent Christmas boxes. We never knew if it was meant for Christmas past or the one coming up! It didn't matter. The first introduction I had to Mickey Mouse, created, and introduced in 1928, was from a shirt that came in a care package from Illinois. I decided that is why missionaries have so many children – they pass all the clothes around to share. Besides, there is not much else to do, anyway.

Jean's Baby Doll with Bad Spirit repelling cap for baby
Silver belt and opium Pipe

Potatoes

Potatoes were bought in bulk and stored in the attic. When we kids came of age, our job was to sit up in the attic and remove the eyes from the old potatoes. When they sprouted, we were to remove all the sprouts, the eyes, and toss out the rotten ones. We had a good view from the attic and whenever Joey Beebe walked by, we would pelt him with rotten potatoes and make him cry. We were not nice at all, kid stuff. Mr. Beebe was the minister and liked to preach. When we took our baths in the laundry tubs, we pretended we were preacher Beebe by slicking back our hair and preaching like Mr. Beebe. There was not the closeness of our family with the Beebe family as there was with the Goodenbergers.

Medical Supplies

My father ordered all his medical supplies and equipment from London two years in advance of delivery. We could hardly contain our excitement when we heard the approaching caravan with the medical supplies and other ordered goods. Most important to us kids, were the funnies that were sent along with all the things ordered from Montgomery Ward Catalogues. Tinned items, such as butter and flour, all came from New York. Not many, but some of the things came from Bangkok. Everyone learned to study the catalogues in May and order in June, to hopefully receive the goods sometime before Christmas. Although we went barefoot most of the time, we had shoes for special occasions. There were times we outgrew our shoes before new ones arrived. All mail and catalog orders arrived at the station by mule caravan at least three months after ordering, if not more. Since no TV, phones or electricity existed, this was our only communication with the rest of the world.

Sometimes, my brother and I went up to the hospital that was situated about a half block from our house. Due to the heat, the windows were usually kept open. That is where we sat to watch Father do his work, including surgery. Of course, we were sentenced to silence, not one peep! I know it doesn't sound very sanitary, but the patients needed to feel as comfortable as possible so they would come to receive help when necessary.

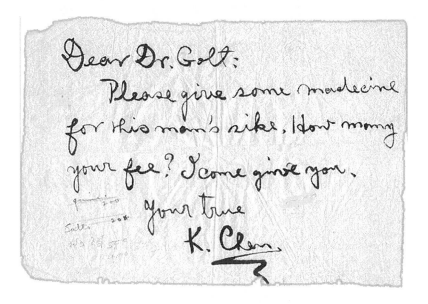

A note from one of the patients

Although it was comforting for them to see Dr. Galt, the surrounding physical area resembled a dungeon and needed to be made as comfortable as possible. Most of their comfort level came from the way my dad treated them, letting them know what was going on every step of the way. He chose his helpers from former patients who learned a great deal from his teachings.

A note about the man pictured above

This is a man that Curtis took cataracts off his eyes, he was blind in one eye, and almost " " the other one this was taken after he was well, and Curtis had gotten the glasses for him from Dr Patton at Omaha Nebr. that is his son and a part of their native village

Dr. Galt was given a foot pedal machine, instruments, and a tutorial for dentistry. One time, mother had a bad tooth. He set up the machine in the schoolroom and the kids knew it was a major event. Al and I peeked in. Besides the whirring of the machine, we heard mother cry. Daddy had no choice but to extract the infected tooth. Thank goodness afterwards, she was her "good ol' self" again.

The way people in our area of China did things was very ingenious. Because they didn't know what was coming down the pike, they made do and came up with creative solutions. Somehow, they devised a method for printing their own pictures, much like a printing press. Luckily, we still have somewhat faded but viewable photos that they printed themselves.

School

There were no native schools for the local people. Many of the boys who wished an education, went into the priesthood. They lived in the temple, wore the robes of the priest, and learned reading and writing.

Memories of China are many, but one of my first was being taught the Calvert Course, a correspondence grammar school course out of Baltimore that focused on the arts, reading, writing and arithmetic. Pencils, papers, rulers – everything was provided. Mother became both mother and teacher. From approximately 9:00 am to 12 noon each day, no matter what balking I did, nor tears I shed, learning came first. I loved to "high-brow" my dad at lunch with stories and myths and even some science that his education lacked.

The things I learned at my mother's knee from the Calvert Course are just mind-blowing. That course was definitely another *cookie*. I took advantage of all I could learn. The Goodenberger children were homeschooled by their mother as were the Beebe children. Every day of every week, we had to write something. Writing was easy. I had great music to listen to and books galore, most of which were part of the Calvert Course. I had to learn and recite poetry. I don't recall other people having learned poetry like I did.

Recently on a cruise with Kathy and Milena, we met Billy Collins, a two-time poet laureate, and Garrison Keeler. At a poetry workshop, members from the audience were asked to recite favorite poetry. Many of those recited poems I remembered, which brought back fond memories. I have some favorite poems and although I cannot fully recite them beginning to end anymore, I fondly remember them.

My mother did not school the Tai children. They only came to play games with us when invited. I remember one time at around age five, playing "barber shop." The results on this poor, unsuspecting and young Tai child, who thought it might be nice to have hair like a white person, were not lovely. I got in big trouble that resulted in my not being able to leave our little patch of yard for a whole week. Just hearing I couldn't do *that* for a whole week made the punishment difficult to endure.

As children, we walked to the village but never fraternized or mixed in with the local children. They always had to be invited by us to play kick ball or anything.

Health

Common Illnesses included malaria, dysentery, worms, and leprosy. Kidney stones were common, abdominal surgery were rare and there was no OBGYN. Ladies took their soiled garments to the river. In general baths were taken in river or streams that were used also for washing clothes. Quinine medicine was used for fevers. Lepers did as much as possible to be self-sustaining. Families were small and highly valued. If children were adopted there were plenty of wet nurses.

Death was philosophically accepted. Malaria killed many children, who were wrapped in a bamboo mat and buried the day they died. Mourners were hired to wail. Villagers gathered for births, deaths. Spirit house on high stilts was present for offerings.

Malaria was present in our area, and we slept under mosquito netting. When I was born, Mother was sick with Malaria. My brother was born on May 4, 1927, during a horrible monsoon. Several days later, part of the roof tore off and floods of water came down on mother while she was lying in bed with newborn Alan by her side. When Alice was born on August 4, 1931, I remember how excited my brother Alan (three years) and I (five years) were with the brand-new baby. All in all, no major accidents or health traumas that I recall. I don't remember having childhood diseases, so they must not have bothered me much.

Weather

Weather in our part of China was similar to California but hotter during the summer season. We each wore pith helmets outside to protect our heads from the sun. We were at 20 degrees latitude. July through Oct was subtropical with rainy, hot, humid weather and mold. Winters did not go below 40 degrees and were foggy. March was the hot season.

Summer Heat in Mountains

Author Pearl S. Buck often talked about going away during summertime in China because of the heat. As it was in the summer, we too packed up our goods and tents, got the horses and took off for a couple of weeks on a little camping trip up in the mountains where it was cooler. We always picked a time when all of us could go, even though Daddy could not spend the entire number of planned weeks. Because of all the foodstuffs and provisions, we had to bring, the journey going took a full day before we reached our destination. Before summers began, we gathered loose pieces of string, wound them together into a ball we used for baseball up in the cool of the mountains during summer. The bat was a stick with the little knob at the end built to resemble a bat. Every once in a while, someone got in a really good whack that unraveled the ball. Our time was then spent rewinding it and laughing. We also saved old newspapers that were sent to us and turned them into kites.

Dinner with the New Magistrate

We exchanged many wonderful dinners with the new magistrate, Mr. Shi, and his family. The children, myself included, enjoyed the magic tricks put on by the nephew.

Since water was not served with the Chinese meals, Alan and I always brought our canteens full of water. Mrs. Shi really liked my mother. When Mrs. Shi's mother died, Mrs. Shi could only wear cotton during the mourning period. During that time, she gave mother a genuinely nice, heavy silk dress. She was also responsible for me having a silk, coat-trouser Chinese suit. When my baby sister Cornelia was born on December 1, 1935, the Shi family presented her with a complete baby outfit including the spirit-repelling cap that was worn to ward off evil spirits.

The thing that may have pushed this next incident a little bit was that every once in a while, Mother and I were invited for tea. There were times when I could go, and mother couldn't and vice versa. When I went without my mother, the Chinese wife just sat there. She had a son about high school age; I was around eleven. We played, had a good time and were given all kinds of good things to eat.

At the next visit, the Chungpai's wife said to my unsuspecting mother, "I think our son would make a wonderful husband for your daughter." Arranged marriages were a part of that culture. If my mother could have turned white, she would have. As for me, I was terrified. I got out of there and ran home as fast as I could. I know the mother meant it as a compliment, but what a shock. I thought, 'After all, mother DID give her the sewing machine.' I was in no way ready to leave my mother and father, and I don't think they were ready to have me leave their side either!

As soon as Mrs. Goodenberger received her organ, she checked to see if my feet would reach the pedals. At about eight years of age, I could finally reach the pedals of the organ. Mrs. Goodenberger taught me to play just a few simple hymns that I probably played with one hand.

The Banner

The government gave my father a banner that can be translated hero or savior of the people. Here it is in 1936, when young people dressed up in Omaha Nebraska at a church for Daddy's "lecture." The Banner says, Savior of the People 救 (saving) 民 (people).

▲ Omaha, Nebraska, 1936
▼ Jean Holding a banner with a tribute to her father,

My First Music Lesson

When the Goodenberger family left in 1935, two years before we left China, we began to wonder who would play the organ at the Sunday service. No Tai had learned. For a year or more, Mrs. Goodenberger had taught me to play the organ. Mother kept a check on my practicing. Although Mother did not play very much, she had an ear for mistakes in notes and timing and didn't hesitate to call my mistakes. Thanks to the two ladies and to my native ability, I made good progress and still today can play simple pieces. I later continued with piano lessons in Manteca on the baby grand Steinway piano that came with the Manteca house where Daddy had his office.

Dressed up for the Masquerade Ball

When an emergency came while in China that took Mrs. Goodenberger away from the station, I rose to the occasion and played the church organ. This was not an easy assignment since we had folding organs with bellows that had to be pumped by foot all the time. The church organ the best tone but was the most difficult to pump. It did become easier, and the rest of the time I did very well.

Daddy's Church Bell

Curtis and Mabel Galt with their three children: Alice (born 8/4/31), Jean 12/27/25 and Alan (5/4/27) in Kuchingkiang, Yunnan, China. (Later Corny born 12/1/35)

Cornelia's Birth

Cornelia was born December 1, 1935. My dad gathered all of us and said, "I'd like you to come up and meet your new sister." We walked up the stairs into the bedroom where mother was lying in bed holding the baby. One by one, we walked by and looked. My brother said very seriously to my mother, "Where did you find a white baby?" He had only seen Chinese babies and, at eight

111

years of age, had not yet heard the tale of the "Birds and the Bees." I get a good laugh every time I think of that.

Jean holding Cornelia with Alan and Alice.

Friends and Visitors

There was a young Tai woman, a widow, who came to our village with her young son. She was above average in intelligence and in time, became an elder in the church. She was the one who accompanied our family of four to Bangkok when dental work became necessary, looking out for my brother and me. I probably learned a great deal of Tai language, customs, and gossip from her as we washed and ironed clothes side by side. My father handed Corny to her when she was born.

From what I hear, a male visitor from the North who claimed to be a Romanian Consul returning from a term of service in the Chinese Capital, told how his goods and chattels were taken by his carriers. He stayed with us for about ten days. When my father gave me quinine for a fever, fearing malaria, this visitor said that all one needed to do was eat plenty of garlic and throw out the quinine. Later, we learned he became quite sick and, in spite of the good care from our Chinese friends, he insisted on moving out and died the next day. My father always said he perhaps did not use enough garlic.

Mr. Ralph Wells, my father's boss, was another visitor. We did not really have a guest room but made one available by the time he arrived. I guess I told him we had spent most of the past week getting his room ready. He was a jolly fellow and told us kids many stories and showed us magic and tricks.

Mr. Bantli, a Swiss professor, accepted my parents' offer to send down horses and men. He and Mr. Schuller, a German druggist, both from Bangkok, arrived for a three-day visit. Following their stay, they both wrote to say that few places were as far from any water, motor, or rail transportation as our station at Chingrung.

A couple walking around the world stayed with us for a couple of days. They had a windup radio. At age 11, I had a difficult time making any sense of that radio.

When I was about three, there was a revolution, a shooting war across the river between two warring factions. Bullets were whizzing and women and children were evacuated up to the leper colony for a week or so. When Daddy and Mr. Goodenberger went back to see how things were, they were captured and interrogated by the Chinese. Fortunately, being American, they were of the only nationality in good favor of the revolutionaries and held just long enough to have their American status ascertained. They were lucky to get out of there alive.

Pastimes

There wasn't a whole lot to do out where I grew up. No phones, radios, no communication with the outside world. That made us a self-contained unit with lots of activities within the family.

Daddy read to us for hours. We played a game called Rook, listened to records, and danced, read encyclopedias and sewed. Our playmates were the Goodenberger kids and some local children. The Beebe kids were older and kept to themselves for the most part.

Once or twice a year, the various nearby stations got together for festivities. Daddy and I worked hard and loved putting on skits. We were quite the team. Depending on age, we played croquet and touch football. Sometimes a couple of the men took the croquet set and played a game called "Holy pastures" or "Cow Pasture Golf," a mixture of golf and croquet and heaven only knows what else. The adults had also built a tennis court for themselves. Bamboo partitions were moved to accommodate the game areas. We were allowed to play with the native children as long as we let our parents know where we were and when we would return. I'm sure I learned much of the local dialect from those children.

Most of our time was spent studying and doing the work of the day. We often traveled upriver but prepared ourselves for being a "sideshow" for the locals as we passed.

We also had a Victrola. There is hardly a song that touches my heart that I didn't hear on that Victrola they brought to China, along with many, many records. For decades, I have loved Garrison Keillor's "Prairie Home Companion" radio show. Many of their songs are the same early Christian hymns my parents' congregation sang. Music again was a big part of our life. Both my parents sang in the choir at Hastings College, which gave them a whole repertoire of songs to sing. When asked by Sue if I sang, I answered in a very melodious voice, "Ohhh Yesss." Kath says, I instinctively harmonize to music I've never heard before. We children loved being gathered around our parents' feet while they sang. Most of the time, no accompanying music was necessary since they knew the songs. I have no idea what happened to that wonderful machine, our Victrola. It could have been worthless by the time we left or perhaps they gave it to the Chungpai.

Each year my parents gave each other the next volume of the Encyclopedia Britannica, which we devoured! My parents also corresponded with their college friends, the Burkes during all their years in China.

Food

Every two weeks "Cook" bought rice, meat, fruit, and vegetables. He was in charge of bringing home whatever was needed to prepare our meals. Other necessities were ordered from the Sears Catalog and took many months to arrive. At that time, money meant nothing to me. Our meals were quite simple, dependent entirely on what could be bought at the local market. We raised chickens for eggs and for eating. Rice with plain vegetables of all kinds was our main staple along with greens, pineapple, tangerines, and bananas. Chickens and pigs didn't take up much space to raise, so for meat, we ate chicken and pork. Cows were a sign of wealth and were never killed for food. Every once in a while, for a special occasion, a simple cake was made. Flour, sugar, and cans of butter were sent from New York.

Have you ever seen a rice pounder? It is worked with both the hands and the feet. It is a big bamboo wooden bowl that is sunk into the earth. Dig a hole and step on the end of the rice pounder, which raises it up. Let it go, and it whacks down into the wooden bowl full of recently harvested rice. Step release, step release, and a rhythm is created, pounding the rice. Then the rice is taken out and poured into a great big, round bamboo tray where the hulls are removed. It is something they did with rice that I have never seen duplicated. They then steam the rice inside of bamboo. The membrane that is inside the bamboo encircled the rice. Rice was a part of every single meal.

For the pork, a big pit was dug, and a fire started inside the pit. The pig was slaughtered and suspended over the fire pit. As children, we loved the drama and squeals of the procedure.

We had wells from where we drew water. Since my sister Alice was allergic to cows' milk, we raised both goats and cows for milk. The goats were smelly and were kept as far away as possible in one section of the station.

Missionaries

The three missionaries, especially Mr. Beebe and Mr. Goodenberger, were there to bring religion. All three men had graduated from Hastings College, a Presbyterian college both then and now. Following graduation, they all went to the Presbyterian center in New York to learn the ins and outs of missionary living and giving. Although they were there as doctor, minister, and linguist, that was only a portion of their duties because they were part of the larger group, Presbyterian Missionaries. Many locals accepted the religion and came to church each Sunday. We all set our watches once a week at the prayer meeting.

The church service was conducted by two Presbyterian preachers and sometimes by the missionaries. I still have the hymnal that has my name in the front. Underneath it, Daddy wrote my name in Tai.

I don't think any of the Chinese themselves understood terribly well what Christianity was all about since, when most became ill, they put a little offering in the crook of the tree to whatever God or evil spirit might be affecting them. Whenever there was an eclipse, they went down to the banks of the river with pots and pans, firecrackers and made noise to scare away the dragons that were eating the sun or the moon. The river near the town on the Mekong around where we lived was called, "9 Dragon River." These dragons were apparently doing their thing when an eclipse happened!

When people of that compound died, they had the choice of either a Buddhist or Christian funeral. The local people always stayed at or near a Buddhist temple when traveling. Sometimes a temple was nothing more than a wall.

Family working and playing around the house and animals

Christmas gift exchanging was very foreign to the local people and only took place when everyone got around to it. We had Christmas trees. For our first Christmas, the tree and gifts were set up in the church. I got a bunch of tangerines and a number of cigars throughout the years, which I didn't understand at all. Daddy told me, "You must always remember to look at a gift through someone's heart and not as a gift." They wanted to say "I love you" with a cigar because that was probably all they had to give, according to Daddy, it was the most acceptable gift ever.

My Horse Named Billy

Each of us had our own mode of transportation. My pony was named Billy and my brother's donkey was named, Hunky Dory. My father got permission from mother to name his mule Maude after my mother's sister.

When Alan (two years younger) and I were old enough to ride horses on the level parts of the roads, we went for little trips. My father enjoyed my "prattle" as we conversed in both Tai and English.

Jean and her horse

I loved my horse because it was my only way to get from point A to point B. But having your own horse brought responsibilities. After a ride, I wiped my horse down and fed it. I learned so much without ever knowing I was learning anything. It was just how life was. If there were wild animals around to be fearful of, we were not told. I think the wild animals kept farther away from the civilized areas, stayed out in the open spaces where they foraged for food and, therefore, didn't pose a danger for our surroundings.

A Horrid Memory

Each house in the compound was surrounded by younger bamboo that wasn't growing very high. A path for horses and people going down to the river separated the houses. Every once in a while, I heard a funny sound, kind of a ring-a-ling, clanging sound. We asked our parents about that sound and they were reluctant to talk about it until we were old enough. But as it was, what with so many strange sounds around there, the ring-a-ling was the clanging of chains around prisoner's legs and arms as they were being taken down to the river to be shot. From what I heard; justice was swift. There were no courts outside the magistrate. Other than for very petty crimes, the sentence was death by gunshot. We heard them being walked down to the river. Would you like to be a mother or father explaining this to your child?

The Leper Colony

I am not sure how old I was, but on a trip north from Bangkok, we were investigating the possibility of missionaries beginning a leper colony. A packhorse carrying our cots, table, and chairs, became frightened and took to the jungle. The packhorse was found, but not the pack. For the next fourteen nights, we slept on temple floors with very little padding under us. One night a stream of ants awakened us. The ants originated from the oil mother used to anoint my brother Alan's scalp.

The leper colony was about a mile and a half from our station up in the mountains, just a little way across from an exceptionally large creek, making it easy for us to reach. All the houses in the leper colony were on one level, like shelters, so they didn't have to climb stairs. They didn't move much out of their station. Provisions were delivered to them and church was brought to them, but not every Sunday. Occasionally, we took a bible to them. Daddy gave the lepers medical care.

Leper Colony

I went up to the leper colony about once a month and played the organ for them. That was when I was introduced to what lepers looked like, very different from us, some with no hands. Not many mothers wanted their children to be exposed to them. I was never frightened by their looks, nor was it something I had to get used to. I was with my dad, and he was much more solid than God. Daddy explained things to us for as long as we would listen. What we learned from him took away the fear. There was nothing to be afraid of when seeing the disfigured lepers. It is the unknown that is so frightening. Many children, then and even now, don't have the kind of Dad to teach them those kinds of things.

We went to church to worship God, Jesus and all the good things in life. It didn't matter who your audience was since we all worshipped the same God and were living the life that was talked about.

On these trips to the leper colony, my father was always along to provide medical treatment and Mrs. Goodenberger furnished the music. I explicitly trusted both Mrs. Goodenberger and Father and had no reason to question everything they wanted for me. Some of the lepers only had a stump left but were so happy to see us.

Leper Colony

They never rushed forward to hug and welcome us, knowing what the rules were.

I was there to play the organ in the little open-air chapel.

Goodenberger Family Leaves

In 1935 the Goodenberger family left. Goody was taken ill, suffered a nervous breakdown and was carried by Haam to Bangkok. A Haam is a small bamboo stick-like playpen used for transporting the ill or the young and placed on two bamboo poles carried on the shoulders of four men. One reason for his breakdown: like anyone else bound up in a bureaucracy, you have to prove that what you are doing has an end result. In Goody's case, the end result was based on how many souls he saved. It mattered a lot to Goody, but Daddy didn't get caught up in that since it wasn't the main reason why he was there. Daddy was there to minister medically to the local people. We were very close to the Goodenberger children growing up in China. The Goodenberger sons became Presbyterian ministers and their daughter is a schoolteacher.

The following is an amazing coincidence that happened fifty years after the Goodenbergers left China. On one of our trips with my sister Alice and her husband Gordon, we ended up in the Vancouver area. A guide had taken us through a local museum. The guide mentioned that the minister of their town had grown up in China. I quickly asked if his name were John Goodenberger and when she said yes and that he lived here in town, I could feel real excitement building. She contacted him, and he came down to greet us. We had the most wonderful reunion after roughly fifty years. We knew our parents would have been delighted.

Alice and I stayed back with mother while Dad and Alan, who was eight years of age, accompanied the Goodenberger family on their trek out of China. Chingrung station was never to be the same, for our family would soon leave in 1936. We put a plaque at the corner of the Goodenberger's house after they left.

I don't know what happened to the Beebe kids. Their parents had a different outlook on life, and I had a sense my parents were not that close to them.

Going Home

American Missionaries were being told to leave China because of WWII, and specifically, the fighting between the Chinese and Japanese was the reason my parents felt it was time to leave China. It became too dangerous for us to stay. About Christmas time 1935, new missionaries arrived, and we began planning our trip home to America. I was ten years old then and had also completed the Calvert School course that usually takes eight years of regular grammar school to complete. Since I had completed my schooling, the options were to either send me back to a family in the states or to England or India for school. My parents were not open to any of those options.

So, on April 6, 1936, our family headed for the United States. The leaving was sad. Ninety-nine percent of the village escorted us to the Nam Ha Riverbank. It was a stream, not the Mekong River, where we said our goodbyes. Some village people who were carriers went with us. Because she was small and only four months old, Corny was in a Haam. The rest of us were on our own horses. Alice, at three or four years old, rode with someone; she was too small to ride alone. Alan and I were accomplished riders by then and rode our own horses. Dad wrote, "The sun was hot, but the roads were good and the streams, shallow."

We ran into a problem, however, when we stopped by a stream to rest before going up the hills. It was lunchtime and we just sat and relaxed. Then suddenly, we heard the yipping of dogs and soon saw dogs and women running down the hill as fast as they could. While up the hill looking for firewood, the ladies dislodged a beehive, which caused all kinds of havoc. The bees attacked us. We crunched them in our mouths, had them in our ears and under our pith helmets. Once out of danger, we inspected our wounds." I won first prize with eighteen bee stings. Thank God, none of us were allergic to the stings. We went back to a village we had just passed through. They put together a poultice from river moss that seemed to do the trick. Since then, the word "bee" means only one thing to our family!

We first went to Bangkok and visited with my mother's youngest sister Edna who had married a doctor, Horace Whitlock, and lived in the civilized part of China.

From there, we boarded a ship for the trip home to San Francisco. Since I wasn't prone to seasickness and was up and about exploring the ship, I soon came upon the very different world of gambling. A part of the ship was set off for gaming where the grownups played cards, mahjong, poker and games like that. I was rich beyond words with two nickels that burned a hole in my pocket. Another girl and I were fascinated by the one-armed bandits. When the arm was pulled, tinkling money was disbursed. We watched long and hard, only to learn that there were times when you did not win, which made us shudder. Of course, I tried it and, of course, I lost both nickels. That did it for me. I never became a gambler!

Jean (right) and travel friend on the trip to
the United States in 1936.

Curtis and Mabel Galt
(Pictures taken on May 17 and June 1, 1936, when Dr. Curtis M and
Mabel Moore Galt, with Jean, Alan, Alice, and Cornelia visited Dr.
Horace H and Edna Moore Whitlock)
▼ Baby Corney

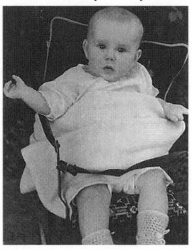

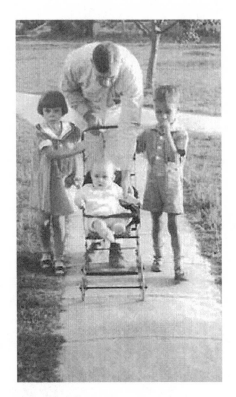

Galt and Whitlock children May 1936: Jean, Alan, Alice, and
Cornelia at the Moon Gate with John Irwin.

One Journey's End

Here, in regard to our leaving China, I would like to quote again the last part of my father's tribute to my mother as it gives a great example of who and how she was and why I, her daughter, am proud to be identified with her.

"Journey's end: We had crossed our last mountain, ferried and forded our last stream, waded our last mud hole. We had dismounted and unsaddled for the last time. We had taken down the mosquito net, folded the cots, rolled up the bedding and packed the food and pan basket for the last time. Farewell to pith hats, to burning sun, to lukewarm, smoky-tasting boiled water, meager meals, candles, and lanterns, to horses and haams. All these were now behind us. Altogether I have watched Mabel travel the caravan trails of China, Burma, and Siam for more than one hundred days. To her, burning sun, frosty nights, mountain rocks, and jungle mud were all part of the game. She has slept on bare board beds in Chinese inns, on concrete Buddhist temple floors, and on cots in stables, in tents and under the stars. She has put up and taken down beds late at night and early in the morning. She has eaten lunches standing or sitting on a rock, and suppers surrounded by dozens of curious people. She has retired and risen with the same eager audiences. She has nursed and changed babies by the roadside and washed their clothes in the streams. She has been hot, hungry, thirsty, dirty, and tired. There were no toilets but the woods, no baths but the streams. Sunburn, windburn, saddle sores, bee stings; she has known them all, yet I can truthfully say that never once have I heard her complain. Fellow traveler: I salute my Superior!"

Mission Philosophy

I once asked my parents how they could be the kind of Presbyterians (or Methodists) or just Christians and have enough faith to go out as missionaries to the Orient.

Daddy, who was always very pragmatic about things said, "Well, you know, it is really interesting. There are certain things that you believe in your heart that are probably better left in your heart. If you cannot translate what you believe into actions rather than words, well then, you shouldn't bother. It doesn't make any difference how I believe, theologically. What I set out to do, I was able to do because of my medicine. We lived out there long enough to come to the absolute conclusion that we may not have been 100% right. The locals had their traditions and beliefs, and there were lots of things they incorporated into their lives that I considered to be really quite brilliant and I think made them better. So, who are we to impose this very strict theology or doctrine or dogma on somebody who most probably would have a very difficult time understanding it."

Daddy often said he thinks he became more a Buddhist than he left them Christians.

My nephew Steven, now head of the Philosophy Department at Rice University in Houston, had this observation because of my upbringing in China:

"One of the biggest impressions that I have of Jean originated from the stories my mother Alice would talk about

their time as children in China. My mother was born there and was young when the family returned to California, but she would often sit with me and point to pictures of that time in one or another of the albums that she carefully preserved. Jean, of course, was there in those pictures, a good bit older than my mother, and Alice would tell me how Jean always seemed like one of the "grownups" even then. Not surprising, then, that she naturally became the matriarch of the Galt clan with the passing of my grandmother, Mabel. She was born to the role."

—Steven Crowell

…and in Jean's words,

"Just by being near the right action was how we learned that our parents were good people. It was quite easy to love them. They never spoke badly about anyone. We learned to be kind and to give back. You learn a lot based on the people you spend time with. "

"I remember some funny things. But of long conversations of the past or details about things we did, I only remember little patches here and there. It is frightening what I have forgotten. I can't honestly remember a single moment when I was bored. My mother said, "To be bored is an insult to yourself." I believe this to be true. Boredom is something I have never known. It follows then, to seize the moment!"

—A Favorite Saying

This Clan is Your Clan

This includes excepts from This Clan is Your Clan a photo album and brief history from a 2007 gathering of the descendants of Curtis and Mabel Galt. Photographs by Annie Kuzminsky, Ken Galt, and Rebecca Galt East. [2]

[2] For additional copies of the original book, This Clan is Your Clan, A Gathering of the Descendants of Curtis and Mabel Galt, please contact Rebecca Galt East Rebeccageast@gmail.com or (714) 447-4123. Bremen, GA 30110.

Curtis met Mabel at Hastings College in Nebraska. They married in the early 1920's and went off on life's adventure together. First to Puerto Rico to study tropical medicine, then to China to work with those afflicted with tropical diseases. While in China, they had four children, Jean, Alan, Alice, and Corny. This in and of itself was quite a feat, considering the primitive conditions and absolute lack of any sort of creature comforts. The children didn't seem to mind and were taught and nurtured by their parents.

At the threat of World War II, Curtis and Mabel returned to the States and settled in Manteca, California where Curtis was town doctor for many years. The children all completed their schooling there, went off to college, and got married. Among the four of them, they produced 15 grandchildren of Curtis and Mabel and those grandchildren have, in turn contributed an additional 23 offspring, carrying the family legacy.

The 2007 reunion had many more participants and a whole new generation to welcome to "the clan!"

2009 Galt Clan

Jean Galt Coblentz is the oldest of Curtis and Mabel's four children.

Kath (Jean's oldest) was happy to re-connect with family members after having spent so many years in Italy.

Jean listens intently to what Alice had to say about Curtis and Mabel.

Jean married Harry Coblentz. They had four children, Kath, Janis, Marty, and Scott. Her family was well represented at the reunion with oldest daughter, Kath and her daughter Milena in attendance. Scott, friend Jolene Harlos, and daughter Stacy attended, as well as Stacy's mother, Karen. Harry's presence was missed by all.

Marty's son Chris rounded out the Coblentz guest list. Milena made a special trip from Milan, Italy to get to know her American side of the family even better. Unable to attend were Marty, his wife Laurie, daughters Trina and Jessica and Scott's daughter Kelly.

Jean spoke about her experiences as a child in China, and as a teenager in Manteca. She fondly recalled the relationship with her parents and siblings and remarked about how well they all had stayed close to one another throughout their lives.

Kath (Jean's daughter), her daughter Milena, and Alan Moore Galt (center) talk at the reunion.

Alan Moore Galt was second of the four children to be born in China. As the only boy among three sisters, he had to fend for himself a lot. All four of Alan and Wanda's children, Janet, Rebecca, Kenny, and Cynthia, attended the reunion. Cynthia's entire family came. They are husband Peter, and sons Peter, Matthew, and David.

They live in Fresno, California. Ken, wife Gin and daughter Erika live in Rocklin, California. Erika could not attend. Janet and husband Tom and children Amanda and Chris live in Corte Madera, California. Rebecca's

137

husband Allan was at the reunion, but their daughter Elaine could not attend. They live in Fullerton, California. Alan told the gathered clan about the very close bonds his ·parents had to each other by reading a passage from Curtis' autobiography.

Several nieces and nephews commented that it was the most they had ever heard Uncle Al say all at once!

It was a delight to all.

Alice chatting with granddaughter Charlotte Kuzminsky.

Alice Griggs, the third of Curtis and Mabel's children, spoke about the guidance and love of her parents as a child growing up and how those lessons had served her well as a parent. The main elements being firmness and fairness. She mentioned that she learned a lot about sibling relationships by watching older sister Jean and brother Alan interact with each other. Alice attended with husband Gordon and three of her five children (Steven, Katie, Annie, Karen, Richard) made it to the reunion. Annie Kuzminsky and husband Larry made the trip from San Diego, California with children Steven, Charlotte, and Jack. The boys were glad to see other boys their age at the party. Karen and Gary Wagner made it from Manhattan Beach, California but their two boys, Curtis and Philip had other commitments. Richard and Alison Crowell from Pacific Palisades, California and their oldest daughter Nora enjoyed the day, but daughter Jessica was unable to attend.

Cornelia (Corny) Galt, the youngest of Curtis and Mabel's children, married Jack Leach. They had two children, Eric, and Allison. Eric and his family, wife Lisa and sons Alexander and Maxx, attended the reunion from their home in Ransom Canyon, Texas. Alison resides in Modesto and attended with her friend Wade.

Jack and Corny's performance provided the setting and organization for a perfect day. The icing on the cake was the live entertainment with enthusiastic participation from the gathered clan.

Bruce Galt, cousin of Jean, Alan, Alice, and Corny attended the reunion with his wife Ann, and his grandchildren. They made the trip from Burbank, California. Bruce and Ann have forged a close relationship with their generation of Galt siblings, and they were pleased to get to know a large portion of the rest of the extended family.

Galt Family: Mabel, Curtis and the two older children
Jean and Alan.

"Don't be afraid to ask for help when you need it: That's what smart people do."

—A Favorite Saying.

Life Continues After China

After growing up in a remote area of South China where horseback was the means of transportation, seeing Bangkok as we were leaving China, full of neon lights, traffic, crowds of people, strange noises, electric lights, and movies was such an overload that nothing I have seen since has had the same emotional impact!

From Hughson, California we traveled by train to Alexandria, Nebraska for Christmas. Come the First of February, we moved to Omaha, Nebraska, where my mother, Alan and I kept house while Dad did post-graduate work in medicine. At age three, I amazed my Sunday school teacher by what I could learn at such a young age. In April we took Grandma Moore on a trip to Ohio where we visited mission-minded people who dubbed Alan, "Perpetual Motion."

Visiting Grandma Moore for a Year

After returning from China in 1936, we lived with Grandmother Moore, a widow in Alexandria, Nebraska. Did we let Grandma Moore know much in advance that we were coming or even ask permission? Probably not, since from China it took thirty days for mail to be received in America and more than thirty days to get an answer back to China, though there must have been a way for emergency information to be transmitted.

Three of Grandma Moore's six daughters lived with her and then my mom came home with her four children. Wow! Dad went to the University of Nebraska Medical

School to get caught up in order to take the state boards. Alexandria, Nebraska, was a very small town of about 500. There was only one bank in town, started by Grandfather Moore. So, we lived with Grandma Moore, a wonderful little lady, in the house where all her six daughters were born. Poor Grandma, I didn't realize how difficult it must have been for her. With six children, daughters at that, she grew her own vegetables and had her own chickens out in back that she slaughtered now and then. Grandma was everything a grandma should be. She was quiet, short, and funny. We four kids from China had a million things to learn, and she was the perfect teacher. The whole world there was different.

My mother's second sister Hazel never married and

Missionary Sisters: Edna and Mabel (left)

lived at home. Edna, the youngest, later married and went to North China. Another sister became a math teacher and taught at a local college. Maude lived at home and ran the bank. While we were in China, Aunt Maude, the oldest sister, was the person who gathered up the funny papers and sent them to us, which we received about three months down the line with great delight.

Moore sisters Edna and Mabel (center)
and their families.

Moore sisters in 1970: Mabel M. Galt, Edna M Whitlock, Nellie Moore, Blanche M Kroll.

So, here is Grandma Moore, who has lived in peace and harmony for all these years, saddled with another daughter and four grandchildren. My brother and I were the oldest and walked about two and a half blocks to school every day. We kids slept up in the attic, and when Nebraska got hot, Aunt Hazel came up with a sprinkling can and sprinkled us. I don't know how they stood it with all those children around. I never heard a cross word.

The only time I saw anything that looked like "being pushed to the brink" was the time when I pushed my mother a little too far. I wanted to do something, and my mother said, "No." My mother never raised her voice, but she said this "No," loudly. I was sitting on the steps and then went downstairs and said, "You're an old meanie," something I think I picked up from the cartoons, where a secretary said that to her boss. With that, my mother slapped me across the face and turned her back. She said, "You had my answer." Obviously, I did not get to do what I wanted. She never struck anybody.

At around age twelve or thirteen, I had tonsillitis and was sent to a hospital in Omaha for my tonsillectomy. The day after my surgery, the surgeon walked in saying, "Well, how are you doing? How are you feeling? Have you had any food today?" I responded loudly, "I am just fine, and I'll have my regular breakfast." No one told me it would hurt terribly to eat regular food. I told my mother I wanted roast beef and mashed potatoes that night for dinner when I returned home from the hospital. She cut up my roast beef into little, tiny pieces. I couldn't eat it – just couldn't. Since I thought I could eat and do anything, this came as quite a surprise.

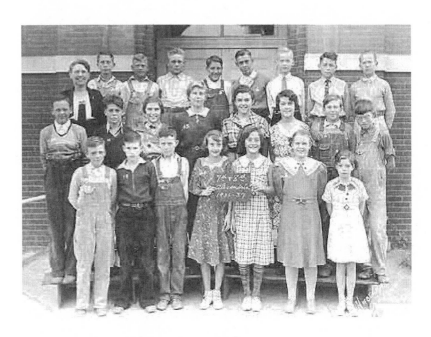

7th & 8th Grade Alexandria in 1936-1937. Jean Galt is front row
second from the right.
(left to right starting with back row)

1. Mrs. Seward
2. Gerald Nelson
3. Gerald Baruth
4. Eldon Harrold
5. Marlyn Huber
6. Gerald Mulvey
7. Paul Cone
8. Bill Thompson
9. Eugene Bawden
10. John Marland McClure

11. Billy Martin
12. Helen Blaum
13. Mary Hazel Taylor
14. Winifred Jacque
15. Leota Jean Thatcher
16. Samuel Summers
17. Marvin Thatcher
18. Fay Ross
19. La Verne
20. James Cortney
21. Neola Joe
22. Ruth Harrold

23. Jean Galt
24. Nellie Ross

While in Omaha, I was also taken to see the opera
Carmen. Imagine an opera being my first musical. I also
met the family I had been corresponding with for four or
five years through Child Life, a young person's
publication, kind of like a pen pal. We went to their house
for lunch, where I encountered my first artichoke.
Following lunch, they introduced me to all the kids who
were at the picnic. It was quite a day what with so many

new things to experience. We played croquet and other age-appropriate games. We stayed in touch for a few more years and then lost touch.

I learned to sew while staying with Grandmother Moore that year after China. Fortunately, she was a kind and loving teacher like my mother. Later when I was a mother, I made all my children's clothes and mine as well until I started working full time, which was when my kids were almost out of high school or in college. I taught both my girls how to sew and they still remember the fun of picking out fabrics and patterns (Butterick, Vogue, Simplicity and McCalls come to mind.)

One vivid memory of that first year in Nebraska was having my new bike stolen from the schoolyard, a dreadful event for any child.

Parents

Here at Grandma Moore's, my brother and I had our first allowances of $.25 a week. We were taught to balance our expenses and produce the number of pennies left over after all outlays had been accounted for. A sobering experience.

Because of the opportunities offered to my parents at Hastings College, I came from a more diverse background than most of the kids with whom I later went to school. I was too young at the time to appreciate what that really meant, but knew I had an advantage due to the Calvert School of learning and teachings from my mother. I learned everything one needed to know about English. Today, the Calvert School of Home School teaching is still going strong, especially a favorite for overseas families wishing to homeschool their children.

Mom and Dad were phenomenal. I never heard a cross word spoken between the two. It didn't matter what the circumstance was or whose fault it was, I never heard an argument. I also don't remember hearing the words, "I love you" being spoken, but we all felt that special bond between them and between them and us kids

Once back in America, I saw how other families interacted. It was like having cold water splashed in my face. I wondered, "How could they talk to each other like that?" My parents used their great sense of humor. There was always a lot of laughter. Till the day he died, Dad thought mother the greatest person who had walked the earth. No reference during my childhood was ever made about the time when mother was so very sick with fever when she delivered me.

The story from Mabel's bio follows:

"My mother, very ill from malaria with a temperature of about 106 degrees F., went into labor and delivered me on December 27, 1925. I was born without too much difficulty but there followed an intense ten-minute period when I refused to breathe. Daddy stated, "Efforts to establish respiration were successful and from then on, everything was fine." The new routines of diaper changing, heating water for bottles and changing my clothes and bedding two or three times a day soon became normal, the drudgery of those chores dimmed by the thrill of having me, their first child."

In periods of reflection, after both my parents died, I was left with a huge sense of gratitude. I can't even imagine what I would be like, how I would have turned out, what I would have thought important or how I

would have reacted to life, had a different set of parents been mine. I incorporated what my parents gave me into my own life—things like my moral basis, my sense of humor, my love for music and my character. I was given a start, and like with anybody who gardens, if you put the right plant in the right place and keep it watered and fertilized, in the end you will get the best. But if you neglect it, perhaps put it out in a corner where it gets too much sun or forget about it, the results will not be as positive. Who I am is a compilation of many things that include how my parents treated me and what they left me. My parents did not lecture us at all but rather, set an example. I wanted to BE like them. They were wonderful examples and role models, though I knew I would never want to become a medical missionary. Luckily, that possibility never materialized.

I also loudly stated, one day that I knew I did not want to marry a farmer and be a "hick" from Nebraska

Those two things I knew! Yes, it is good to know what you don't want to be while life's journey helps you find what you do want to do.

Jean, age 16 ½

If I were an apple, I did not fall far from my mother's tree. It seems that she was also known for her insatiable curiosity. If she did not know an answer or wanted more information, she had an uncanny talent for finding answers in books, the "go-to" medium of her day. My children all remember the dictionaries we had in every room of the house and in each car. When they asked me the meaning of a word, I sent them to a dictionary to look up a definition of the word and share the meaning with the rest of the family.

Manteca

When Dad completed his advanced studies and graduated in 1937, we left Grandmother Moore's house. My parents decided to come to California since the people Dad interned with, Dr. and Mrs. Burke, had opened a practice in Alameda, California. Nothing had been said about how Grandma Moore was holding up with the addition of our family to her already established household. My parents just decided to take all their belongings and children and head for California. We were on our way to the Burke's but stopped at a drugstore along the way because my brother who had not had breakfast said he was going to die if he didn't get something to eat. Dad crossed the railroad tracks, arriving in Manteca, California and found a drugstore where he said he wanted to buy something to feed his son. He bought him a candy bar and inquired of the clerk if he knew of any doctor in the area wanting to sell his practice. The guy said, "Matter of fact I do. He's two blocks down there." In three hours, the decision was made, and Dr. Galt was the new doctor in town. We were going to live in Manteca, a definite *cookie* for Dad. Manteca was a small San Joaquin Valley town about ten miles from the town of Hughson where his father and several brothers had opened a bank, a hardware store, and a newspaper office.

Family in Manteca

Our family settled in Manteca where I first attended junior high school. Since my education from the Calvert course was so mixed, the powers that be thought it best for me to start in 7th grade to make sure I belonged there. I completed junior high in short time and went over to high school where I excelled. If you go to a place where you've already been and if you paid attention at all and were interested in what you were being taught, your mind will soak it up like a sponge.

Manteca was another world, a definite *cookie* for me. The things I did and the lessons I learned were really ones I had never thought of … like being a newspaper stringer (freelance journalist) for a year from which I learned a lot or being able to play every sport offered at Manteca High, at that time.

Mom was super smart and knew more about my dad than he did. He would never have signed anything without first talking it over with her. When the Manteca opportunity arose, I'm sure she asked a lot of questions and got a lot of answers. Both were probably happy about the whole thing. She became civic-minded and worked at the library. Both were very active in the local Manteca community.

We went to a protestant church where Dad became a member of the vestry, and we children who were old enough, attended Sunday school. Dad was also involved with both local and state medical groups.

Dad ending up in Manteca made it possible for many *cookies* to be offered me. With only seventy-five in my high school graduating class, I was not up against much competition. I loved doing everything and took advantage of the following: volleyball, basketball, speedball, tennis, ping pong, school plays—anything. I had opportunities galore to do everything, which most kids did not. I also was involved with the school newspaper, on the yearbook staff and President of Girls League.

The background of some of the students did not allow them the opportunities I had had. Coming from China, everything was new; I wasn't pushed by anyone to do anything. I was curious, had a fighting spirit and wanted to take advantage of every opportunity. If it didn't include murder, I think my folks were really tickled with everything I latched onto.

Mother was very interested in writing and was a very good writer. She loved poetry, and we talked about it. I thank her for that. She never said anything in public that might put any person in a bad light. She was also very humorous and funny, quick with answers. I recognized all her wonderful qualities early in my life – perhaps because in China, she was not only my mother but also my teacher. Throughout my life, I could hardly wait to see what she would say on any topic. How exceptional was that relationship!

Sewing

Mother made all my clothes, including my wedding dress, which I still have. She was a great companion and teacher too when it came to my learning how to sew, and as she continued to guide my sewing into an area of expertise. We were friends and spent a lot of time sewing together, making all our clothes. Alice and I were both taught how to sew by Mother. I made all my clothes when we lived in Manteca. The ironing board and everything was always set up.

She was a wonderful teacher who never got mad but was always cheerful and funny and fun to work with. She never criticized my sewing, even if it was awful. There was no such thing as a mistake, just a particularly good way to learn!

Mother was a home economics teacher who didn't like to cook. We laughed about that. Nevertheless, she taught us to cook. We, kids, took turns cooking, but mother was always there.

Friends and Suitors

During high school, most of my friends were boys. I had only one romance, which didn't continue into college. He was Student Body President and his entry in my 1942 Tower yearbook took up two pages, signing off with, "Thanks again for all you have done for me. You treated me swell. You are the best girl I'll ever have – no fooling!" Near my senior year, I attended a church summer camp in the Santa Cruz Mountains where I met my first boyfriend. He was from San Jose, California.

A group of us were sitting at a table where the guy sitting across from me moved aside the flowers on the table saying, "You're cute. I want to be able to look at you." That's how we first met. After camp, he wrote to me every day addressing the envelopes: My Girl.

In those days, the postman knew all the families, making it easier to deliver mail such as this. Time passed, and we invited his parents to drop by if ever in the area. They did! When it was all over, my dad, who is really a sweetheart, said, "Diamond in the rough." That said it all. He could have gone on and on about how they weren't from the same class as we were, but he didn't. He left me to figure it out, which wasn't difficult.

Fortunately, that was one of those romances that faded away. Another suitor before I started Stanford was George Montgomery, who was 6'3", a pilot stationed in Stockton, California. He used to come visit and loved my folks. One time he came to visit me at Stanford and brought along a diamond ring! I thought, "I'm sorry he felt that it had gotten that far." He was very upset but understood when I turned him down. We kept in touch.

Later, when I was employed by Stanford, I got a call from him saying he and his wife were going to be in town. He explained how his wife was still jealous of me and how he thought it a good idea we four meet up for dinner. We did so and had a lovely time. Hopefully, that wiped away her fears.

More High School

For almost all my life up to that point, if I had wanted something, I got it. I had to work for things, but because of the Calvert schooling I received in China, things came easy for me. In high school, if a class wasn't of interest to me, I could take it, get an A and have nothing stick with me following graduation.

Manteca High School was actually another *cookie*, which was a long way from the mission in China. I took every course and test and was in competition only with myself. I was used to winning, and since there wasn't much competition per se at Manteca High School, it all worked out. I perhaps only competed with six people who even thought they might attend college.

A Stanford graduate and teacher of chemistry at Manteca High School, Stanley Hawkins, took a liking to me and said, "You know for a woman, you are going to have to get going in this world. You are going to have to learn how to type and take shorthand and get the most out of everything you can. Don't cheat yourself." He then let me know that he taught a typing and shorthand class on Saturdays that wouldn't earn me credit but would be an invaluable skill to learn. He proceeded to say, "I have been paying attention to the big audience out there and what they want from young women. Shorthand and typing will always be necessary and the first thing those who are hiring will look at." So, of course, this fifteen-year-old junior grabbed at that *cookie* of opportunity. I wanted to do it. The instructor entered the students into typing speed contests, inviting schools from all around to participate and send their best students. I mean, how many people then had somebody pushing them like that or giving them such an opportunity? How else do you know whether you can do something or not? I had to try. Of course, I had to be the fastest and everything. Competition did that to me. I was spurred on and became a lightning-fast typist at 80 words per minute. That opportunity turned out to be another one of the *cookies* of my life. That teacher guided me along, particularly in relation to my college choice. As we talked about college, I told him how I hadn't thought much about it but stated, 'I do not want to go to Hastings College and fall in love with some dumb farmer and live in Nebraska for the rest of my life.' This was said in the presence of my parents who laughed. I'm sure my teacher was thrilled, for that put me one step closer to Stanford, which was where he had his sights set for me.

"*From the mud grows the lotus: Just watch! Often a difficulty becomes a victory.*"

—A Favorite Saying.

Beginning at Stanford

My parents had both gone to Hastings College. There was an unspoken understanding that I would attend college, but Stanford was not a place for which I had been yearning.

Aside from learning the importance of typing and shorthand from my high school science and chemistry teacher, he guided me towards attending Stanford. Actually, I had never heard of Stanford. He was probably responsible also for my receiving a scholarship to Stanford.

Although I don't exactly recall the process he and I had to go through for a scholarship, (which I am sure has changed since then) I trusted him. It seemed to be all his doing. He knew the ropes to pull and whom to contact. He did a great sales job, holding my hand all the way through the scholarship and admitting processes. But since I was working for Kaiser Permanente at the Stockton Depot, a good job that paid well, I told him I felt I was too young at age sixteen to start Stanford. He checked with Stanford to see if I could hold off the scholarship for a year. Stanford officials said, "Yes, no problem."

High School Work

I graduated from high school in 1942. I was fortunate to have a teacher who took such an interest in me and helped me obtain that scholarship to Stanford. I was set!

During my high school years, one of my first paid jobs was working in the local ice cream parlor and also as a "stringer" (like a freelance journalist) for the local newspaper. I wrote stories about what was going on at our high school for them. I also worked for my dad in his office for a very long time. I was like a "Girl Friday" and did everything that needed doing, from keeping the office clean to balancing the books. Although he did not require a +/- money report, I did it anyway. "Old habits die hard." Dad always said, "If you spend all you have, you'll have nothing left to spend." Hence, it was natural for me to cover this area as well. I remember patient visits were $2.50.

I also worked in the cannery and Kraft Cheese factory during summers. The cannery was back-breaking work, having to bend over the conveyor belts that accommodated the shorter Portuguese women. From this experience, I realized how important it was to get good grades so I could go on to receive higher education. I certainly didn't want to do that backbreaking work the rest of my life. The free commute ride to Kaiser Permanente I was offered by a friend helped me save even more money.

My high school work history gave me the opportunity to work for many different kinds of bosses. I learned the value of promptness, how to be clear about duties and balancing books. All of those experiences and duties came in handy when right after high school graduation, I took the job with Kaiser Permanente in Stockton, working in their purchasing department. Anyone who needed anything had to go through our department. Although only sixteen, my typing and shorthand skills pulled me along, as they did partially through Stanford where much of my work was spent using these skills. I will always be grateful to Stanley Hawkins who taught me shorthand and typing.

At high school age, we liked music and had our favorite songs. Vinyl records were the popular music of our time and what we wanted most, so we shared our records to save money. America's participation in World War II started when I was in high school. We lost one of our classmates, which was very sobering. We found it important to have available a number of things we high school kids enjoyed, like records, since we were pretty much homebound. There was no gas for driving into Stockton for entertainment. My dad created a dance floor in the room at the top of our garage and put in a jukebox. It was a wonderful place for kids to dance and have a good time. Next to his bed, Dad had a switch for the lights over the garage that he flicked on and off when it was time for everyone to go home. Most did so right away. They knew if they broke the rules, they would not be able to return. My friends had a great deal of respect for my Dad.

I graduated from high school at age 16 as valedictorian. My father was head of the school board and passed out the diplomas. Daddy was very proud of me. He always liked to say I had my mother's great intelligence!

Now picture this: Graduation night at Manteca High School where many "goodies" including my favorite, chocolates, were offered. I talked so much that by the time I got to the chocolate plate, it was empty. Hindsight says I should have taken that *cookie* when it was passed!

As I mentioned before, I spent that year between my high school graduation and my first year at Stanford, at Kaiser Permanente near the Stockton airfield in the purchasing department and saved my money. Because of my typing and shorthand skills, it was an easy job. Working that year allowed me to pull together quite a college nest egg. My social life consisted of boyfriends from high school and boys from the Air Force Base at Stockton. That appears to have set the tone. I have often stated throughout my life that my best friends have almost always been men.

Had I been older, I might have been tempted to get married but knew perfectly well I wasn't going to marry just then. At that time, many young men around me were doing exactly that. By the time the year was over I was ready for college.

Stanford Life

In September 1943, I matriculated to Stanford. The war was still going on, which made it an entirely different experience. I graduated in 1947 without any debt. Stanford University made it easy for me to be involved in as much as I wanted to be. My parents drove me from Manteca to the dorm, Casa Ventura, the "overflow" dorm.

It was still during the war and more women than men came to Stanford. Roble Hall, where all freshman girls were usually housed, was overflowing. It seemed like the "rich" and freshmen daughters of alumnae were assigned to Roble Hall. My family from Manteca basically had no pull, so I was assigned to the dorm, Casa Ventura. In hindsight I have said, 'It pays to be poor,' as this too turned out to be a *cookie*. Boys were scarce on campus but began coming back after the war during my Sophomore year. Most of the fifty-five women housed at Casa

Ventura had no idea they were chosen for that dorm because they were not socioeconomically the cream of the crop, did not go to the right high schools. Not knowing the campus, I didn't care where I lived as long as I had a place to put my head down. At Casa Ventura, I met some genuinely nice friends. My roommate was Wiz Wiggins, whose mother was so fearful of Wiz losing things, that she put Wiz' name on every item she brought, including bobby pins.

My dad helped me get to know almost everyone in the dorm. It was on the day my parents brought me to Stanford that I learned something about my dad I didn't know before, about how clever he was and how well he could read people.

Dad said to me, "I have a present for you." He brought out a chest about two feet high filled with everything anyone might need to move into a dorm room: tools along with other essentials such as tape, crayons, everything imaginable. With great laughter he said, "Let it be known that you have all these things, and you will know everyone in the entire dorm by the time the sun has set." There wasn't anything he forgot. He was right. I met many of the gals and was happy to loan anything from my treasure chest.

I wasn't chosen for a sorority, but that didn't interfere in the least with my grades or campus community involvement. I can't remember ever thinking the competition was too much. Nothing kept me from doing as well as I thought I could. There were many times when I was up against something entirely new to me, a "first opportunity," and in doing the best I knew how, I was confident in my efforts. I knew how to study, had definitely put the effort into mastering study skills throughout my earlier education. Mastery of anything takes effort if you want to excel.

That first year at Stanford, we didn't compare grades much. If you did well enough, you moved on. It was when you didn't get good enough grades to move on that you heard about it! My classes were never too overwhelming. I knew I wanted to work a little bit harder than I was used to, so I got through fine. I was mostly pleased with how I did. My expectations were reasonable. Getting all A's didn't matter to me since most of my friends were not going down that route. They just said, "Let's just finish our freshman year and not get thrown out, and then we'll go to the sophomore year and see how it is." In the meantime, there were also sidetracks to go down, classes I could take that offered me a larger diversity to what I was taking. Truth be told; however, I might have been more interested in boys at Stanford than in my studies. As stated before, I was there during the war, so there weren't many young men in attendance. Some of the boys in attendance during that time were actually chosen from their military ranks to attend Stanford. Platoons of boys occasionally held marching exercises on campus, which was always exciting.

Classes That Made a Difference

Aside from the Industrial Psychology class taken my senior year, which I will talk about later, there were a couple of other classes that piqued my interest.

Everybody remembers the History of Western Civilization class and many complained while taking it. But years later when people met up with each other, what they remembered and talked about was the Western Civilization class.

I also found the Comparative Religions class fascinating. As is often the case, the professor made the class all the more interesting.

Dating and Drinking at Stanford

Dating at Stanford, now that is an interesting topic. Nobody had any gas, so we mostly just used our thumb to get to the movies in Palo Alto, down Palm Drive onto University Avenue. If something big, like the theater, were happening in San Francisco, we would get on a train and go there. I had a good time and dated all over the map. I liked men. How many hearts did I break? I know they did not break mine; I'll tell you that much! I don't think I ever got serious enough with anybody for that.

Fortunately, drinking never became one of my pastimes. I didn't have anybody in my background that drank. Liquor was neither available nor served on campus but readily available off campus. It is worth a story that will be told in detail later when I met my later-to-become husband at a fraternity beer bust.

Stanford Univeristy Presidents

I was one of the few people who had a chance to meet all of the wives of the presidents of Stanford, starting with Jesse, "Mrs. David Starr Jordan. Stanford University was founded November 11, 1885. Here is a list of the presidents of Stanford University and their wives.

1891–1913	David Starr Jordan
	Susan Bowen Jordan, Jessie Knight Jordan
1913–1915	John Casper Branner Not married
1916–1943	Ray Lyman Wilbur
	Marguerite Blake Wilbur
1943-1948	David B. Tresidder
	Mary Curry Tresidder
1949–1968	J.E. Wallace Sterling
	Anna Marie S. Sterling
1969-1971	Kenneth S. Pitzer
	Jean M. Pitzer
1971-1980	Richard W. Lyman
	Elizabeth Jing Schauffler Lyman
1980-1992	Donald Kennedy
	Robin B. Hamill Kennedy
1992-2000	Gerhard Casper
	Regina Casper, M.D.
2000-2016	John Hennessy
	Andrea Berti Hennessy
2016-	Marc Tessier-Lavigne
	Mary Hynes Tessier-Lavigne

John Casper Branner: When Jordan retired as president of Stanford in 1913, Branner was elected President of the university. Jordan retired January 1, 1916, due to an age limit established by the university and was named President Emeritus.

Robert Eccles Swain: Acting president during the time Wilbur took another post, 1929–1933 with his wife, Juanita Jaffe.

Alvin Eurich: Acting president between following Tressider's sudden death in 1948.

Robert J. Glaser: Acting President following Sterling's retirement in 1968 with his wife, Helen Hofsommer, M.D.

Job Opportunity: The Cookie Casa Ventura

Since I had worked in an office in Stockton the entire year before entering Stanford at age seventeen, I wanted to work. In this regard, one of my very first *cookies* came during my freshman year at Casa Ventura. I was too naïve to realize that being assigned to Casa Ventura was not considered the best thing, but it did turn out to be the best for me.

During my second week there, the housemother approached me and said, "I'd like to talk to you for a minute. Do you have some time?" I answered, 'Of course." She then proceeded to say, "I know you are on scholarship and that you are interested in a job. I think I have the perfect job for you. Could you come with me now?" She took me by the hand and walked me not very far from Casa Ventura, up some steps to a little road where two houses stood. She rang the doorbell at one of the houses. This tiny little lady who looked like a sparrow – so little, petite and smiley, opened the door. The housemother said, "Jean, I'd like you to meet Mrs. David Starr Jordan. She needs a chauffeur and somebody to help her with her writing. We thought you would be perfect. Mrs. Jordan said, "Well, what I need is somebody who will take me to the grocery store once or twice a week and maybe help me with some stationery and some words I need in letters here and, and, and…

I thought, 'I could do that.' Since I didn't know who she was, I wasn't as overwhelmed by this wonderful offering as I was when the housemother told me just who she was and why she was so special. She was the second wife and widow of the first president of Stanford (1891-

1913) who had died about two years prior to our meeting. She still lived on campus.

Once or twice a week I took her shopping and on errands, to wherever she wanted to go. We frequented mostly the Safeway store then on University Avenue, and also the nearby garden store. After our time together, we ended up back at her home where she brewed tea while I handled whatever typing she had for me to do. We then sat and chatted. I loved my time with her. She was delightful, a chirpy, little, sparrow-like thing of about 75 years and sharp minded. I remember she sent postcards to me.

My typing came in handy for letter writing and other secretarial duties. I generally helped her out my entire freshman year. Now, how many people would have considered that a *cookie*? I recognized that happening as a definite *cookie*. It came along, and I grabbed it.

Another former President, perhaps number three (3) or four (4) and his wife also lived on campus. All former Presidents' wives were honorary members of Cap and Gown. I got to meet and engage so many of them in conversation when at Cap and Gown functions.

I worked for Mrs. David Starr Jordan until my sophomore year when she began not to have the energy for our little outings. She died shortly after that. The housemother at the dorm came to tell me of her death. I did not attend any service for her since it was not held on campus. From her I learned to not judge a book by its cover.

I also hashed (waited on tables) in the Cellar, a popular hangout, typed endless papers for other students. I babysat for Mrs. Branner's grandchildren and other faculty. Often Mrs. Jordan and I visited Mrs. Branner, wife of former Stanford President (1913-1915).

Mrs. Jordan's cook was her friend, who was also friends with another couple in Palo Alto. Since I had been touted so favorably, the son of that couple, Ray Bangle, Jr., called and asked me for a date. I went out with him a lot, but we were not as serious as his mother thought we were. Towards the end of my freshman year, his parents invited my parents to come down from Manteca to go to dinner with them. We went to dinner where everyone was discreet and charming. We wrote a thank-you note following the dinner. Ray Bangle Jr. called after about a week or so and said, "My mother is so upset that we're still dating." I said, "What for? I thought my parents were wonderful." He said, "No, they are upset because you did not pick up the tab for dinner." They expected my parents to pay for the dinner and didn't want him dating me because of that! I told him, 'Let's just let it dribble down and see if it's meant to be.' It wasn't. I did like him, but there were other guys I was dating. For years I got a Christmas card from him and an introduction to his new wife whose name was also Jean.

Residences at Stanford

My freshman year, I lived in Casa Ventura, which turned out to be a special place and offered me that unique first job, a definite *cookie*! I lived in Juniper dorm my Sophomore year, which used to be one of the men's fraternity houses. That was when boys were beginning to return to campus. One night when we all got into bed, there was a loud scuffle that raised us all from our sleep. We encountered a dead-drunk "brother" who wandered into the house without knowing or realizing girls had taken over the fraternity. We guided him to a place where someone could take care of him.

My junior year, I was selected to return back to Casa Ventura to be dorm manager for the junior transfers. My senior year, I was the head sponsor of all the corridor sponsors at Branner Hall, a huge hall for all incoming freshmen. There were five corridors with a senior sponsor assigned to each one. As head sponsor, I was the liaison between the house and the university, a definite *cookie*. If something came up or needed attention, I was to take care of it and/or report back to the responsible senior administrators of the university. Although I didn't get paid to be a head sponsor (corridor monitor) or manager, I gained a lot of experience. Being the liaison also allowed me to interact with many more people in different capacities than I would have, had I just been a resident.

I was senior sponsor in corridor #1, and Sandra Day O'Connor was a freshman that year in corridor #4. The housemother and staff wanted us to look carefully at her. She had grown up on a ranch and had experienced schooling different from others. It was important for us to watch that she was making friends and that her schooling was not becoming a problem. She was very busy and very smart. We saw that she acclimated very well and fit right in on "The Farm," Stanford's nickname. As a junior, she was tapped to be part of Cap and Gown, which was a lovely addition. Many years later, at the Cap and Gown centennial in 2005, our very own Sandra Day O'Connor, a former United States Supreme Court judge, was our keynote speaker. Many years following that, she coincidentally on a plane, sat next to my son Marty on one of his business trips to Arizona.

Fond Memories of Jean from Former Classmates

"In addition to saying thank you to Jean for decades of giving to the Stanford family, I would like to say a special thank you for the special undergrad years 1943-47. This was the time our lives intersected, from that first year as residents of Casa Ventura and a second year at Juniper Lodge. Jean later went on to be a sponsor at Ventura and Branner. Those World War II years were a special and different time for the Farm. There was a smaller student body, but plenty of activities and it seems bicycles were everywhere, Jean was one of a few who had access to a 1930's coupe and I recall some fun get-a-ways to Pacific Grove. Also, one time on the softball team, we had a uniform of boy's jeans, the only kind then, with legs rolled into cuffs calf high and topped by plaid shirts. We must have spent a lot of time around the Women's gym. I'm grateful there are alums like Jean who have been such an intimate part of Stanford through the many changes that have occurred over the past 70 years. She has been an exceptional representative for our generation. So many thanks to you Jean for mutual memories."

—Byrl Warrick Ward

"Jean and I first became acquainted as first-quarter freshmen, next-door neighbors in the Casita wing of Casa Ventura in the fall of 1943. She roomed with Mary Jane Skillman of Watseca, Illinois. We referred to ourselves as the trio from Manteca, Watseca, and Seeeedro-Woolley, all small towns. It wasn't long before her cheerful good nature became evident and she became a friend to everyone.

As sophomores several Venturans moved to The Row into Juniper Lodge, a fraternity converted to a female residence during WWII. Jean and I became roommates and good friends, and it was a memorable year. At years end, Jean decided to move to one of the larger dormitories for girls, to become a resident adviser for the younger students, thus beginning her career of service to Stanford, which continued throughout most of her life.

One of the early and long-lasting impressions of Jean was her devotion to her family and, in particular, her love and admiration for her energy-bunny mother who stayed amazingly active well into her advanced years, a model that Jean seems to be emulating. This trait became evident in the annual Christmas and non-Christmas correspondence received from Jean over the years, duly noted by me, leading to my present resolve, "If Jean can do it, I can do it." This, along with Fred's untimely death at age 56 in 1981, made me realize that every day of life is a gift and that I'd better make the best use of it I can. These combined thoughts propel me through each day to do as much as possible."

—Barb Ward Thompson

"Jean was the first person I met when I arrived a day early with my luggage at Casa Ventura in September 1945. In spite of my inopportune arrival, she was kind enough to let me dump my belongings – the dorm opened officially the next day. She was a wonderful addition to the rather stern housemother who ruled with an iron hand. Of course, she moved to Branner before the year was out, but she remained a very special person in my memory bank.

We had more opportunity to meet when Casa Ventura reunions were planned in later years. Jean was prime organizer and always behind the gatherings, contacting the dorm mate and lending expertise. Ben and I were guests for dinner at Nome Court on one occasion. The dinner is memorable because Jean served sliced strawberries for dessert. It was the first time I had ever seen them sliced rather than quartered or whole. I have always sliced them since. I frequently think of Jean because now that strawberries are available year-round, I have sliced strawberries almost every day in a medley of fruits for my breakfast."

—Anadel Law

"I remember Jean with great fondness. She was my sponsor at Branner Hall my freshman year, '46-'47. We had many memorable times, lots of laughs. Good memories."

—Peggy Zukin

Cap and Gown Senior Year

Before Cap and Gown was established in 1905, the campus was made up mostly of men. Women felt they were being overlooked. Four or five coeds went to women in "high positions" at the university to talk about their feelings of being overlooked. Together, they came up with the idea of Cap and Gown just for women, an honor society that choose members based on community and University involvement, as well as academic achievement. Of course, changes have happened over the years, the model for "tapping" in particular.

Longtime members of Cap and Gown

Brainstorming together

Tapping Ceremony – How Women Were Chosen

When the honor society first began, women were chosen by members and it was very hush-hush. During my years at Stanford, the non-sorority women had assigned dining areas, so you always knew where to find someone at mealtime. As Cap and Gown members came to one of our dining halls in their Caps and Gowns, a sudden hush came over the dining room, and you could have heard a pin drop, as members walked around in a line until they came to a deserving coed. One member then put her hands on the coed's shoulders and tapped. The newest member then rose to march around with the others until all deserving new members were tapped. They all then went to a reception at the President's house. In time, University Presidents' wives were invited to join Cap and Gown as honorary members. The application process changed over the years to accommodate more students and recently, Stanford women could apply for membership in Cap and Gown on their own by filling out a form they either asked for or retrieved from one of the department heads. At the start of the 2016 academic year, the university will adopt new, more "inclusive" guidelines. Cap and Gown will no longer be an exclusive women's organization. Even more changes are in process.

Because the honor society has grown so, two major events are held each year with an open invitation to any and all interested in attending. Fascinating university and public figures are featured speakers at the Faculty Club for the Spring brunch and the fall event especially welcomes freshmen to the Stanford campus.

In my day, the Cap and Gown honorees consisted of a very select group chosen by the membership. I was tapped for Cap and Gown before my senior year at Stanford, a huge honor. I'm often asked to share the story of my tapping with new members. It went something like this:

The cap and gown members, wearing their caps and gowns first met up at Herbert Hoover's office in the tower. Ten women going into their senior year were to be chosen, although an outstanding junior could have filled the spot if necessary.

I remember I sat in my respective dining hall sometime during spring quarter when all of a sudden, a hush came down over the dining room. Whispers of, "Cap and Gown" were heard. As the members quietly walked around, we silently prayed, "Let it be me, let it be me, let it be me." When they stopped behind me, one member put her hands on my shoulders (the tap), the signal to have me join the parade line. I was beside myself when chosen. I also strongly believed during my high school years, that doing something more than just going to school would someday bring rewards. I just stood up, joined the parade and was very happy. Because I had worked hard and felt I should be chosen, I wasn't too surprised, but really pleased. When everybody was "collected," we went to a little tea party up in Hoover Tower. Herbert Hoover's secretary was an honorary Cap and Gown member, so we were allowed up there. The President of the University when I was tapped was Donald B. Tresidder.

The Cap and Gown Board at Stanford

I cofounded the Cap and Gown Alumnae Board in 1953. When the board first began, it was small. We gathered the names, retired to the Herbert Hoover tower where again the secretary in that position was an honorary Cap and Gown member, which enabled us to meet in this prestigious location. We sat in chairs until a decision was made regarding who was to be tapped before coming downstairs. As a side note and as fate would have it, in 1962 when we first moved into our house in Sunnyvale, Herbert Hoover's granddaughter, Joan Vowels, lived right around the corner. We became the best of friends.

You are invited to join the board if you have some kind of talent or have a friend on the board that thinks you would be a good member. It is very loose. I have been on the board off and on since it started. I was chosen but don't think it a good idea to have a lifetime on the same board. Sitting on the board, you can give as many suggestions as you want.

Even now that prospective Cap and Gown members can either be nominated by someone else or apply on their own, the Cap and Gown Board still chooses the new members to be tapped. The new members are called on the phone and invited to a special "Tapping Tea." This is a wonderful way to recognize those who don't "make a lot of noise" but have added much to the campus.

Because University Presidents' wives have automatic honorary admittance into the Cap and Gown Society, I had an opportunity to meet many of them; the others I met along the way. I have met the wife of every Stanford president since the university's beginning.

Friendships were developed with a few, not because of what I did, but rather from my opportunity through Cap and Gown to meet all these wonderful women and engage them in conversation.

Meeting Harry

Each corridor sponsor's room in Branner Hall had a phone with a little clicker attached. I was a corridor sponsor. If the phone rang and the call was for me, it would knock over a hairpin that I had carefully tied to it. It just sat there on the little bar and if and when it clicked, I then picked up the phone and took my call.

Invite to a Beer Bust

One late afternoon, I got a call from a gal I had lived with the year before saying, "Hey Jean, we're going to go on an exchange beer bust with the Fijis, and we want you to come along." I wasn't wild about beer, but since Jordan House, the place where I lived my junior year, was right next door to the Fiji fraternity, and I knew who the big Fijis were, I said, 'Sure, what the hell.' When the time came, I took my trusty car "Shaky" and went over to the frat house. I parked the car and walked across the street to the Fiji house, which has since burned down. My friend looked up the steps and said, "There's your date."

Handsome Harry

I really thought that this was just an exchange where a bunch of people got together to just drink and mingle and where nobody had a date; but I looked up and there was this tall, gorgeous, blue-eyed blond, just home from the war and wearing his uniform flight jacket.

He later told me the only reason he was there was because he was the only one with a car, a brand-new Ford.

When he signed up to join the Air Force, he started a savings account so that when the war was over, he would have money to buy a new car. We chatted, had a good time and one date led to another. Studying was not a priority for me then since I was a senior and pretty sure I would soon graduate. Harry turned out to be the love of my life, but I didn't know it yet.

Harry and I later attended what was called a Jolly-Up dance. Harry was quite a bit taller than me. When we danced and the music stopped, we just stood there. Harry said, "I could eat a bowl of soup off the top of your head." Sounds silly today but endearing at the time.

The Ring

Sometime later, one of my freshman corridor girls came to me and asked what I knew about an ad in the Stanford paper of a person named Harry selling a diamond ring. I told her, 'I know nothing about the article and will not pursue finding out anything more about it. If something comes to me that gives me a clue and catches me at the right moment, I may tell you what it is; but right now, it is just not important.' I was not about to ask Harry about it. Probably a month later, a different freshman girl approached me and said, "Look at this!" On her hand was the beautiful diamond ring that was for sale by Harry. One of Harry's fraternity brothers bought the diamond and gave it to the freshman girl. Harry and I dated almost every night, but he never once mentioned it, and I refused to ask any questions. The girl with the ring, a freshman in my corridor, just happened to be heir to the Stauffer Chemical Company. This couple were engaged and later married. The ring was really not meant for me.

About 20 years later, I learned that Harry had tried to get the diamond ring back from the girl he had once been engaged to in Baltimore. Harry had asked the girl for the ring. I don't know what her answer was, but it was probably something like, "Up yours!" She just flat out told him to forget it. He then went to her mother, told her what was happening and asked for her help. The mother talked to the daughter, and he got the ring back. Harry then sold it to his friend.

I understood why he became engaged, going off to war and all that. I never knew nor asked details about that engagement. The mother obviously had a way if she talked her daughter into giving back the ring.

Much later in life, his former fiancé, Jackie Heck Feeley sent Harry's wings to me, thinking perhaps one of our sons might like to have them. Son Marty has them beautifully mounted in a shadowbox, positioned above the picture of Harry's B29 flight crew. She and I are friends now. She sent me a more recent photo of herself saying that the only photo I might have seen of her was when she was in high school!

Harry proposed to me during my senior year. If he asked my dad for my hand in marriage, neither one mentioned it to me. It was between the two of them.

Industrial Psychology Class

During the last quarter of my senior year, working toward a social science degree, I took a class called Industrial Psychology. The outside world was going to be mine pretty soon. Little did I know that this class would firmly plant my feet on the ground. The professor of the Industrial Psychology class was "bananas" over this new company that had just been started in the area, Hewlett Packard (HP). He talked of how their attitude towards employees and customers would become the gold standard for all companies to come.

HP was proud to say that the people who worked for them were their most important resource. From there, the professor went on and on, outlining all the things that made them so unique in that post WWII market. The company believed strongly in people giving back to the community by donating time and effort toward worthy causes. Since many HP workers were Stanford graduates, much of HP's payback was to the Stanford community.

I was newly engaged and wanted work. Post-graduation and fulfilling a job promise to a friend, I decided to check out the "gold standard" company, Hewlett-Packard, which was just down the road from Stanford. So, on a Saturday morning, in my naivety, I went over to 1501 Page Mill Road to see what it was all about. Of course, most people don't work on Saturday and there were no cars in the parking lot; but somehow, I thought the whole world would be there... but they weren't! Curiosity got the best of me, so over to the doors I walked. The entire HP building area was locked, but I proceeded to peek into windows of locked-up rooms until someone peeked back, came out and said, "Well, hello, what can I do for you?" I proceeded to tell him why I was there, and he said, "Come on in, let's talk." For about fifteen minutes we talked at an empty desk before moving to a desk with a typewriter. I was asked to type. Then all of a sudden, he picks up the phone and says, "Frank, I just hired my new secretary." He was the VP of Marketing. I was hired on the spot after chatting with my new boss, Noel Eldred. My typing and shorthand skills got me the job. In addition to the nice salary, HP had benefits, which I had first heard about in the Industrial Psychology class. Interestingly, years later when my husband worked in Employee Benefits for Marsh and McLennan, he consulted with HP and put together their employee benefits packages.

The *cookie* was first of all the Industrial Psychology class I took, followed by my intuition and being in the right place at the right time. The people I met and everything about my time there was serendipitous. Happenings occur, even if almost 100 miles apart. I'm referring to the distance between Manteca where I took typing and shorthand in high school, and Stanford, California where I took the Industrial Psychology class and learned about Hewlett-Packard who later became my employer.

On Volunteerism

People don't realize that volunteering is an amazing way to create, hone skills and think about things differently. You never know where the experience will lead. I learned a lot about volunteerism from my work at Hewlett-Packard, a company that championed volunteerism and is still today reaffirming their commitment to volunteerism and raising awareness. Every HP employee is given four paid company hours a month to volunteer or do pro-bono work.

Change Anything in Life?

That title suggests I need to put a circle around this kind of behavior or this kind of effect on somebody else. What would I change? Nothing, I guess. I mean, I could have probably been nicer about breaking a date, but—that is not what is being asked. Looking back in retrospect sometimes makes things seem simpler than they were at the time—and mostly, that passage of time helps us gain insight and wisdom.

—Jean Galt Coblentz

Harry's Family

Harry and his brother Madison basically grew up in the Baltimore, Maryland area but moved out here after the war to attend college after their father took a job in San Francisco, California.

The two brothers completed their wartime tours of duty and returned home to their parents in San Francisco. From there, both applied to and were admitted into Stanford. The brothers were very close, all through their wartime service, college years and as fathers of young families. Both worked in the insurance industry and got together often while they both worked in San Francisco, California. Harry later moved to San Jose where his new office overlooked the San Jose Airport. With binoculars on his desk, he was in his element as he watched planes take off and land.

During the war, Harry's parents had been sent to Amman, Jordan, where his dad, a chemical engineer, was part of a government team helping with the country's infrastructure. They later returned to the states and lived near San Francisco in Daly City, CA for a while. They then moved down to Menlo Park and in their later years, lived close by, here in Sunnyvale. Harry's brother Madison also attended Stanford and married an heiress to the Gillig Bus Company and made their home in Piedmont, California.

Graduation

In June 1947, I graduated with all my family in attendance. My sister Alice was also to graduate from Stanford. Years later, my youngest sister Cornelia was also enrolled at Stanford. What started out in all innocence about college choices, Stanford eventually influenced all the girls in our family. Our brother Alan, on the other hand, chose Hastings College in Nebraska where my parents had attended.

Marriage and Cookies

We married on June 12, 1948 and lived "happily ever after." An engagement ring was deemed inconsequential at the time, what with our marriage to each other being understood as primary.

Knowing I was from Manteca, one of Harry's fraternity brothers asked where we were having our wedding reception. Harry said, "We have been thinking about it but haven't made up our minds yet." The frat brother said, "Well, I've been talking to my folks and they would love it if you would have the reception at their house. They lived in Burlingame in a very good part of town."

This happened and brought all the frat brothers together not only to help out but also to celebrate.

Harry – Head Hasher

Harry, head hasher at the Fiji Fraternity House, served, took directions from the cook and was in charge of all the hashers in the house. When the announcement was made about our engagement, the house just went berserk. As head hasher, Harry became exceptionally good friends with Louise, the cook who adored him. She said to him, "When you get married, I'll take care of the food. Don't worry about it. Every time the Fijis' have chicken for something, I'll throw another one in the freezer, you know." She did the same with dough for baking. She brought her own workers, and they did a marvelous job feeding all our guests. Harry's fraternity brother, Bob Smothers (who we recently saw at a delightful Stanford Reunion,) tells this story best:

"I was a Stanford Fiji, (Phi Gamma Delta) fraternity brother of Harry Coblentz and got to know Jean when they met at Stanford and started going together. He brought her to our fraternity parties and we also double dated a couple of times. Needless to say, we all loved her too and thought Harry was one lucky guy to have "pinned" her (when you ask your gal to wear your fraternity pin). Over the years, we had lots of fun together.

The evening before Harry and Jean's wedding, the Fiji's took Harry out for his bachelor party. We encouraged Harry to drink and then drink some more. After all, you don't get married every day. Even after he had had enough, his considerate brothers got him to drink a little more. So, Harry was having a great time but soon became oblivious to what was really going on. After he was essentially "passed out," one of our brothers, a pre-med student, installed a full-length cast on one of his legs. Harry was totally out and so far gone, he had no idea what was happening.

When he awoke the next morning, not exactly feeling his best, he was stunned to realize he had a cast on his leg. He was told he had had a bad fall and broke his leg. Too bad, but don't worry, you can still go to your wedding but on crutches. Between his hangover, his leg cast and the impending wedding, poor Harry was fit to be tied. During WWII, Harry had flown his B29 bomber and had dropped bombs on Tokyo, but that was nothing compared to this! Finally, in the spirit of brotherly love and fraternalism, Harry was told the truth. The cast came off and the wedding went off without a hitch. Jean was a gorgeous bride, and it was one beautiful wedding. Little did most of the wedding guests know though about what that handsome groom had gone through to be there."

—Bob Smothers

Choice of Church

Harry had grown up around an Episcopal Church where the preacher and his wife were in charge of high school kids, offering them all kinds of activities: dancing, play acting, etc. It didn't matter whether you were a Christian, Buddhist, or any other persuasion, it was the love that went out to these kids that was important. Since the Episcopal church was familiar to Harry, we got married at All Saints Episcopal Church in Palo Alto, California.

Marriage Ceremony

I remember my maid of honor was Betty Davies, not THE Bette Davis! She and I went down to the church at 7:00 a.m. to put ribbons on the pews. A guy at the church saw me with my hair all up in curlers and said, "Aren't you getting married today?" I responded, "If I get around to it" and assured him that I had plenty of time. Champagne flowed at the reception. My father had never tasted champagne and commented, "I don't ever have to taste it again."

When it was time to leave the reception, I went upstairs to change into my going away clothes. A photo was taken of me throwing my bouquet over the balcony. We got in the car, but not before noticing lots of shoes, cans, and things like that were tied on the back. Harry was one step ahead of them and got his brother and friends to untie the stuff so we could ride in peace.

When we returned from our honeymoon, we were talking to a friend about the wedding and he asked, "Are you guys really in love?" I responded, 'Well, I'm not sure I know what love is, but I would like to say that I'm in love.' I told the guy that he could certainly ask Harry. He asked, "Do you guys expect your marriage to last very long?" I told him, 'I don't know that anybody has asked that question straight on, but I can't see any reason why it won't.' We had high hopes at that moment. I asked him what had prompted that question. He told us how we had driven off with no clanging noise or anything and how Harry drove so fast to get out of there, one would have thought he didn't like any part of it! Also, this fella and others followed us just in case perhaps someone had used a timer to delay the appearance of shoes, cans and noisemakers. "When we reached you and looked up, Harry was driving, and you were reading the paper." The comment at that point said by one of the guys was, "This marriage won't last."

Sidenote: We ended up being married for fifty-five years before Harry died.

Honeymoon

Friends of my parents loaned us their beach house for a week, high on a cliff south of Carmel, California.

At the end of our week, we looked at each other and said, "Do you suppose it's long enough?"

I found you did the same things married that you did when you weren't married. Things had to get done. I had to cook, sew, garden, pay bills just as always.

The only difference was living with someone else when I wasn't used to such.

However, since we both were working, it wasn't like we were bumping elbows every minute.

Marriage and Raising Children

I'm not sure how to analyze my marriage. It was not an up and down emotional roller coaster ride. Not being sure what love was, I watched my parents and used them as a role model. When they differed on anything, there was always a civil way of dealing with it. I was taught by example that you don't always have to have your way every time. Life is so much more fun if you're not always fighting about something. I'd like to say Harry and I did the best we could. Not one single child out of our four had a normal marriage, they've all been different.

What is normal? My parents' union could be considered normal for their era as was ours for the time we were married.

My children take good care of me and consider it quite an honor to watch over me. I don't expect anything from them. When we are all together, we just have a good time. Kath and I have the benefit of a close mother/daughter relationship as she has full responsibility for my care and well-being in my last years.

Work and Family

I loved my job at HP and was more concerned about having it end because of my pregnancy than anything. I wasn't thinking beyond that – about my career, or anything. During those days, it was the norm for women to quit before being asked to leave when their pregnancy began to show.

We married in June 1948, and not until I thought my pregnancy might start to show, did I go to Noel Eldred, my HP boss. I was beside myself, literally in tears. He asked, "What's the matter?" I said, 'I'm pregnant. I am so mad and furious and don't know what to do.' With that, he put his arm around me saying, "Sweetheart, don't worry about it. This is today's way of dealing with that: You come to work every morning, go home every night. You can work for me until I have to either take you in the ambulance to the hospital or pick you up under my arm and find the best place for your baby to be delivered."

Becoming pregnant was one of the biggest surprises of my life. We had not talked about birth control – not sure why not. All of a sudden, I was pregnant. And would I trade Kath now for anybody? Not on your life, she is now saving my life.

Jean on HP and Pregnancy

In my time as a young mother, we didn't have many options for childcare. It was assumed that mothers had babies and raised them until they were all through school. The job that I left was as a secretary for the marketing engineer for Hewlett Packard when the company was only two years old. Who knew HP would go so far! I have no regrets about leaving that job to raise my children. I think part of it had to do with the fact that I had had a lot of experience watching people raise their children and what the results were. Some of them decided that they would try to have a career, and they just didn't have the tools to make a "splash" at that time, so it was a disgruntling of sorts. Going up the corporate ladder was not a "for sure" recipe for success, but raising children is as close to doing what I would have enjoyed. I was able to say YES to a lot of things that I would not have been able to do as a full-time, working woman. Nothing in this world is a guarantee. You never know what little moments will lead to major opportunities later on!

Working with "the HP Way" taught me to volunteer for Stanford and give back to our community, and that your staff were your most valuable resource.

My pregnancy with Kathy was easy, no morning sickness or anything. All I did was get bigger. My boss, Noel Eldred, was such a forward-thinking person and must have liked my work, my spirit and me. He gave me a chance at the very beginning.

Had I been working anywhere else, I'm sure I would have been let go. Noel had explained the situation to both Bill Hewlett and Dave Packard, told them what was going on and that what we would like to have happen – me continue my work. That posed no problem whatsoever. I worked right alongside Packard and Noel, my desk right at the very front of the door, not in some back room. To my great relief, my medical costs were covered. Life couldn't have been better.

I left work on May 27, and Kathy was born on June 1, 1949. I was definitely "showing." I did not go back to HP after she was born. Again, another nest egg was produced with money in our account for an occasional babysitter.

Kathy's Birth

At the time Kathy was born, Harry was working for an oil company, managing a gas station, doing bookwork and just about to graduate in June of 1949 When we went to the hospital, he was in a big hurry. When I asked him why he was rushing so, driving so fast, he laughed and said, "I would like to be going so fast that the cops will stop me and I can finally say, 'Look at my wife. She is going to have a baby right here!'

That never happened, but it was a funny story. The birth was easy, labor not awfully hard. Of all four children, Kathy's birth was probably the longest and most difficult, but not really anything that difficult. We went to the hospital late morning and she was born midafternoon. Because men were not usually allowed into the delivery room then, I don't think it ever occurred to Harry that he might possibly be welcomed during the birth. We had not decided on the name beforehand but there was a favorite song my father often hummed "I'll take you home again, Kathleen." We liked the name; she was a girl –that's all we needed.

After three or four days in the hospital, Harry and I couldn't think of any good reason for me to stick around. I felt great, hustled, and bustled about and felt childbirth was just one of those natural life-cycle occurrences.

Harry and the girls

194

My parents were very casual about it also – no fluttering around. Since I was nursing Kathy, there was no need to have someone there helping me figure out formula and all. We became close friends with my OB-GYN, Dr. Downing, who adopted us and answered easily all the questions we had with a first baby. He delivered all our children at Stanford.

A big wooden bassinet that had folding legs (for whenever we went anywhere in the car, was Kathy's home. It was easily transferrable to the car.

Living Spaces

We first lived in an apartment in Redwood City that had been rented by one of Harry's fraternity brothers who was graduating and leaving. He introduced us to the people who had turned the top part of their garage into an apartment. Once upstairs, there was a big living room, a kitchen, dining area, a bedroom and bathroom. It was perfect and the owners treated us like we were their children. We were truly fortunate to be recipients of such generosity. We lived there about a year and a half before it came time for Harry, Kathy, and me to move from the apartment in Redwood City to a Park Merced apartment in San Francisco. Harry then worked for Marsh and McLennan, a huge insurance company in San Francisco. The weather there was cold and foggy, and the upstairs tenant lifted weights and banged them down on the floor over our heads, waking our baby. I was pregnant with our second child. It was time to move.

Menlo Park

House hunting was done with a real-estate fraternity brother of Harry's. For a spell, every Sunday was spent driving around looking at locations where we thought we might like to live and raise our family. Since he was finished at Stanford and ready to relocate to the South, a nice young man sold us his home in Menlo Park. Our savings and Harry's job in San Francisco (he rode the train from Atherton) all added up to a yes that we could afford to buy the house in Menlo Park. We could afford it and deposited our down payment before receiving a phone call about how other people had come in with a higher bid, plunking down their money. Although the realtor said it was ours, he said he would see what he could do. With a little help from my parents, we went down to the Fiji in charge, signed the papers and got the house. My parents were paid back within six months, and we lived happily in that house until 1961. Our neighborhood in Menlo, Suburban Park, was next door to James Flood Park. The home there and the surrounding neighborhood was our "village." Local mothers and I joined forces and convinced the school board to create a school on the property of the park because of the number of kids bussed to school. Our house was within walking distance of the newly created elementary school. Flood Park had wonderful play equipment and the homes were convenient to both Bayshore freeway (The 101) for driving and Atherton for the train.

When we returned to the Peninsula from San Francisco, I did work as a temp with HP until I decided I wanted to raise my children myself, and not leave that job to babysitters.

More Babies: Jan, Scott, and Marty

Jan was born May 16, 1951, Marty came two and a half years after Jan on October 19, 1953, and Scott was born three years after Marty on November 18, 1956. With two girls, we were not concerned about the sex of our babies; I just didn't care. However, since we had two of one sex and one of the other sexes, we decided to see if we could get another boy to go with Marty. We did!

Dad Dying

It was around the mid-1950s, and we were still in Menlo Park, when Daddy, due to ill health and aging, decided he could no longer perform his duties as a doctor. The first thing he did was close his office. The practice was later taken over by another caring physician, Dr. Taylor. Daddy recognized the onset of dementia, what later became Alzheimer's, and he understood the course of the illness. I remember we bought him a nice, olive green recliner-type chair. There he sat in the corner of the kitchen where all the activity was centered, near the window. His last formal outing was my sister Corny's wedding in 1957.

Mother had a male nurse come every morning who got him ready for the day. When no longer ambulatory, he either spent his day in his chair or in bed. Mother did what she could and accepted the rest. My father in his bedridden state, died at home in Manteca on March 10, 1966, where my mother had been caring for him the last two years. She lived another twenty years after Daddy died.

The Galt clan Thanksgiving 1969 in Modesto, CA

Jean's Mother Post Father

After Daddy died, Mother had no intention of living in a retirement community with lots of people. She rented a nice apartment for herself in Modesto. My younger sister and her husband lived about two miles away. Mother again became interested in many things. Every time we visited her, we went to the library to see the new books before visiting the "old library" from where people could borrow paintings for a week or a month from their lending library that covered more than just books. Her curiosity was insatiable. Mother was sweet and always had a way of sharing her wisdom in most every conversation.

Before she passed away, Mother was staying in Pasadena at my sister Alice's home. While at Alice's, we were all there laughing and talking. My brother Al and his wife Wanda told of their upcoming trip and, one by one, we children and our spouses went off to where we were staying nearby, and Mom stayed at the house. Mom mentioned she didn't feel well, and Alice didn't like the way she looked. She said, "I'm going to call the doctor. We will put you to bed and find out what is going on here." She was later taken to the nearby hospital where we all were visiting until we left. Mom was laughing and telling stories about her recent drive down to Pasadena. None of us ever thought there was anything seriously wrong.

At 2:00 in the morning, June 29, I got a call. Mother had died. Wanda said, "How considerate of her. You know perfectly well she would want us to go and have our trip." We all agreed. I think Mother set the stage there and chose her own time to die, having had a chance to visit all of her children.

My brother Alan wrote this heart felt tribute to our mother soon after her passing.

Florence Mabel Galt, a Son's Tribute

To All Who Loved Her:

During the night of Tuesday, June 29, 1982, this world lost one of its truly great women. Great, not in the sense of historical acclaim or worldly accomplishment, but for living a life of unparalleled exemplification of all that she believed and stood for.

She was unique in many ways, educated when women were not deemed worthy of education, selfless in giving up what could have been a comparatively comfortable and easy life for the term in China in primitive surroundings for betterment of the less fortunate. When her husband became an invalid, we really got a complete lesson into what the wedding vows meant when she said, "until death do us part".

This wonderful person raised a family, first in a Chinese jungle setting and later in the American jungle. She always stood on her principles making her yeas and nays the final authority in all matters of right and wrong. Each of her four children produced for her moments of pride, and as each of us individually know, moments of shame and despair because she cared.

Her four children also produced a plethora of grandchildren, each of whom hold a special place in their thoughts for "Granny Galt". She always knew how to please them with some little gift, story, book, poem, and most importantly, some very personal and heartfelt time and attention. She was "theirs alone" for that time and they knew it.

Her sense of community was strong, and she knew that she could make a contribution, thus her functioning on planning commissions, etc. She was always friendly but had few really close friends, but those she did have were of like spirit and were each unique in their own way. She always enjoyed meetings and study groups with those friends, and I know she cherished them as individuals she loved right to the end.

She was a religious person without any need for the social side of religion. She knew and studied biblical writings in the sense that she was a real scholar, delving into the histories, concordances and reading extensively the literature of Bible study. The world lost one of its unsung scholars in the field. Nor were her interests limited to this field.

Her thirst for knowledge carried her into virtually every literary field but that of the technical and mechanical trades. History, philosophy, the social sciences were all followed in the quest for a little better understanding of this complex thing called society. Her fund of knowledge was truly amazing and what was compiled in her mind is now lost to us. A real shame.

She lived a long, full life and was the impersonation of the Puritan work ethic. Even when she could only move with difficulty in her last days, she was looking for ways to make herself useful and contribute something. Nothing useful was ever thrown away, even though she had no use for it. Her family made fun of her saving string and cottage cheese cartons just because they were still good. She should have headed up the Cabinet post of "Conservation of Resources."

We who remain, her family and friends, will remember her from our last contact as there will be no formal eulogies. She was embarrassed in life by people making any kind of a fuss or formal preparation for her sake, and so in death the pattern will not be altered. No one who has ever known her has left that *relationship unaffected by her composure and sense of inner strength.*

As her only son, I have put down these personal observations in an attempt to capture the feelings and thoughts that are going through my mind. There is no sense of real personal sorrow, but one of regret for not having been a little more attentive or having given her a little more of myself. Let's all try to take what we can from her life for our own. I know that "Mom", "Granny" or "Mabel" would have shared unselfishly in life that which we may choose as ours now.

Alan Moore Galt July 1, 1982. [3]

Although this is a side story, it is worth telling. My former doctor sent me a short story of a woman who was picked up by a taxi driver from her home where she had lived for a long time, taking her back to where she currently lived. She pointed out to him, "Oh, you know, I used to do this here and this here." By the time, the day was over, they had put about three hours on the meter. She asked, "How much do I owe you?" He replied, "Nothing, it was such a pleasure and a privilege to bring you back as you showed me all the memories you have." My former doctor then wrote at the bottom of his email to me: "I am honored because since we talk a lot, I have lots of memories from you.

If there was anyone in my life I'd like to thank, it would be my mom for the way she looked at the world, the way

---

[3] Donations can be made to the Mabel and Curtis Memorial Scholarship Fund at Hastings College in Nebraska as a way of acknowledging their unselfish contribution to the world and keep their memory alive.

she treated people, how she used her brains and the example she set no matter where she went and who she was with. That is just who she was. I am honored if anyone compares me to her. I, like my mother, don't make judgments of people. Instead, I try to walk in their shoes

Throughout those years in Menlo Park, I was involved in our school PTA and felt I learned more than the kids did at school. Aside from the business and political mechanics of PTA, I learned how to work with an adult group. I became president of that PTA the last year before we moved, led a girl scout troop, began teaching both girls to sew and made many life-long friends. However, three bedrooms were beginning to feel small for us. We had outgrown our little Menlo Park home and decided it was time to start looking for a larger house to meet our needs.

New Home in Sunnyvale

We were serious about finding a bigger house. Friends told us of newly constructed, large homes being built by an outfit called Brown and Kaufmann in Sunnyvale. Harry said, "Sunnyvale? There's nothing but orchards down there," which was probably true since we used to picnic in that area as Stanford students. We visited and fell in love with the area, forcing us to get out the pens once again and do the math. Could we afford it? Things were in our favor. Suburban Park homes were in demand and no money was owed on our Menlo Park home. Harry had done well with Marsh and McLennan, and we did not have "Champagne tastes."

The home we wanted to build was in a large, new subdivision. All the schools were within easy walking distance. This was at a time when parents never dreamed of driving their kids to school.

On that important morning in 1961, the day that we were supposed to sign for the house in Sunnyvale, I went out for the paper and ran back in saying, 'Harry, you will never believe the trouble God has gone to, by saying what a good thing this is for us to do.' I knew this was a clear sign and was being told that this was our house, and we should have it. I told him to come and look. There it was—snow blanketed our yard. We had certainly never seen snow in Menlo Park, and it would be another fifteen years before the Peninsula would see a ground-covering snowfall again.

Jean and Harry

Our family lived in Menlo Park until we moved here to this house in Sunnyvale in 1962. Having four children and one bathroom and knowing friends who had moved there prompted this move. It was January and the lot in a former apricot orchard was where we knew we wanted to build our house. We did build. The whole family drove down on weekends to watch this house being built. Our kids brought lunchboxes and had a ball talking to each other about bed placement.

We moved in during the fall of 1962 and have lived here ever since. It has been a wonderful journey. All four children went to Homestead High School.

After moving in, our job was to make sure each child was settled in school before I became a "citizen" of this new territory. Kathy went to the junior high school and the other three to Serra Elementary School. I became involved in Girl Scouts again and quickly became a part of the Sunnyvale community.

I was so grateful that I had learned to budget both time and money as a young child and able to participate in a number of volunteer activities in the community as well as various school athletic events.

While the girls were growing up in Sunnyvale, I still made most of their clothes, even shirts for the boys. I taught Kathy first how to sew, then Jan. The kitchen area was for both eating and sewing. That table went from being our dining table to sewing table and is now used in my office to house the computer. It is the same table that previously served as the dining and sewing table in Manteca.

In 1962, I was invited to join the Woodside Atherton Auxiliary that later under my leadership, became the Allied Arts Guild Auxiliary. This auxiliary supported the

Lucille Packard Children's Hospital at Stanford and my relationship with the auxiliary brought many friends, opportunities, and a commendation 50 years later from President Barack Obama for Outstanding Volunteer, Community Service.

Each Family Member Unique

Was each of my children a *cookie*? Heavens, yes! There is no reason why they shouldn't be. Each one was a hugely different cookie, different looking and acting, different in gladness and sadness. Life is what you get. When the sad hits, my children and grandchildren and great grandchildren deserve more than for me to just fold into and stay with the sadness. I guess the *cookie* doesn't fall far from the tree since I received from my parents the great example of how to perceive life. They set an example and passed that on. It was amazing how that happened, almost like osmosis.

You just don't know what path your children are going to take; you just can't predict. I think it is better that way. I felt my job was just to make sure they were safe and to love them for who they were/are.

> *Children most like Jean:*
> *Martin Rush and Kathleen*
>
> *Children most like Harry:*
> *Janis and Scott Alan*

Kathleen

Kath is very bright, knows what she wants and works to get what she wants. She did very well in school and has worked a number of jobs. Following high school, she attended UCLA. We got a call one early morning about 2:00 a.m. from Kath who said, "Mom, some of the girls and I are sitting here chatting, and I wanted to ask you something. "When summer comes, could I take piano lessons?" I answered, 'It's 2:00 in the morning but if it is something you think you're going to follow through on, then yes, yes.' Kath said, "Yes." 'Well then,' I said, 'if you're certain, I have no problem with you taking piano when summer comes.' She then turned from our conversation and said to her friends, "See, I told you."

It seemed they were talking about their parents and Kath had said, "Well, I could call my mother at any time, any time, ask her anything, even if it is something stupid, and she wouldn't get mad and blow up or yell at me."

One of the girls said, "Oh my mother would never do that. She would be so mad."

One never knows, does one?

Kath was always interested in trying something new. She decided to leave UCLA and go to Europe with what little German she had learned at UCLA and her high school French, to focus on foreign languages.

She knew if she was going to major in foreign languages, the classes would be easier if she were already fluent in German and French.

While working during the summer prior to her trip to Europe, she was introduced to the idea of skydiving. A friend from Chico State was home for the summer, and Kath got very excited about learning how to jump out of airplanes! Kath did indeed learn to jump and pack her own parachute and had a short but exhilarating career of it as the trip to Europe was already planned. She did not follow the jump scene once in Europe.

In preparation for her first trip to Europe, I asked her, 'Do you have any money?' Kath knew she could earn enough and went to work in Libby Canning Company. Her Dad was happy to help her with his Teamsters connections. Along with other work, she was soon able to buy her ticket on Icelandic Air. I was worried she would not have the nerve to go, but she wanted to attend the Goethe Institute in Bavaria. While there, she was thrilled and happy, lived with German families and started to learn about the German culture. She later told us she had met this wonderful, young Italian man. We were hoping to one day meet him. We called friends of ours who were traveling in Europe and asked them to check him out! Kath was studying in Bavaria, and our friends were staying in Munich, so it was easy to arrange a meeting. They gave him the okay! We exchanged photos by mail, and before we knew it, Kath and Renato called us to say they were getting married. Although I would not have chosen to do it that way, I watched her grow up and knew she was always full of adventure and successful at her endeavors.

Kath and Ren finally married in Italy in March of 1971 and came back to the states that October to live with us for two years. They both had swing shift jobs, while Harry and I worked days, giving us all our own space! Kath then got a job driving a school bus for Redwood City School District. Her husband Ren worked as a gardener/caretaker for a San Francisco attorney who lived on an estate next to Filoli in Woodside, CA. Kath and Ren lived in a quaint annex to the main house on the Phleger Estate. She became pregnant with her only child Milena, born in 1977 at Stanford Hospital where all four of my children were born. When Milena was one and a half years old, Ren and Kath decided to go back to Germany and buy an ice café (ice cream parlor) in Aachen where Germany, Holland and Belgium have their common borders. When the ice café was closed in the dead of winter, they stayed with Ren's mother in the Dolomites of Northern Italy. Come spring, however, when the ice café was open, they worked up to 15 hours a day. Kath said while in Germany, she spent most of her days on her feet, managing the ice cream parlor/bistro. Once Milena started school, their daughter went wherever her parents were, studying both Italian and German simultaneously. She seemed to be very bright and had no difficulty switching between the two languages and cultures. Her teachers went out of their way to make sure she wasn't being left behind and she excelled. She grew up speaking English with her mom and our family, Italian with her dad and all his Italian friends and family, and German at her German school.

Milena completed her university studies in Milan and obtained a master's degree in public relations and started working almost immediately for DKNY in their Milan international sales office. After several years in the Milan office, she saw an opportunity to move to California to be closer to her mother and grandmother and see what life in California was all about. She was here for three and a half years. During that time, she also worked for the designer, Donna Karan, and did a lot of traveling. Kath and Milena lived quite close by and we spent a lot of very precious and memorable time together during those three plus years. Then one day, Milena received a call from DKNY's HR office in New York inviting her to come back to Italy to work and "move up a notch." Why not? She was very ready to return to Italy and that sounded like a good idea.

As of this writing, she is still living in Italy, working for Donna Karan, and traveling to all the major cities in western Europe where DKNY merchandise is sold.

Renato and Kath never divorced but separated in 1998. Soon thereafter, Kath came back to California and immediately went back to school, starting her career in Health Sciences as a Physical Therapist assistant and massage therapist.

I wrote the following poem to congratulate Kath on graduating with her PTA degree. She was a full-time student at DeAnza Community College for three years with a straight "A" average.

She loved being back in school in her late 40s and made many friends, especially among her teachers who were the same age. Through those contacts, she landed three different jobs that were all in health-care related areas – clearly her passion.

Kath got all my "extra genes," which has now in my later years, given me the opportunity to sit down and relax. I know that she can and will take care of any and all circumstances that arise now that we are living together, I appreciate all the work she does for me. Since Harry's death in 2005, Kath has always been close by enabling me to stay in my home for the rest of my days.

Congratulations, dearest daughter Kath
It's been a long, long journey on this detoured path
You've worked so hard and done your best
Tho I doubt very much if you'll now take a rest.

At this spot in the journey you've earned a degree
What happens next, we'll all wait and see
But of this I am certain, spoken like a proud mother
Whatever you do will be of help to another.

I love you very very much
And am immensely proud of your loving touch
Please take these bills and do as I ask
Spend them only on YOU – not too hard a task.

Enjoy this very special chance
and take some time to roam
I'll miss you loads and shall count the days
Until at last you're home.

M
XOX
M

Janis (1951-2010)

Jan was always one of those who thought of others first. She would no more have hurt a person's feeling on purpose than shoot them. She was not loud or boisterous, more like her dad. I might even characterize her as shy or timid. She was a straight-A student, did her chores without complaining and babysat a lot. She never boasted but was incredibly quiet about all her attributes. Jan was a senior in high school and had a boyfriend we had not had a chance to get to know. I had laid eyes on him only two or three times, and that was all.

One morning while my mother was visiting and everyone was in good spirits, Jan announced she and Eric had moved in together. By this time, Jan had graduated from high school and had taken all her belongings from the house. She announced that she and Eric were living in a tiny house down by the church on the other side of the street and that they were having an open-house tea and hoped we all would come. That was it. When Jan went to live with Eric, it was one of the most difficult times for me.

Eric's parents were divorced with his mother still living in the area. His father was a vice president of something to do with lumber and lived on the East Coast.

Jan, an avid cyclist

On the day of the open house, Harry and I put on our Sunday best and attended. I don't know who else was invited, but we were the only parents there. They took the time to show us the little things they had done both inside and out. When it was over and we were leaving, we told them we hoped they would drop in often. I don't think they did as they were busy doing their things. They moved from Sunnyvale and went up to the North Bay where both attended and graduated from Sonoma State.

Eric was very clever with his hands and machines. They got an old school bus, painted it blue and lived in it. When they bought their house in Fairfax, the bus, more like a mobile home, was parked in their driveway for friends who came to stay.

In the years before they bought their house, they both worked and parked their bus (mostly in San Francisco) wherever it was convenient.

Jan became known as the skirt lady and on weekends sold all the skirts she and Eric had sewn / assembled during the week. She also gave dancing lessons, and both worked in the cafeteria. While at Sonoma State, they never once asked us for money.

Sometime after their Sonoma State graduation, Eric's father said he would give them a car if they came and got it. I think it was a company car, a big, blue Mercedes Benz. So, they hitched a ride with a friend of theirs to North Carolina and drove the car back to California. They also spent an entire summer camping in an authentic Teepee on the banks of the Russian River. They were entrepreneurs to be sure. After living several years at Larkspur Landing, they bought a house close to the center of town in Fairfax.

House needed a little work and they made it beautiful. By that time, they had lived together for 20 years. After 25 years of living together, they decided to marry. They eventually put in a pool where we spent many a happy hour on weekends. Her nieces and nephews would often come to play. Jan was a generous person and loved to share things with people.

THE WORLD OF MOUNTAIN BIKING

WOMBATS READY FOR COMBAT.

The first all-women fat tire organization (at least that we know of) has been formed by two time National Champion Jacquie Phelan (who else). The group, the Women's Mountain Bike And Tea Society (WOMBATS) was formed with the purpose of encouraging the use of fat tire bikes among women.

Although the WOMBATS originated in Marin County, California, Jacquie says she's anxious for other chapters to start up around the country. Memberships are open to women of any skill level "as long as they're willing to sweat, able to ride a bike, and like to socialize with other off-road women." Yearly dues are $12 from which you'll receive the monthly calendar and shop discounts when in the San Francisco area.

The group was started, in part, because of what they describe as a poor job on the media's part of promoting women in the sport. Although we like to think that

MOUNTAIN BIKING has done okay, we'd have to agree. With the rate of women bicyclists increasing at a faster rate than men, we think it's a great idea.

So, gals, get off your tails and join in the festivities. For more information contact Jacquie Phelan at P.O. Box 757, Fairfax, CA 94930.

Jan always looked like she had just stepped out of a beauty parlor or off the cover of a magazine - her clothes always stylish, neat, and tidy. She was very athletic and became involved with a bicycling group called the "WOMBATS," which stood for, "Women on Mountain Bikes and Tea Society." She was invited to work in a friend's bicycle shop. I have a picture of her then.

She was also invited to be a part of the bicycle racing team. Eric was also invited to take over maintenance, in charge of fixing bikes and giving good advice. He was essentially her manager. She then was asked to give a speech at one of the local middle schools about bicycle safety and the need to wear helmets. The kids had become excited about what she had done, and she was asked to join the staff at Mill Valley Middle School. She was told that if she had a degree, she could bring in three times the pay she was receiving and be eligible for health insurance. So, she went to Dominican College, was head of her class in a one-year program for her teaching credential and graduated with honors. Harry and I of course, were present for that memorable event. Both of

our daughters benefitted by returning to college later in their adult lives and were straight "A" students.

Janis Coblentz at the wheel, Bicycle Odyssey 1989

Jan had acquired friends all over the map and one day she called me and said, "Mom, I have cancer. I have talked to my doctors and they gave me the name of someone at Stanford. I'd like to come down, and have you, go with me." I went with her and she mentioned, "You know, I think that I would just as soon talk to the doctor alone." I responded, 'Well, that's all right with me. Look at all the time I've had to visit with you back and forth." The doctor gave her the straight scoop and it didn't look good. Jan never batted an eye. We drove home. She was in her mid-fifties when she contracted colon cancer and it is still a mystery to us. She had been a vegetarian for 40 years, was very athletic, grew her own vegetables and herbs, was a wonderful cook, did yoga and meditation, had numerous black belts in Karate and had not needed to work for several years. She led a very stress-free life. Jan may have done a lot of planning and thinking before she announced her cancer to anyone other than Eric. After aggressive treatment and a good year of being cancer free, it did unfortunately, return.

After the doctor explained the sequence of how the disease might progress, she invited all her best friends, one at a time for a visit. She lay on the couch in the living room where peals of laughter were heard as each one talked about the memories and good times. She then gave back to each one the items they had given her. She told everybody, "You can cry if you want to, but I'm not going to." With Jan, one chose laughter rather than tears. She and I laughed and made fun of each other. In a way it was a very quiet time, but also a cheerful time.

She was very generous with her time and thoughts. She not only gave people back the things they had given her, but also gave them things they had liked of hers, like this ring I wear with her (and my) J.C. initials on it. It was a ring Eric's dad had made for her and the same for Eric.

Hospice was involved then. Kath or another family member drove me up as often as they could to visit. She never looked sick or gaunt and one time asked me, "Would you do a sleepover?" I said, 'Sure.' We had dinner and laughed a lot, went to sleep, got up in the morning and gave each other a goodbye kiss as I left. This whole time, there had not been a sniffle nor any hanging on to each other – not a word about death or plans, etc. My ride came to take me home and two days later I received Eric's call. He said, "This is the call you've been dreading." That was the end of it, February 9, 2010.

I was very glad I got to spend that special time with her. Harry had died five years before Jan, which was a blessing in some ways, because without even knowing it, she had to be his favorite. She was quiet and perfect, could handle herself in any situation.

In her short life, she took the bull by the horns and in her own, noticeably quiet way, got what she wanted without hurting anybody. Being a bicycle racer, she wasn't as private as one might think. But she and Eric were noticeably quiet. Everything about their romance and life was quiet and private, behind the scenes, so to speak. She wasn't an emotional or fitful person but gentler, more the sober type. She was very pretty and had a lot of friends, but they were never raucous.

The hardest thing I had to contend with was when she moved out during high school and went to live with Eric. She was barely 18 and it just came as such a surprise.

Jan – A Not So Funny Story

At just about kindergarten age when we were all just playing around at Uncle Madison's house (Harry's brother) up in the Oakland Hills, Jan ran into the closed sliding glass door. The glass was reasonably thick and for her to fling herself through it and not go over the balcony was lucky.

I can remember Dad drove to Oakland where the doctor was with all of us talking to her in cheerful voices. All Jan did was apologize for breaking the window. The doctor told us it was okay to drive her home before taking her to the hospital. He didn't think there was any problem to wait to stitch up her leg. Jan's scar (mid-shin and calf) remained visible but never hindered her athletic pursuits.

To Our Beloved, Indomitable, Big Jan

The Gods are really angry – it's very plain to see
The polar cap is melting, and Big Jan's Big C
The Middle East's in turmoil, greed in industry
Our leaders are pathetic, and Big Jan's Big C

Stercus

We worship the God Oil, a worse choice cannot be
Our moral compass, it is broke, and Big Jan's Big C
The supermarkets overflow, while Africa goes hungry
There is no justice it would seem, check Big Jan's Big C

Accidit*

But don't lose faith there is great hope
which come in many a guise
Modern science, alternatives, loyal friends
– the good vibes rise
With all our love and all our prayers
and Big Jan's strong brave spirit
We'll form a force to lift her up, and she will overcome it.

Fight Fiercely! Mom and Your Sibs

*Shit Happens

Friend and Fellow Bicyclist, Jacquie Phelan Writes

"March 8 is Women's Day. There will be articles, and in Europe people give acacia blossoms to the women in their lives...but this year, I want to recognize one woman. Janis Coblentz—of the original dozen or so Wombats—died this month, after a three-year-long cancerous siege.

Her brave life partner and tandem/bike/Airstream adventuring man, Eric Johnson, stood by her during the siege, and kept her comfortable last month as Jan ran out of steam.

My first sight of Jan was in 1987 at a Sausalito health food store, where she came over and introduced herself...and shortly after joined that charter bunch of fat-tire women in Marin County, California. New Year's Day 1988 was a drenching downpour of a winter's day. Jan, Eric, and only a couple others headed into the hills...

The following summer she and Joan Nilsen were "best women" at Charlie and my 'wedding bells' nuptials. I got the (used) dress, the (semblance of) pomp, and the genuinely delicious food aspects of a Solemn Occasion right. ...but since weddings in general seem like dress-up play-acting, I couldn't resist tweaking other givens—no one was asked to don fancy clothes. Having attendants was good enough, and Jan, Joan and "Jerome" (Charlie's dude-of-honor) gave us that pinch of style.

Jan's panache arose from an inimitable blend of forties Hollywood glamour and late century organic Earth-Woman. When she told stories, she'd often punctuate them with extra vigor, italicizing what she'd just seen or done, like when they witnessed the 50th birthday of the GG Bridge.

"You could not believe what it was like!" she told me of their day. "Fireworks raining, pouring! down off the deck of the bridge, with the bay reflecting this golden light. A magic night— thanks to the bikes— with front row seats up in the hills..."

I took notes.If you ever catch me in lipstick, it's thanks to her.

If you ever have some of my home-grown vegetables, Ms. Coblentz, master gardener inspired that, too.

From the bike to the food, to the dignified carriage on any of her bicycles, she embodied the cycling way of life. She must have a wall covered with trophies (she managed to be eight years older than me, but look younger than me, and raced like a twenty-year-old). They, along with a garden, a broken-hearted mate, and a hole in the Fairfax community, will mark the presence of a remarkable woman who faced the end without flinching, complaining, or weeping.

Janis, you inspire me." [4]

---

[4] Jacquie Phelan Blog
https://jacquiephelan.org/2010/03/08/requiem-for-janis-coblentz/

Marty

Marty is more like me. I don't know how to describe him. If I were somebody who wept a lot, I would have wept buckets over that child. From day one, I knew he was brilliant. Marty got things done but drove us nuts. He had to know what made anything run. His friends were many, and he was a gifted storyteller. I am including some of his stories.

A Marty Story – Marty speaking... "Being blessed with abundant energy and curiosity (not always understood nor appreciated by my father) my early years were sprinkled with "Not So Good" (NSG) events. Another event I recall happened at around age three when my curiosity got the better of me and I decided to see just exactly what made the gas meter attached to the side of our home, tick. I proceeded to methodically disassemble the meter (with my father's tools which, without his knowledge or approval, he had donated to the cause.) I'm not sure if I got far enough along with the process to actually begin disbursing natural gas into the atmosphere before my mother discovered what I was up to and brought an end to the dismantling. She recalled to me years later that she contacted the local PG&E office to inform them that there was a small problem with the gas meter. She didn't mention that the 'small problem' was her three-year-old son! When the technician arrived and saw what had happened, my mother pulled him aside and requested that he, under no circumstances, admonish me for what I had done. She requested that he allow me to watch him reassemble the meter and explain what the parts did and what the dangers would be to an inexperienced technician (yours truly!) were the process not conducted correctly.

Were it not for my mother's intervention, the experience with PG&E would have most assuredly had a different outcome. I firmly believe that Jean's intervention in this event helped to preserve my curiosity about all things mechanical. This curiosity and subsequent ability have served me well all my adult life. I have made a successful career in the field of mechanical maintenance engineering in the mining industry, working my way up from a mechanic welder to hold senior management positions with some of the world's leading mining companies.

My life could easily have gone in some other, less productive direction if it were not for Jean's uncanny knack for understanding the long-term ramifications of decisions and seeing *cookies* as they pass by. Lucky for me, she was wise enough to grab this one."

Marty Story – Jean's Condensed Version

One time when I had the Girl Scout troop at our house, Marty and his friends closed the garage door, opened the refrigerator, and helped themselves to all the cupcakes I had made for the meeting. When it was time to serve refreshment, the boys had to apologize to the girls. We took up a collection and bought more cupcakes. I fixed steak that night for dinner, something I rarely did. Marty sat at the table but did not get anything to eat. He still laughs about that.

Marty's Story of Same Incident:

"Jean was always volunteering for something! It's obvious she was never in the Army! One of her volunteer jobs I recall was Troop Leader for my sister's Girl Scout troop. I fondly remember one event (another "Not So Good") that occurred when my mother was preparing for an exceptionally large troop meeting at our home. Part of the preparation was to bake approximately three dozen really tasty cupcakes (one of her specialties, along with the world's best ginger snap cookies) and place them in the refrigerator in our garage for the next day's activities.

This must have occurred on a Friday (no school the next day) because my friend down the street and I decided to make a tent and camp out in his front yard. As the evening progressed, and we started to get a little hungry, I remembered that there was abundant goodness just down the street. We proceeded to liberate said cupcakes from the fridge, call over some more friends, and enjoy every last one of them in our makeshift tent. Well, the next day, as preparation for the event began, you can imagine my mother's surprise when she opened the fridge. Now, it wouldn't take a genius (although she is one!) to figure out what happened to the cupcakes but at that young age, I was amazed at how fast she figured out who the pilferers were. My friend Paul and I were confronted regarding the missing cupcakes and we confessed immediately. I think...maybe not immediately...'the dog ate them' comes to mind, although we didn't have a dog. I don't remember the mad dash to replace the cupcakes, but I will never forget the dinner my family and I had that night. In honor of my pilfering, we had a special treat...steak with all the trimmings, yum, yum, my favorite! Not being a wealthy family, I remember steak was a special treat and I eagerly watched the preparations. Imagine my surprise when the prepared plates were being handed out and mine contained not a juicy steak, but a piece of plain white bread. A glass of water accompanied this sparse meal. I vaguely remember my father telling me that bread and water is what they feed convicts in prison, and if I continued to take things that didn't belong to me, that is probably where I would end up. So now was as good a time as any to start getting used to the food I would be eating. Not sure how my mother was involved in this creative punishment, but I'm sure, like all good parents, they conspired to teach me yet another lesson about right from wrong. I wish I could say that from that point on, I always did the right thing, but I can tell you that I never, ever took anyone else's cupcakes!

I wrote the following for Mom's 83rd birthday. The taste of the scrumptious Girl Scout cupcakes that were enjoyed, in excess, by friends and me whose names I have forgotten. I'm certain Michael Durr talked me into it. I do not, however, remember the taste of the steak that was consumed by the rest of the family that night! The bread was good, and the water had no discernable chlorine taste.

My mother's cooking and especially her ginger snaps were so great that her recipe made it into the local paper."

"A Soft Answer Turneth Away Wrath." I have always tried to diffuse tense or angry circumstances by remaining calm and speaking softly, often pointing out something positive about the situation."
—A Favorite Saying.

The dessert is the special thing about the picnic menu from Mrs. M. H. (Jean) Coblentz of Sunnyvale, Membership chairman.

"The strawberries, sour cream and ginger snaps are a rare treat and should be eaten together for maximum enjoyment," Jean says.

Jean's ginger snap recipe has been used by her family for almost a quarter of a century. She says that everyone who has tried the cookies has asked for the recipe. Here it is:

GINGER SNAPS

3/4 cup shortening
1 cup sugar'
1 egg
1/4 cup molasses
2 cups flour
1 Tbsp. ginger
2 tsp baking soda
1 tsp cinnamon 1/2 tsp. salt

Cream shortening and sugar, add egg and molasses. Shift remaining ingredients and stir. Form balls about the size of walnuts or smaller. Roll balls in granulated sugar. Place 20 on an ungreased cookiie sheet. Bake at 350 degrees until flattened, cracked and lightly browned; approximtely .8 to 10 minutes

Recipe from local newspaper

Cookie: As a child, Marty was on the move all the time and had difficulty sitting still. Basically, he just wouldn't conform to the rules most teachers expected. We somehow got him into high school and during his senior year, we heard of a speaker coming to the school who had just opened a welding trade school. I knew he could always get a high school diploma, but this was really an opportunity. We talked it over with Marty and the staff at school, who I'm sure were happy to see him move to a learning environment more suited to his ambitions. We made an appointment to visit the school, where the owner showed us all around. Marty asked all kinds of questions, and the owner was happy to answer them because we were listening. The guy said to Marty, "What do you expect to get out of this?" Marty looked him right in the eye and said, "I want to be the best damn welder in the whole world." The guy opening his shop said, "And I think you're going to make it, too."

Cookie? You bet. This guy saw the potential in Marty. Marty finished the training and certification process a full two months ahead of the established timeline. Since we had paid for the full course, Marty stayed at the school where he practiced what he had learned and also helped other students with their proficiency. The instructors saw that he had a talent for teaching his new-found skills and asked him if he would consider becoming a student instructor for his remaining time at the school. He accepted the offer and was paid for his tutoring. I suppose this was his first paying job as a welder.

He then fell in love, married Alma and moved to Nevada where he began his mining career. They had two children: Christopher Rush Coblentz, 8/8/79, and Jessica Rush Coblentz, 1/7/83. Rush is Harry's mother's maiden name. Susan Rush was a direct descendant of Dr. Benjamin Rush, signer of the Declaration of Independence and medical adviser to the Lewis and Clark expedition, though he didn't travel with them. At that point, Marty's career just took off, learning this and that, being promoted and invited to join company after company. Welding is only part of it, but welding opened the door to an exceptionally good future. The rough and tough miners listened to him when he spoke and followed his instruction.

Alma and Marty were later divorced, and he married Laurie Ann Bogue in August of 1985. They currently live in the Applegate Valley area of southern Oregon.

Marty writes: "When I married Laurie, the Coblentz family received an additional blessing in the form of another granddaughter, Laurie's daughter Trina. Laurie had been a single mother since Trina's birth and the two of them had overcome numerous challenges together in the 14 years before we met. I was immediately impressed by this 14-year-old who was not only pretty and well behaved but thoughtful and respectful of others as well. I had little experience with teenage girls and Trina never really had a father figure in her life, so we worked together as father and daughter and both learned a lot from each other. Watching Trina grow to womanhood was one of the many wonderful memories of my children that I will always cherish. The journey was not without some strife but nothing good ever comes easy and I can say without a doubt that the love between us grew stronger with each passing day.

Trina fell in love and married Shawn Sorrell and they had two wonderful sons together, Jean's great grandsons Zackary and Torren. Sadly, their marriage did not last, and Trina eventually married her high school sweetheart, Curtis Norris. They settled into life in Boise, Idaho with Trina putting herself through school and becoming a dental assistant. Her sweet and gentle nature was greatly appreciated by her patients!

Trina's story and our lives were forever changed in early 2010 when she was diagnosed with stage four lung cancer. Laurie moved in with her family to help her through all of the treatments and to supply the encouragement that only a mother can. Trina put up a valiant fight but succumbed to the cancer in October of that year. She had all of her family around her including her grandma Jean as she drew her last breath. The sadness I felt on that day has not diminished and the tears flow whenever I think of it. The sadness that Jean had to endure, losing a daughter and granddaughter in the same year can only be imagined. The memories of both will live on inside of us forever."

Marty worked in Indonesia from 1997 until 2000, Peru from 2000 until 2003, Honduras from 2004 through 2006, back to Peru in 2007-2010, Morenci, Arizona from 2010 through 2014 and back to Peru for the last time as a consultant in early 2014 until October 2015, where people picked his brain as he worked as a troubleshooter.

Alma returned to the Bay Area and lived with her parents for a while. I helped her get a job at Stanford, a definite *cookie* for her since she worked there for 29 years, was very well thought of and happy and now glad to be retired.

Did I know Marty would ever become successful? I did not and prayed in every single language I knew that this kid would find his way. It was very tough to see someone you knew had ability, struggle in life. How was he ever going to get through high school? He didn't want to take the normal path. He just didn't care about most of the high school curriculum except for the shop classes.

Scott and Marty

Marty adores me because as he says, "You didn't kill me when I was little." We both survived. Harry was not mellow about it at all but willing to celebrate what could be celebrated and gloss over what we had to wait for … the good that might come from all this. Harry and I didn't always agree on how to handle Marty, but what I think made it work was my willingness to take the decision for him to attend welding school. Harry came from the East Coast blue-blood society who never would have thought of welding as a great career. It was our understanding that I would take responsibility for Marty. Harry just washed his hands of it, which caused no resentment on my part. Harry and Marty became very good friends long before Harry died and Scott and Marty, although very different, are close and good friends. They each have different personalities that don't often conflict with the other, no competition. It is not 'big brother' idolatry on Scott's part.

Marty said this about his father: "My father was a conservative man and raised to not display too much emotion. I was the polar opposite. My father was a college educated, white-collar executive and hoped I would follow in his footsteps. Once, while my father was away on business, I removed the engine from his lawnmower to power a minibike. He was not pleased at this accomplishment and ordered the engine returned to the mower. He had a difficult time seeing how taking everything apart to fix it or just to see how it worked could ever manifest itself into some lucrative career. My father played golf, and I rebuilt cars in his driveway and sold them for a profit. My relationship with my father was a bit rocky until about age thirty-three. That was when he told me for the first time that I could recall that he was proud of me and what I had been able to accomplish without a college degree. That was after I had worked my way up from the ground floor in the mining business to be chosen for a position with the Detail Engineering Team (one of six candidates, the other five had degrees) to develop our company's 1.2 billion (1995 dollars) offshore copper and gold mine on the island of Sumbawa in Indonesia. He continued to praise me the rest of his life for my continuing achievements and we developed a relationship based on love as well as mutual respect. I learned much from my father, but it was more by assimilation than by direct tutoring."

Marty still runs into people that were affected by what they learned from him. Although recently retired, he is on contract to be called back in case they need only what he knows.

Scott and Marty

Another Marty Story from Jean: He must have been junior high-school age when I went to the garage one day. My olfactory nerves told me that something had died in the garage. There was a horrible smell. On my quest to find what might be causing such a stench, I came upon a drawer full of sandwich bags.

The conversation went something like this:

Jean: Sweetheart, what is all of this? Why are these things here? You're supposed to eat them for your lunch.

Marty: Mom, it's not cool to take your lunch anymore.

Jean: Well, all you had to do was tell me it wasn't cool to take your lunch. I wouldn't have minded.

Marty: Yes, but then you wouldn't have written me a poem every day.

There was nothing more I could say to that. I had put a little something in his lunch every day. During lunchtime, the kids all gathered around and asked what his mother had said. In another box in the garage, all the poems were gathered.

I also sent Scott notes in his lunch. It was just a way of communicating with my kids that ended up being a big hit. One example: Good Morn, Blow Your Horn. Here's Your Lunch, Munch, Munch, Munch.

Marty Tells the Same Story: This story highlights just how much this woman loved her happy but somewhat troubled son.

"Every morning my mom would dutifully get up early and prepare healthy, brown bag lunches for her children. In each one of those lunches, she would write a poem on the napkin. The content varied daily with either whimsical or somewhat serious content but, always constructed in a way so as to engage the reader's mind. Now, when you're trying to be cool in high school, you just *don't* bring brown bag lunches to school. If you are cool, you eat junk food from the newly installed vending machines. Wanting desperately to be cool, but not wanting to disappoint my loving, caring mother, I adopted the practice of depositing these lunches made with love and care into an old dresser that was in our garage; however, not before extracting the napkin with said poem. My mother discovered early on what I was doing but never mentioned it to me. She just kept making those lunches and writing those poems. How's that for a deep understanding of a teenager's mind! I was reading one of the poems one day at school when a friend of mine asked me what I was doing. I was slightly embarrassed but decided to show him the poem. It happened to be a cleverly crafted (always...you know Jean!) poem about something (hers were never mushy or too sentimental) and my friend thought it was great! It didn't take long before my friends were asking to see the poem of the day!

Marty, Chris, and Harry. Three Generations of Coblentz'

I thought it would be the farthest thing from cool in the world but boy, was I wrong. I have assimilated a small helping of my mom's poetic prowess and use it from time to time. I am no longer overly concerned about how cool it may or may not be. Some aspects related to getting old are really nice!"

Marty has a very smart and handsome son named Chris. He never really embraced the academic aspect of school, kinda like his dad. He worked his way through high school and then took some course studies at the local junior college. He now works for a civil construction company and has worked his way up to supervisory positions. Marty is sure to remind him how proud he is of what he has accomplished as he knows the importance of his support. I don't know how important it is to make a mother proud as you march to a different drum. Mothers just seem to be proud of their kids no matter what. I was just happy everything worked out for Marty because as he put it:

"If there was ever a child who tested the patience of their parents, I was/am that child! No sense denying it. Worthy to note here that, thanks to them and their tireless (again, no pun intended) patience, I have never been incarcerated!

Marty adds: "In addition to being my best friend and my mom, I also mention that Jean has been (and will continue to be) my most trusted confidant. I have lost track of how many times I have sought out her guidance. Although her major in college was not Psychology, maybe her minor, it should have been. Being who I am, I have faced numerous events in my life (probably more than most) that required someone's council other than my own. Never was this help refused and never was it not the best course of action. Jean's real-world experience, her intense desire to help others, her amazing intellect and her powers of perception have been a gift of guidance for me that I can never hope to repay.

Scott

Early one Monday morning, the doorbell rang. We opened the door and were surprised to see Joe Davis, our pediatrician. He said he just wanted to "see those babies." It turned out that "Baby" Scott had measles, which the older kids twice brought home from school. Joe Davis said to get Scott to the clinic at once! While we were in the waiting area, another doctor in the hospital walked by and questioned the medical staff as to who was taking care of that baby. She felt he was dying! Seems he had an infection that needed immediate attention. That was about the scariest medical moment we had with the kids when they were little. Also, when Scott was a toddler, his appendix burst. Again, there was hospitalization and thankfully good medical attention with a positive outcome.

Scott is easy-going and handsome like his dad and as easy to like as was his dad. When Scott was a baby, I used to tuck him under my arm with my tennis racquet and go play tennis with friends. He sat inside the fence with a big basket of Dinky Toys and was happy as a clam. Scott may have been about five when he contracted a communicable disease like measles, something the other kids brought home from school before vaccinations. One day we came home from tennis, and he had developed one of those diseases. The doctor wished him to be seen by a doctor at the hospital who said, "Who's taking care of this baby? He's dying." Due to an infection, he was immediately operated on, which began his speedy recovery. He was a very sick little boy for a couple of days, didn't even recognize us.

He loved Dinky Toys, and when he began to act more normal, we brought him a new Dinky toy each day he showed a sign of getting better. One day our pediatrician said, "He can go home now." I walked into his room telling him such and he started crying because, "If you take me home, I won't get a Dinky toy every day." We have all laughed with him about that.

At one time, Scott, around 12-16 years of age, had a paper route. I would often help him by putting down the back end of the station wagon, and as I drove, he rolled up the papers and tossed them out. We worked well together. One Christmas, we had friends visiting and things were topsy-turvy. I helped him once again. We had a nice rhythm. He often expresses appreciation for all my years of driving him on that route. (See below)

Scott recounts: "When I was 12-16 years of age, I had a morning paper route delivering the San Francisco Chronicle. Mother would help me deliver the papers with the station wagon we used to have. I would sit back, on the tailgate, and throw the papers from there. One morning I threw one of the papers into the bushes and jumped off to get it and Mom kept going ... without me. She knew the route by heart from helping me so much that after the third house or so she did not hear the papers hitting the driveway, looked back, and I was gone! She had to backtrack until she found me waiting. I climbed back onto the tailgate and we finished the route.

For a Christmas present one year, Kath, Renato and Mom decided to do the route for me so I could sleep in on Christmas morning. Well, when delivering papers by car, you zigzag a lot going from house to house. That caught a Sunnyvale policeman's eye and he pulled them over to investigate! After he found out what they were doing, he let them go with a warning"

Scott says, "One year when I was about 12 or so, Mom asked me what I wanted for my birthday dinner. After giving it much thought, I turned to her and said, 'Would it hurt your feelings if we went to McDonald's?' Back then they were not on every street corner and it was a real treat to go there. And, of course, she chuckled and said, 'yes.!'

Marty wasn't around much to play big brother to Scott. With a three-year difference, they were not vying for the same girls or any of that stuff. As far as school went, Scott graduated from high school and didn't give us any trouble – a real sweetheart. He's handsome and fun, the easy one and so much like his dad but does not have Marty's fire.

Scott married Karen Lindahn, and their children are Kelly (Crittenden) and Stacy (Nichols). He and Karen divorced, and he now lives in the Gardnerville area of Nevada with his fiancé Jolene who has two adult children. Scott is employed as a Data Analyst for a software company out of North Carolina.

Harry

Harry was really very easy-going. In that respect, Harry was much like my dad who also had a great sense of humor and didn't take himself too seriously. Our son Scott is much like him. Talk about apples not falling far from the trees, whether genetically or by marriage!

Harry didn't consider himself a great golfer, but he loved golf. He began golfing at a young age when he was old enough to caddy. They lived near a golf course, and he and his brother shared this golfing experience. Harry also golfed while at Stanford and later, golfing fit right into his business lifestyle. He continued to play golf well into his 80s on a regular basis. I was very happy he enjoyed and was engaged in this sport.

He was in the insurance business and was offered one of his first jobs right after Stanford with a San Francisco brokerage firm. He stayed with the firm, Marsh and McLennan, until he retired as a VP at age sixty-four. Even though his commute to and from work at the time seemed long, from Atherton to San Francisco, he always managed to read the newspaper during that train commute. As long as we lived in Menlo Park, I drove him to the train station every morning with all the kids in the car.

Harry never set out to change the world nor be the highest on the ladder. He just wanted to be challenged and enjoy his work. He was very good at his job and that was enough for him. He enjoyed his family. When it came to the children, Harry sometimes didn't want to put in his two-cents worth because he figured it wasn't worth an argument.

He did, in all due respect, however, support my discipline decisions.

Tribute To Harry

Harry passed away at age 83 in December of 2005. I especially remember two of his birthday celebrations that required more planning than usual. The first was for his 70th. Being such a milestone, I wanted all his children to be there to celebrate, no matter what it took. This meant that Kath and Milena flew in from Germany for five days and the other kids made any necessary changes to their schedules to be here on the big day, June 30! The kids had fun planning their entrance for a maximum surprise effect. I was still working at Stanford and told Harry I was heading to San Jose for a meeting and suggested we plan on having lunch at home to celebrate.

We were standing in the kitchen when the garage door opened and in walked three of his four children. He was flabbergasted as everyone began wishing him a happy birthday.

Then as planned, about thirty seconds later, Kath and Milena walked in and Harry practically "lost it." He experienced disbelief and joy at the same time as tears welled up in his eyes. We all expressed our love and admiration for handsome Harry. The celebration lasted long into the evening. Scott still had his boat, so we all went up to Folsom Lake the next day for a party on the lake. Kath and Milena especially wanted to fit in as much fun as they could on this short California trip before returning to work and school in Germany.

The second festive occasion took place for his 80th birthday and here again, I insisted all children and grandchildren be present. That meant Trina flew in from Boise, Milena from Italy and Marty and Laurie from

Oregon. We had gone up to Jan's in Fairfax to celebrate. Harry had congestive heart failure and wasn't feeling all that well and was happy to just sit around and watch his children and grandchildren. I told everyone that the only present I wanted given to their dad/grandfather was for each one to write down something special about him. I gave each a piece of paper to finish either or both of these sentences:

This is something I wish I had told you before ...
This is what I think of you ...

I told the kids that these comments are usually said at memorial services but that I wanted him to hear it right now. I want his heart to be warmed by your kind and humorous expressions of your love for him. It was a kick and a half, and he loved it. It was easier to say things that way, like reading from a script, than speaking them directly while looking into his big blue eyes. Everyone had their own style and feelings and knew what was important to communicate to Harry and we all appreciated each other's efforts as we told story after story.

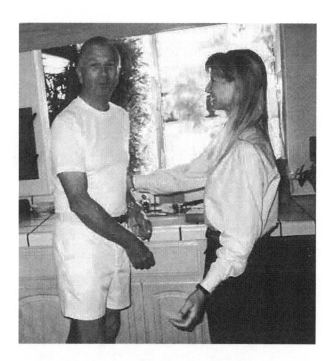

Harry (70th birthday) and Jan

Coblentz family together on Harry's 80th Birthday

Jean and Harry at Nome Court

Nome Court House

On Technology

"As far as technology goes and it's doing away with some of the finer practices of old, it depends on what it is. I sometimes watch Kath use technology and the internet to readily obtain information she needs. Because of this smart technology, she can accomplish a remarkable amount of work in a short amount of time. This continues to amaze me. I was working at Stanford when computers first came into our offices and was continually being retrained as new software arrived.

I used the computer while working at Stanford and even now have an up-to-date computer in my office at home that I used mostly for email and word processing. I found ways that worked well for me. A big help, of course, have been my dear, thoughtful, and technologically adept personal assistants, Janet, Laura, Karen, and Kath, as all helped me stay in touch and involved with Stanford and my other important civic engagements. Especially with AMD - I needed and appreciated the help of these women."

—Jean Galt Coblentz

Harry's 75th Birthday

My Loving Words to
Handsome Harry
80 Years Old on June 30, 2003

My tribute is the hardest of all because it covers the greatest span of time. Why did I fall in love with you in 1946? Because you were handsome, fun to be with, and you had a shiny black car.

Why did I love you in 1948? That was the year we were married, and you danced with me on the night we were married!!!

And in 1949, 51, 53, and 56 why did I love you? Because you were the father of four wonderful kids born in those years who brought sunshine and rain into our lives and who always kept us on track - and together – since the deal was whoever left had to take them.

I loved you in the early 50's because one very cold morning when the lawn was all frosty white, you took the broom and wrote, "I Love You" in the frost.

In 1962 you decided Sunnyvale wasn't too far south to commute and I loved you for that as we bought the Home on Nome, which I really love. We work in the garden together, and once when I wasn't looking you erected a shrine to me – which warms me every time I look at it ... must be love.

On a business trip, checking into the hotel in Boston, there was a card at the desk from you which said, "I Love You" and once in New York there was a lovely bouquet of flowers from "Roomie" boy! that made points for you with my colleagues. Many are envious of the relationship we have and much of it has been built on tiny acts of love and kindness (even such simple things as keeping one's mouth shut when the first instinct is to correct or criticize.)

There were times when you resented the time I spent on Stanford and the job and experience which gave my life a whole, wonderful new dimension. You hid the resentment well, supported me in every endeavor, and enjoyed the fringe benefits which came with the territory and which have provided experiences and friends we could not trade for anything.

Over the years, I have loved you for sharing household chores and the wonderful way you have taken over everything when I was laid up with backs, knees, hips, ankles, and shoulders, and then decided to be the house husband when you retired. One in a million.

Your love affair with golf tickles me. The way you rationalized getting new equipment you want, the dedicated way you have run the tournaments and the clubs, the camaraderie you have built with some very interesting people, and the way you shake off a bad score because there's always tomorrow, it's only a game, and YES, you had a good time!

I admire the way you have pulled up your socks and dealt with the cause and result of your health problems. The self-discipline you have shown after the diagnosis of both heart problems and prostate cancer, in every element of your life including exercise, medication, diet, and moderation in all things, is a model for all of us. You refuse to be held hostage to your "bad heart" and you live because you are alive, and plan to be for decades.

You are gentlemanly and unfailingly courteous with store clerks, drivers, phone solicitors, and people who finally come on the phone after you have been holding for an hour. You have also learned the power of written thanks. Our children and grandchildren have been beneficiaries of your enormous generosity – in a crisis, in times of need, or "just because I love you," a $20 bill slipped in for gas, a plane ticket (or two), loans without number and without interest, business advice and management – the list goes on and on. Your temper you keep in check, yet you can allow your deepest emotions to show and you have that rarest of talents – the ability to laugh at yourself. Yes, you are truly a nice man.

And why do I still love you in 2003? In addition to everything I have said up to now, it is because on really cold nights I have found a hot water bottle for my feet in the bed, in the morning my cup is out and coffee is down, and for Christmas I got dish towels because you knew that's what I really wanted. Mostly though, it's because you are still handsome, still fun to be with, we laugh and kid a lot, our kids are great and have given us wonderful grandchildren and amazing memories, and we still have a shiny black car.

Happy Birthday and cheers to the love of my life from the love of your life, Roomie!

Jean.

Music

Few would have thought that at age nine or ten, sitting with dad for hours listening to music was a cookie, but it was. Music was important to my folks and, not until later years, did I realize how important it was for me. Listening with my Father gave me an appreciation for classical music. I also learned to play piano. The songs my parents sang became my songs. Now, as I enter my 90th year, this older music has a greater place in my heart and soul, often bringing me to tears when I hear the pieces. I often say to Kath, 'That was one of Daddy's favorite songs."

—Jean Galt Coblentz

Family Celebrations

Our most memorable family vacations took place at Capistrano Beach where my sister Alice's family has a wonderful beach vacation home right at the water's edge. We looked forward to those summer trips with great anticipation. We, like many young families in the 50s and early 60s had a station wagon. As Harry drove, I kept the commotion down in the back. The four kids got creative with their travel games and stories and made plans for the moment they arrived at the beach. My sister Alice's kids were very close in age to mine and they all treasured this time together. My two girls were the oldest and did endure lots of teasing and taunting from their younger brothers and cousins. It was all done in good-natured fun, which fostered a closeness that grew each summer among the cousins as they body surfed and had a good time.

Harry and Uncle Jim, Alice's husband, learned to read the surf and watch for the best waves. We indulged in summer novels and collected shells and rocks on our numerous walks along the beach. The excitement also of the passing trains along the Pacific Coast Highway is something that will never be forgotten by any of the cousins.

Those times at the beach house figure in many of my children's fondest childhood memories. I'm pleased to say that even today, there is a special unique bond between these two families that exemplify some of the special elements of the Galt Clan.

Steven, Alice's first-born son is my nephew. He wanted to share some thoughts about our relationship over the years and it starts with our precious memories of time spent at Capistrano Beach.

"Jean and Harry were part of what felt like a mass of adults who surrounded us kids like a cloud, enveloping us with the care and love that gave us the freedom to be ourselves. This enveloping love was also felt down south, at Capistrano Beach, where the Galt clan would often amass en masse for a couple of weeks each summer. In the "Crowell's Nest" we would all stay, parent and children somehow managing to eat and play together mostly without serious incident. From my child's perspective, Jean and Harry made a remarkable couple: knowledgeable about all kinds of things, stately, fun loving, and understanding. Of course, this was also a time of unpleasantness for Jean. For years, I remember hearing of her persistent back problems, and I remember the grace with which Jean bore her troubles.

Once Jean reconnected with Stanford, a whole new side of her emerged. And with it, something new in our relationship emerged as well. She became something of a confidant. I think this change became evident to me at the end of my high school years. As the years went on, my feelings of closeness to Jean only grew, and I think that in large measure this was because Jean is a writer. You've all experienced her wonderful "Christmas in July" missives, but I'm talking about letters she would send to me when there were transitions in my life or the lives of those dear to me: when my dad died, when my first wife and I divorced, when my mom was on her own for so many years; but also when good things happened like when I graduated from college, when I got my PhD, when I got remarried. Jean would always write something encouraging, reflective, and full of wisdom and warmth.

I think of Jean somehow as the one who saw herself most clearly as carrying on the Galt family legacy. My mother embodies many of the virtues that my grandmother and grandfather stood for and passed on to her, and I like to think I may have absorbed a bit of that too. But as the eldest Galt child from that generation, Jean had, I think, received from Curtis and Mabel something like a mandate to keep the memory of their achievement alive. Her being a writer was an aspect of that since Mabel was an inveterate letter writer practically until the day she died. I have a great many of them, and when reading Jean's letters, I could almost imagine Mabel looking over her shoulder. In the end, they all said the same thing:

WE'RE ROOTING FOR YOU,
YOU ARE A FINE MEMBER
OF A GREAT FAMILY, YOU CAN DO IT!

So, did I take my cookies when they were passed? Well, I took a lot of cookies. I guess the real question is, did I pass any to others? Here, I'm not so sure. But what I do know is that Jean did. She certainly passed them to me, without hesitation, and with love."

—Steven Crowell

Steven is the oldest of the Crowell children, and currently heads the Philosophy Department at Rice University. I've loved following his worldwide travels as he presents at various international conferences. I was very touched when he dedicated his first book, a philosophical treatise on HEGEL, to my sister Alice, his mom. She joked that about all she understood in the book WAS the dedication.

As the years went by and our families grew, the four Galt kids and "Granny/Gramma Galt" started to refer to Curtis and Mabel's grown kids and their families as the Galt Clan, evoking a strong sense of pride as we think about our heritage and this memory of Curtis and Mabel.

In 2009, we decided it was time for a gathering of the clan. My youngest sister Corney and her husband Jack had an almond ranch in Modesto, simply perfect for entertaining, with lots of shade, lots of open spaces and a pool. All four of the Galt children were well enough to attend, and most of their offspring, significant others and kids also arrived that July from across the country and as from far away as Italy. We made up funny, clever songs about the group, paid heartfelt tribute to the family and our deep appreciation for our roots and all pitched in to make it a most memorable weekend.

Our family vacations at Capo Beach started out earlier in a smaller, rented house nicknamed, "The Pink House." This house had an unusual structure on the sand resembling a crow's nest where the kids loved to play.

Later when my sister and her husband remodeled their one story, it became known as the "Crowell's Nest," since Alice's husband's name was Jim Crowell, and he designed the house.

August 1960 Vacationing at Capistrano Beach

Their home at Capistrano Beach continued to be the place for the four of us siblings to get together and strengthen our bond as members of the Galt family. After our mother Mabel died, we made it a point to gather every year over the Super Bowl weekend to enjoy the game and each other's company, take long walks on the beach and have great conversation.

August 1960 Vacationing at Capistrano Beach

My cousin Bruce Galt lived in Southern California, so he and his wife Ann often joined us for an afternoon. I was closer to Bruce than any of my other cousins and he always did a wonderful job of photo documentation of our time together.

"In high school during WWII, 1943, my principal of the small Hughson Union High School instructed me to respond to a brochure from the Navy urging the signing up for Naval Aviation. So, I went to San Francisco for three days and passed all the requirements. While working for Uncle Stuart in the warehouse I got orders to report on July 3, 1943, to Butte Montana so as to attend college at Montana Mines (now known as Montana Tech). All the openings for pilot training were filled and this was a waiting period. We were all given courses in engineering; freshman for most for us. I received better grades in there than in my lackadaisical time in Hughson High School.

Being a pilot turned out to be not what I was suited for, so I spent the rest of my obligation as a carrier airplane mechanic on the East Coast and on a new carrier shakedown cruise

My parents moved from Hughson to Palo Alto during this time, so that was my home when I mustered out. Before I got discharged, I told my mom to enter me into Stanford as I had nothing else in mind and could live at home. So, based on my completed year in engineering, I was accepted as a sophomore. After graduating I gradually realized that the knowledge that I was a Stanford graduate contributed to my confidence and self-esteem. Dr. Tresseder, President at the time seemed to be no great asset, however Wallace Sterling took over just before I left. He and his successors created an improvement in the Stanford reputation. Stanford was the only university to encourage useful design and innovation leading up to the Internet. Dr. Hennessey was involved in that and received quite favorable reviews on his recent retirement from his job as Stanford president. (While studying mechanical engineering I had no idea what was going on in the making of Silicon Valley)

I don't have a good knowledge of the time periods of the following events, but there seems to be some connection from the long time point of view. (1) Jean had a series of back surgeries. I wasn't involved at the time but was aware of the seriousness. Her brilliant father, Curtis (Curd), was stricken with Alzheimer's. My experiences had to do with a dysfunctional family, divorce, and reestablishing relationships with my three daughters. I see these events as maturing for both of us and producing what I like to think of as mutual respect and understanding. Sometime later I married Ann and got a step-daughter.

There were three time periods when I connected with Jean: The first being Jean staying with us as pre-teens during the time Curtis was looking for a doctor's office for a permanent stay in the States. I was used to only playing with boys—my brother Bob and cousins Ken and Murray. Then slightly younger, Alan joined the group. (The five of us played the five brothers: Maurice, Stuart, Curtis (Curd) Clarence (Cle), and Ellis in basketball for a couple of years). So, not being used to playing with girls, and Jean not about to give way at all; we engaged in various forms of enmity. Only much later did I realize that Jean was in much more of an awkward position than I, living in somewhat a strange house with strange people.

The second being my going to Stanford and living at home in Palo Alto, while Jean attended Stanford, and Curtis' family was living in Manteca. It was convenient for all to get together at our place. In spite of Jean trying to help me to be sociable, I never accomplished much in that regard at Stanford. Never got the hang of it. Studying Engineering and living at home didn't seem to help. It seemed to me that Jean and Harry were always out on the town having a good time. (Actually, Harry was hashing at the time) Looking back on it I did manage to fill time in activities: football, wrestling, concert band, basketball band, brass choir, and German Band. The latter being quite informal; Rosotti's beer garden, a baseball game (the student in charge was very unhappy that we didn't schedule our presence ahead of time), and a couple of concerts at Rickey's lounge.

The third period was when Ann and I were taken in as "Siblings" as part of the Siblings reunions; going to all the functions with a great group of people.

Jean — Bruce and Ann love and respect you." Nov 1, 2015

In February 1998, Kath came back from Europe, she had just two weeks before starting back to college and, as luck would have it, the Super Bowl weekend fell in those two weeks, so she asked if she could join us. Wanting to be respectful of all the siblings, I told her since her presence would change the dynamics, I would have to check in with everyone. All said they would be delighted to have her company. She still says it was one of the highlights after she came back to California, and it gave her a great opportunity to reconnect with her aunts and uncles whom she had not seen during the 20 years she was in Italy. Kath then, in fact, made it a point in the next 20 years to help me keep in touch with relatives whenever possible.

Harry and I went on several ocean voyage trips with my sister and some of their best friends. We traveled to Africa, China, Scandinavia, Canada, and Europe with them and to the Caribbean with the Stanford Travel Program.

2004 Jean and Harry on the 4th of July. Our season's Greeting Card this year

---

On Speaking and Listening

"What one says can make a difference. Even if it is only twenty words, people listen, and digest what you say. I have always tried, first and foremost, to be a good listener. Now in my later years, words from my past unwittingly resurface, getting people's attention.

Some are the few Thai sentences (Chinese Dialect I spoke as a child,), I still remember. Seems that the older I get, the more that comes out of me, and no one can understand it!"

—Jean Galt Coblentz

Married Life

As far as my marriage being a challenge vs. me just absolutely loving him, both were true.

There is not a wedding nor marriage nor anything like that in the world that doesn't have irritation attached to it. What was nice for us was that what irritated me didn't irritate Harry. He was mostly quite easy-going. In all honesty, I think it quite a miracle our marriage lasted as long as it did though a few pages back, you read "Handsome Harry is 80." That really tells the whole story. My children still get tears in their eyes when they read that!

Harry at his namesake
city in Germany

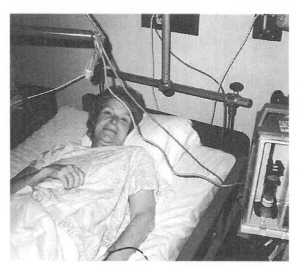

Jean in the Hospital.

Jean and Harry on a cruise

Christmas Cards

Harry's mother thought it awful that we sent out a family gathering photo with our Christmas cards. Being East Coast proper, she wasn't used to seeing a gathered group of family in bathing suits and exposed legs, for example. I think the informality of it got to her. She was much more traditional.

One of my favorite Christmas Cards though, was a photo of us lined up on a bench in front of the beach house looking out toward the water. It was a priceless picture that brings back lots of memories.

After I started working and Kath had moved to Europe, I wanted the kids to still feel a strong family connection. So, I started a family letter, which went out to all my children. This tradition continued for a good 10 years, if not more. It is an offshoot of the ROUND ROBIN my mother had started to keep her kids "in the loop" as we say today. The ROUND ROBIN circulated, among us siblings and mother (till she passed away) and gave each of us a chance to write one letter which all could read. When the envelope came back to me, I'd take out my old letter and write a new one, commenting on the news in the letters from my sisters, Alice and Corney and Al's wife, Wanda. We were a lucky family, appreciating our bonds as "Galt Clansmen" and found this the perfect way to stay in touch.

My niece Kelly asked me where I got the idea to write a family letter and why it was important to me. This was my reply:

'From my childhood. Out in China, you didn't pick up the phone or send a letter, you would keep a journal, and then send out a longer update to your family. Father and Mother's families still all lived in Nebraska, where they both went to college and met. Dad majored in medicine, and mother majored in Home Economics. When I was young, I would write letters and send them to my pen pals in Nebraska. This had nothing to do with the mission but was more about our lives as kids in China. New babies, new wing in the hospital, anything that was new.'

After Kath moved back from Europe, the need for the family letter fell away, and we Coblentz' kept touch over the phone, and lots of visits to Nome Court. Around that time, I stopped working at Stanford but wanted to stay in touch with all the wonderful friends I'd made over those 20 + years, so my SEASON'S GREETINGS was born.

For Season's Greetings or Christmas Cards, I wrote a big single paged letter that covered all the bases explaining what I had done throughout the year, what our family was up to, etc. and send it out to upwards of 250 people. Although my epistle may not arrive during the holiday season, it's still called 'SEASON'S GREETINGS,' and people just love it at any time of the year. Also included was a whimsical picture or two of me taken during that previous year.

I sometimes wonder if doing something like that is selfish, but I don't think so since I have no problem taking the time and showing people my gratitude for their efforts and the love, I have for them. By letting them know this, they hopefully receive a symbolic embrace from me.

I have lived a long time and have known a lot of different people in a lot of different places. I sometimes stop, close my eyes, and have a little memory visit of a time with them. How are they going to know I did just that? They wouldn't, not unless I told them. I also tell them my address is the same and that I have not moved and love having visitors.

2006 Season's Greetings Text

Following Harry's death, 2006 was a year of adjustment to many things in my life, and if you ask me

"How are you doing?" I will say, "I'm doing just fine, thank you."

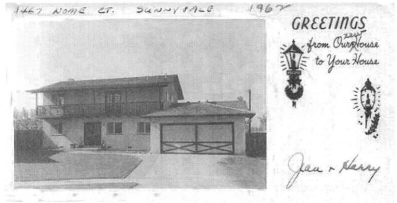

Examples of some of the Season's Greetings

Once I had successfully navigated the world of forms and changes of ownership and established myself as "sole proprietor" in Nome Court, I had time to focus on the commitments I'd made before Harry's death.

Being president of the Woodside-Atherton Auxiliary at this moment in time is very much like being CEO of a multi-million-dollar business complex which has just reopened after a two-year closure for renovations and is trying to regain its place in the market. Except you have no staff and the pay won't buy you a cup of coffee. Ah, but there are rewards.

The neighbor's lawsuit was settled, a very strong board wrought changes (no mean feat with an organization going into its 76th year), several small "personnel" crises thwarted, and the future looks promising for even more money raised to provide for uncompensated care for the children at Packard Hospital. Do come visit Allied Arts Guild, it is gorgeous and often referred to as a hidden gem in Menlo Park.

The Avenidas board is very interesting, not only for the breadth and scope of services the agency provides to the older population, but for the forward planning they are doing for 10 to 20 years down the road as well. Boomers, we'll be ready for you!

The Cap and Gown board and Stanford Associates Governors keep me close to the action at Stanford, and I've agreed to be involved again with planning my 60th (huh? how can that be here already) reunion next October. Fortunately, there is still time for my book groups (one will be celebrating 45 years together in September) and reviewing.

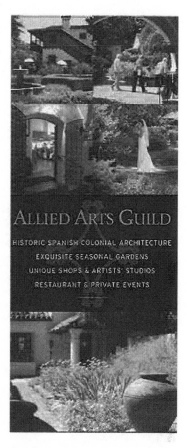

My children are wonderful, right up there among my top blessings. Kath is about a mile away and is busy night and day with her therapy clients and taking classes in anything that sounds interesting. Her daughter, Milena, is coming over early in the year to spend at least a year here honing her American persona. DKNY in Milan wasn't leading to the kind of future she envisions, so stay tuned. She and Kath will live together.

2012 Season's Greetings Text

Season's greetings in June this year because I could not get around to it earlier, just more evidence that I refuse to be held hostage by the calendar. That said, lots has happened since our last "chat", most of it positive, I am happy to report.

Granddaughter #1 Milena has been in the fashion world with Donna Karan (DKNY) for seven years —four in Milan and three in California, where she and Kath lived close by. February she was offered a new position managing the major European DKNY customers. She accepted and returned to Milan in May. I then invited Kath to come live with me (I may "need" all the closets but certainly not all the space.). Kath moved in with me on June 1st (her birthday) 62 years after she first "moved in" with me. It has proved to be a wise decision, especially since I gave up driving (dimming eyes!). Kath, colleagues, and loyal friends, chauffeur me around.

Two more great grandchildren, Katelyn and Beckham, joined CeCe (three-years-old) in that rank. My moniker is GGJEAN and watching this generation gives hope for our sorry old world.

1962—50 years ago was an exceptional year, which made great changes in our lives. We bought 1467 Nome Court, Sunnyvale. I was invited to join the Woodside Atherton Auxiliary (now Allied Arts Aux) to Children's Hospital. I joined two other friends and we created Book Tasters, whose 50 years we shall celebrate in October.

Each of these three landmarks have added undreamed of dimensions to my life—you never know, and in the end, everything correlates and intertwines.

Dining in Toscana

In October 2011, Kath and I along with Jennifer, (Milena's Godmother) went to Italy to visit Milena and we had a glorious visit to Florence, Tuscany and Milan, as well as Voltago, where Milena spent a lot of her childhood with her dad's family. We visited the Stanford campus in Florence and where the new one will be. Weather perfect, the Duomo awesome, wined and dined by Milena's friends and eating and drinking to be sure not to miss any cuisine … a trip to remember!

Jean and Milena in Milano, Italy.

I was surprised and honored to have been selected as one of five honorees for the Avenidas Lifetimes of Achievement Awards. Avenidas is an agency providing a large variety of services for seniors in the Peninsula area.

The event took place on May 20, 2012 in a lovely backyard setting with lifetime "storyboards" featuring pictures, articles, citations, etc. All my family were there, and the great grandbabies were a hit. Definitely memorable!

May 24, 2012

Jean Coblentz
1467 Nome Court
Sunnyvale, CA 94087

Dear Jean,

I'm so glad you agreed to participate in *Avenidas Lifetimes of Achievement 2012*. The recognition was well-deserved, and I hope that in some small way, we were able to convey our appreciation for the time and talent you've given to us through the years.

I know that you'll be glad to hear that the event was one of the most successful ever for Avenidas, thanks to our amazing group of honorees. I've attached a list of the individuals who made special gifts in your honor.

As always, it was a lot of fun working with you, but it was also my privilege to get to know a bit more about you personally. What a remarkable life you've led. In the words of Mae West, "You only live once, but if you do it right, once is enough."

Well done, Jean!

Warm Regards,

Lyn

Lyn Balistreri
Event Coordinator

Enclosure: Donor List

"Lifetimes" Thanks to the Chairs

To Nancy Olson and Anne Taylor, kudos
For guiding Lifetimes so well
I've participated in several of them
But THIS ONE was really SWELL

Somehow you bribed Mr. Wind
Here … go somewhere else to play
Which he did, the weather was perfect
So, Storyboards in place didst say

The drinks were abundant, the nibbles superb
And the crowd got their money's worth
The garden you chose was really a beaut
With wonderful flowers and turf

A LOT of work goes into this day
And a lot of cooks are stirring the stew
But your steady hands and careful guidance
Created a new benchmark for future LT's to view

From one who has been behind the scenes
There were lots of "potholes," I'll bet
So, I send congrats and many thanks too
For a day no honoree will ever forget

The party is over
And what a Whiz Bang
Lots of folks helped out
They made quite a gang

And behind the scenes
The HARD WORK was done
Here's a small token … since YOU were one
Put in your book, be reminded of me
COB sends her deep thanks … a proud honoree

So, now it's on to my Class of 47's 65th Reunion and we
will be inducted into The Cardinal Club on Sunday, the
last day of events. It will be interesting to see how many

people can / will come. It has been easy chairing it since at this point, there aren't many special events, and the staff does most of the work.

2013 Season's Greeting Text

In a drawer today, Dear Friend, I found a "Round To It", so now I can get Around To It.

Season's Greetings from the Court of Nome Court circa 2013! A thoughtful writer (my goal) then provides news in an understandable way for her audience of friends ranging from: Growing up in China, Manteca High, Stanford University, neighbors, all organization members, kids' friends, Harry's Air Force (B-29 pilot) friends plus two widows who asked NOT to be dropped) and finally the careers of Handsome Harry and me. Into which category do you fall? Were you able to match pictures and prose?

Number 1 son, Marty is making retirement noises (mining industry) but is getting interesting offers from "faraway places" which are being thought about. Scott has a new position, and you can see part of his merchandise in the picture. Scott (#2 son) lives near Sacramento so blesses us on a regular basis when he comes down and tackles the "Sonny Do List."

Little did we foresee the major role Kath would play in my life. She has arranged her schedule (she is a Physical Therapy Assistant working for a great boss) so I can get rides to most places with friends filling in. She cooks (doesn't trust mine!) hurrah, so I clean up (my forte).

I find that all my senses above my neck are fading, but thoughtful people play Taxi for me, so I continue with all the organizations and enterprises as before. Thirty years ago, I had a knee replaced which has finally signaled "The End." So, on June 14, I'll have that revised.

If I paid attention only to the news, I might be certain the world was a total mess with greed and avarice in charge, but come closer to home and there are fine people doing good things and trying to make their part of the world a better place … aren't we?

I do count my blessings: An unfailing sense of humor, Faith, Friends and Family!

I am seeking a new project to keep out of trouble. Stay tuned. In the meantime

For Mother's Day I received a poem composed by one of my sons, for which he should be in line for a Poet Laureate. The poem written when I was 88 is something that could never be bought. Reading that poem was one of the most emotional times I have ever had.

C

X O X

B

For Jean G. Coblentz at 88

I know a Gal, lives near the bay
who never has a cross word to say
she greets the morn on everyday
and shares with all, her special way

I've known this Gal for many years
we've shared our laughter, and some tears
when "all was lost", she calmed my fears
how blessed I am, to be one of her "Dears"

When I was young and really quite wild
her mate would say, "who is this child?"
my boundless energy could make folks riled
but this Gal said, "Give it time" and just smiled

Throughout the years, as I have grown
I've found myself lost, but always known
I did no good to whine or moan
tis better to nurture all the seeds she'd sown

Now I'm older and as time flies by
this Gal oft tells me, I'm quite a guy
but well I know that if she didn't try
I'd still be lost and wondering why

Who is this Gal who keeps her calm?
she's my friend, my mentor, she's my mom

All my love on this Mother's Day
Your adoring son …. *Marty*

2014 Season Greetings Text

Season's Greetings from the Court of Nome, where every day this month is May Day and or Mothers' Day to celebrate ... (OOPS! May got away from me!) With this epistle I am celebrating our cherished friendships. While preparing for this I noted that the last two editions focused on weddings, children, grandchildren, and some great ones as well ... so this time I plan to focus on something closer to home ... me!

I have enjoyed good health and have worked hard to maintain it ... Ha!

On Dec 3, 2013, I was doing Theraband stretches, when the band suddenly snapped and down I fell, fracturing my fifth lumbar vertebra. (The walker you see in the picture is now history). My reaction? Censored !#@* But from the mud (bad) grows the lotus (good). The following are the bad and the good ...

Bad (mud): Everything from my shoulder up has deteriorated —which means I don't see well, I don't hear well (eh??), memory ... "now what was I saying?" Have you ever looked in the mirror and thought "Who the honk is that? !#@*. Names are the first to go.

Good (Lotuses) Daughter #1, Kath, a physical therapist assistant, has lived with me for three years and we do nicely together because we want to, and by adhering to the Golden Rule. Upgrades have been made, including landscaping, installation of a Hot Tub, and unbelievable succulents! A new recumbent bike is consistently put to use while I watch the squirrel Olympics on my back fence and sing along with Willie Nelson, Bing Crosby, Elvis, Patsy Cline, and the Limelighters, etc. (no opera).

Normal Life goes on with "taxi service" from all you dear friends, to and from: Book tasters, Allied Arts Guild, Stanford Associates Board, Cap and Gown board, Founding Grant Society and Stanford Historical Society Programs and the Cardinal Club.

The Coblentz Clan, with its wonderful mix of my handsome, interesting children and their spouses; my grandchildren; and my great grandchildren, keep me "young" and feeling that I have everything! ... except, of course a lovely visit or call from you.

I still send a Season's Greetings card to Jackie, the woman engaged to Harry before he met me. They met as youngsters in Baltimore and, although it presented itself as the perfect relationship, the timing was wrong. I encouraged and fostered Harry's relationship with former friends from Baltimore. After Harry passed away, I had the opportunity to meet her. Her story is especially important in my life and I want people to know about it, so I've included it here.

Kath Tells Jackie's Story

This is a very unusual story...the story of two women who loved the same man, and whose lives only crossed many years after he had passed away. They would not have met if my mother had not encouraged my dad to stay in touch with Jackie's parents. Ever the wise woman, Mom recognized the meaningful role they played in Dad's character formation – first as a young teenager, then as a young adult as he was finishing high school, attending Baltimore City College, and ultimately enlisting in the U.S. Army Air Force.

Jackie's father was the pastor of their church, and both her parents were active in the church's youth group, to which both Jackie and Harry belonged.

On a recent phone conversation with Jackie, she told me that they had crushes on each other at the age of 10.

So, when Dad knew he was going overseas to serve in WWII, he presented Jackie with a diamond engagement ring. Throughout his years in the service as a flight instructor on U.S. soil, a B29 Aircraft Commander and first Lieutenant flying bombing missions from Guam, Dad knew the love of his life was home in Baltimore waiting for his return. They wrote letters, of course, as he also did to his brother Madison, who was in the Army Air force as well.

Harry, Jackie, and Madison

Harry and Jackie

Most of his letters to Madison are preserved, in which he often speaks of Jackie. Fortunately, we have several pictures of the three of them together as young adults, before Dad met Mom!!!

By the time the war ended, Dad's parents had moved from Maryland to California, which meant that the two brothers would also head West after the service.

By virtue of the GI Bill, both brothers were able to attend Stanford University. They both joined the Phi Gamma Delta (or Fiji) fraternity and were pretty popular fellows at that!

Mom had already been at Stanford for two years when Dad enrolled after the war. "Not many men on campus then" is how the women of those years remember that period of '43 –'45.

When Mom was asked to attend a Beer Bust at the Fiji house, she was not enthusiastic but convinced to attend anyway. A friend said, "look up there Jean, there's your date"... at the top of the stairs stood this ever so handsome (nickname "Handsome Harry"), blond, blue-eyed young man in his eye-catching flight jacket, and she was glad she had decided to come!

Mom has talked a little about their romance in college and did not know that Dad had a sweetheart in Baltimore, nor that he was engaged to her. That information came to her in a roundabout way later when Dad wanted to get back Jackie's engagement ring and sell it.

Jackie, by the way, was not eager to give up the diamond ring, so Dad appealed to Jackie's mother who, one must assume, intervened. Jackie eventually sent back the ring.

Harry and Jean's story continues, and they marry and have kids, career, and still communicate with the family in Baltimore. Many years later, Mom references a trip Jackie made to the West coast with her husband where they were able to meet up with Dad. Mom had a prior engagement, so never got to meet Jackie.

Pictures were shared with Christmas cards, but it wasn't until after Harry died, that the two women started reaching out to each other at Mom's initiation.

Mom decided to keep Jackie 'in the loop' and send her the much loved, 'Season's Greetings' every year. Jackie wrote back one year and commented on how lovely the arrangement Mom had with her daughter living with her and that it would be fun if they could someday meet.

Mom was touched by that as was I. I started entertaining the notion of flying to Arizona with Mom to let these two women finally meet and exchange stories. Mind you, both Mom and Jackie were in their late eighty's, but Jackie was thrilled at the prospect of a visit from the woman "who stole her fiancé so many years ago."

They liked each other immediately, and it was evident from their conversations, just how much they had in common. Jackie still today comments that Harry had great taste in women! It was a monumental event for both women, and I was honored and thrilled to have been able to facilitate their meeting at Jackie's place in Tucson. Although Mom passed away in December of 2017, Jackie and I are still in touch by phone. I visit her whenever I am in Arizona.

50th Wedding Anniversary Jun 12, 1998

I still hear from half a dozen of those very first parents who were witness to a special yet hilarious occasion one time as we finished up a meeting. Someone said, "Oh, look, we have company." Harry had walked in with an obscenely large armful of red roses. I mean, you couldn't believe there were that many red roses! He said, "I want to apologize for interrupting your meeting, but this is important. Fifty years ago, today June 12, about to the minute, Jean and I were married." The people applauded. "But I don't want you to think for one minute that there are fifty roses here. There are only thirty-six because some of those years were really awful." People didn't know what to do. It was hysterical. I was laughing so hard and loud, everyone else was put at ease. He was right! Some of those years were awful for a lot of reasons. Harry and I overcame our issues and could look back and laugh.

Susan Berg — Bill Berg

Best Wishes for many more wonderful y
Tina and Duffy Oyster "98"

Warm wishes to a wonderful couple —
Chris + Mary Ann Monahan

Congratulations! Best Wishes! Much Happiness ...
Marge + Mat Brady

30 years is a
real accomplishment, and you
both deserve every congratulation...

Best love and
congratulations
Betsy

Sincere congratulations
and best wishes for your
future years together
Tom Cho

Hard To Believe
Congratulations
John Mulcahy

Congratulations
we are so very
happy for your future
Rudy & Margaret Peters

Congratulations and
many many more years
happiness together
Christine · Ralph FRANK

Jean & Harry —
You two are great!
Wishing you a lifetime
of happiness,
Love + the
Durings

To great
role models
we all love
Martha

Wow! England,
Israel and Caryl in
absentia,
Lots & many more
years.

Jean & Harry —
What a great pair! I
still think you should write
a book and reveal all
your secrets of a successful
marriage! — Jill
X

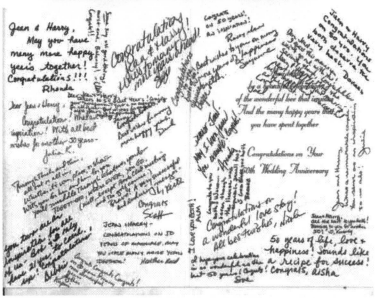

Work and Volunteer Experience

I have been involved in community service over a span of five decades and very recently, awarded The President's Lifetime Achievement Award for Volunteer Service with an awards plaque signed by President Barack Obama.

Congress of the United States
House of Representatives
Washington, D.C. 20515

Anna G. Eshoo
Fourteenth District
California

May 24, 2012

Mrs. Jean H. Coblentz
1467 Nome Court
Sunnyvale, California 94087-4242

Dear Mrs. Coblentz,

Congratulations on being honored by Avenidas for your lifetime of achievement. Your work with Cap and Gown and the Allied Arts Guild have made a difference in the lives of so many. The Lifetimes of Achievement Award is one you've earned and richly deserve and I add my thanks to those of our entire community for all you've done and continue to do.

Most sincerely,

Anna G. Eshoo
Member of Congress

Early on, before my children started school, I presented a case in front of the school board in Menlo Park for the need of a new elementary school, which we got. The "Suburban Park" area where we'd just bought our first house, was filled with young families with soon-to-be school-aged children. The need for a nearby school was apparent and I volunteered to lead the cause.

Regarding the P.T.A. from 1952 to 1962, I did everything and am an Honorary Life Member of Menlo Park. Then as the kids started school, my interest with their education became paramount.

From 1955-1962 as a troop leader (Menlo Park) Both my girls were Brownies and Girl Scouts. I wanted to be able to help on the most experiential level. The girls were very close growing up and scouting was a tremendous experience for all of us. I was also a little league volunteer in Sunnyvale where my two boys played sports.

Allied Arts Guild Auxiliary (AAGA)

The year was 1962, and I had just joined the Woodside Atherton Auxiliary. The event was Tally Ho, a fund-raising event held at the Menlo Circus Club in Menlo Park and run by Woodside Atherton Auxiliary, which later was called, Allied Arts Guild Auxiliary. They raised money for what later became the Lucille Packard Children's Hospital. Back then, Tally Ho was a huge, two-day event complete with horse shows, fashion shows, cocktails, dining, and dancing. Three years later, in 1965, I became chair of the event and received a taste of what a big job that was. I involved everyone in the auxiliary, all my friends, etc., and was extremely impressed by the way people worked, never for a minute worrying that anyone might not follow through. After it was over, I hand wrote thank-you notes to every person (at least 100) who volunteered time, no matter how large or small their task had been. I so appreciated their contribution and wanted them to know it. Since 1962, I have been a volunteer and/or a key officer: President three times—first in 1977 and most recently elected at age 80 and again at age 82, of the Allied Arts Guild Auxiliary. As mentioned before, the group helps to raise money for what later became the Lucille Packard Children's Hospital. I was chair of the Auxiliary's Development Committee for the monumental renovation project that raised the $10, 000,000 needed to renovate the AAGA. I then helped guide the auxiliary into its current operating style with a now distinct business model and new double-sided three-fold brochure.

Coblentz Clan: Kath, Scott, Jean and Marty

Avenidas

I also served on the Avenidas board for six years with many fine and distinguished community, service-minded individuals. It is my joy and pleasure to serve alongside a physician and friend of mine, Dr. Syd Hecker.

When he stepped down, my current primary-care physician and gerontologist, Dr. Peter Cheng, filled his spot. Over the years, both men have become family friends. Syd was interested in my memoir writing, providing helpful suggestions as he had already published a book about his own life, Stories from My Life, by Sydney P. Hecker M.D.

As people on the peninsula know, Avenidas is a community based, non-profit organization that supports and celebrates older adults. Their innovative programs enrich the lives of an increasing number of more than 6500 mature adults and their families each year. The Palo Alto Avenidas facility is currently undergoing renovation and expansion to better serve the needs of the growing senior population of the San Francisco Bay Area mid-peninsula communities.

Ever mindful of thanking people, this is an example of how Jean like to do it best, with humor!

An Ode from Me to You and Avenidas

I served on the Avenidas Board
For six most pleasurable years
And every time I read the list of services
I want to lead the cheers!!
Day Care services for those in need
And exercises for others? Yes indeed
Lessons galore from computer to ukulele
Need a hot lunch? La Comida serves 'em daily
Want to age in your home,
join a group to play chess
Get help for aging parents,
maybe your taxes? Yes
Now why do I send this listing to you?
because your great support,
helps make this come true!

My handwriting leaves much to be desired, but it is important to me you understand how appreciated and valued is your continued support.

Thank You and Best Wishes, *Jean*

Volunteer Work for Stanford University

For many decades, in a volunteer capacity, I have been very active and involved in the all-woman Cap and Gown honorary society. I was Co-founder of the board in 1953 and was still serving in an honorary capacity in 2016. As chair of their 2005 Centennial, I was named a celebrated member. My daughter Kathy was living at home with Harry and me while back in school fulltime. I was still working and had many stories to tell at the dining room table. Kath remembers and likes to tell the story of how I started planning five years in advance for the 100th year celebration of Cap and Gown. I started early because I knew if I had any chance of securing former Cap and Gown recipient, Supreme Court Justice Sandra Day O'Connor, as keynote speaker, I would have to get our event on her calendar early! I was successful and the event was amazing.

Having been involved with Cap and Gown all these years has led to a life of involvement with students from every Stanford graduating class since mine in 1947. This is a huge honor and keeps me connected with the interests and concerns of these bright, young women. Very recently, the Cap and Gown organization presented me with the first Distinguished Service Award for outstanding contributions to the education benefit of students, alumnae and community. They are all exceptional women, and it has always been an indescribable joy to work with them.

From 1988 to 1994 I serve two terms on various committees of the Associates of Stanford Libraries.

Cap and Gown Big Group. Spring Brunch 2014. Photo from the roof by Cap and Gown Board member and photographer Shari Kuckenbecher. Jean is fourth from the right in the front row.

I also served as the chair of the Stanford University class of 1947's 65th reunion and before that, served on every alumni activities reunion committee since 1967.

The following is from a long-time Cap & Gown friend and Stanford professor, Dr. Ruth Cronkite. She speaks about Jean in words that all who knew Jean, can easily recognize and respect.

What sort of impact did Jean have on the Cap and Gown program?

Jean has always been passionate about Cap and Gown and its mission to foster and support leadership among women. She was very instrumental in the phenomenal success of the one-day conference celebrating Cap and Gown's Centennial. The keynote speakers that stood out for me were Sandra Day O'Connor, former Supreme Court Justice, and Kate Kelly, a prominent local journalist (both were Stanford graduates and presumably members or honorary members of Cap and Gown. Jean was a key host/moderator for this event. I think this event served as a major turning point for Cap and Gown members who may not have been that actively involved at the time, most likely due to work and family commitments. I think a number of members, including me, turned out for a very stimulating day and evening and then, became more actively engaged in Cap and Gown.

What is your fondest memory of Jean?

She offered tidbits of advice in humorous, gentle quips, such as something like, "be sure to take some cookies when they are passed around." I'll never forget this advice about recognizing opportunities as a plate of cookies and making the most of such opportunities. To continue with this analogy, Jean often took the initiative to create and share such opportunities – like baking the cookies and passing them around herself. She often tells the story of how she obtained her first job at Hewlett Packard (HP) on a weekend, wandering around and peeking in windows until an executive of some sort came out and started a conversation with her. That conversation led to an on-the-spot job offer for Jean! She was always thinking of ways to generate opportunities for others. When I gave her a set of notecards featuring my son's artwork of buildings on the Stanford campus, she immediately started thinking of places (allied Arts) where his cards could be on display and possibly for sale, as a way of creating an opportunity for more exposure for him. She was always thinking of ways to generate opportunities for others, including men.

How has Jean's influence in the Cap and Gown program been felt? What is her legacy to the program?

Cap and Gown, by its mission, has the potential to create opportunities for women through its scholarship funds and its formal and informal events and activities. Jean has been a steadfast Alumni Board member for decades.

How has knowing Jean influenced your life / career?

Jean has been an exemplary role model and mentor in several ways for how to conduct oneself over the various domains of one's life.

First, she is even keeled, calm, supportive, diplomatic, and consistently positive in her outlook. I have never heard her say a cross word or complain, even in situations where she might have been disappointed or experiencing loss. Instead, she has always maintained a positive outlook.

Second, she is passionate about and committed to the various family, work, and community roles, each of which she joyfully filled with competence and grace. She felt strongly about maintaining supportive family relationships in her role as a caring wife, mother, and grandmother. She was also very committed to her work. I think her most recent job was in the Office of Development at Stanford, where I had the opportunity to observe her competence as she facilitated a donor's wishes. I am most familiar with her passion for Cap and Gown, but she played other important roles as a volunteer in the broader community. In fact, she received a lifetime Award for Community Service a few years ago from Avenidas, which recognizes individuals who have made significant contributions as a longtime volunteer to the Bay Area community.

Third, Jean treats others with respect, encouragement, and support. She does this in a way that you want to do things for her in return. For example, members of Cap and Gown consistently were willing to help her, whether it was a ride to Alumni Board meetings, Cap and Gown events or a ride home. Members have made donations to Stanford Cap and Gown in her honor. We are currently working on establishing a scholarship fund in her memory.

In summary, Jean is a community builder and pillar, passionate about Stanford, especially Cap and Gown, accomplished, wise, supportive, easygoing, positive, and fun. I hope that I can live my life as effectively and successfully as she has.

Do you have any interesting or funny stories about Jean?

I loved her "Cardinal" red outfits, even the shoes!

Words of Admiration for One of Cap and Gown's Longest Living, Ever Dedicated Members

"Jean's leadership was central to keeping Cap and Gown true to its mission. She always came with a smile and a twinkle in her eyes, a sense of humor, a deep kindness, and a no-nonsense perspective to keep us on track, and, of course, wearing her signature Stanford red dress. Most of all though, Jean was kind. Many years ago, when I was at my wit's end with the antics of one of my teenage children, Jean said, "Let's have lunch in the park and we can chat." Jean's kindness that day in taking the time for that little chat, made all the difference to me. She listened, shared her personal perspective and helped me come to a much better understanding of what it means to be a good parent."

—Esther Hewlett

"Jean is my life role model. Since I met her almost 20 years ago, I was drawn to her energy, enthusiasm, and love for all things Stanford. Every step of the way, Jean has been there to guide me and mentor me through my Stanford volunteer career. Her wisdom is immeasurable. Her spirit and wit are incomparable. Jean is a Stanford treasure and I feel so fortunate to call her a friend."

—Kathy Chou

"I met Jean through Cap and Gown and enjoyed her company at countless events throughout the past 15 years. The Cap and Gown Alumnae Board, which has been so very meaningful to me over the years, owes its very existence to Jean. I will forever be thankful to her for that. But my admiration and gratitude for Jean, goes much deeper. To me, Jean was the perfect model of grace, energy, enthusiasm, positivity, and warm-heartedness. My own grandmother back in my hometown in Kansas was roughly Jean's age, and as I watched her struggle with dementia and suffer from deep and debilitating loneliness, I began to fear for my own future. But Jean showed me a

different way to age: staying social and active and continuing to contribute her deep wisdom to fortunate people like me as she grew older. I saw Jean work tirelessly to serve others even in her later years, and she became a very special role model for me. Thanks to Jean, I now know who I want to be in my later years. In an odd twist of fate, my grandmother and Jean both passed away on exactly the same day. I will always be grateful to my own grandmother for the deep love and wonderful memories she gave me when I was a child, but I will always remember Jean with fondness and especially gratitude for the example she set and the lessons I learned from her after becoming an adult."

—Samantha Crow Quist

"Until then, Jean and I were at the top of the "oldest Cap and Gowner" list and continued to enjoy the many events with younger members at Stanford over the years. Our special "qualifying" fields were quite different, but we always enjoyed sharing them with each other and other members. I am sure I'm not the only person remembering her perky, positive attitude toward life. She was an outstanding role model for her personal and Stanford family."

—Mary Hill Skougaard

"Being 'tapped' for Cap and Gown was one of the special highlights of my life and to me, Jean embodied Cap and Gown. Whenever I had a question, whenever I wasn't sure where or when to send in my dues, the person I contacted was Jean. When on campus for something, I could always find Jean involved in some Cap and Gown endeavor. She was a lovely lady and one who was so admired."

—Jane Fetter

"Jean embodied the essence of the Stanford "Cap and Gown" spirit: A classy, engaging, good-humored woman leader who always showed true concern for others. She was an inspiration to generations of Stanford women. We felt privileged to know her."

—Charlene Hsu-Winges

"I met Jean as a Stanford undergrad at a Cap and Gown event and she made such a positive impression on me, which only became even greater when I joined the board after graduating. I unfortunately never got the opportunity to know my grandparents, so I have very few role models from Jean's generation in my life. I can't tell you how inspiring and helpful it was to me as a young woman trying to make sense of a world and where I fit in it to see a strong, dynamic older woman who wasn't afraid to lead, break down barriers, speak her mind, and "take her cookies when they're passed." She shared all her wisdom with such a warm approachability – Jean always had such a twinkling in her eye. I loved her mischievous sense of humor. She was just a wonderful person all-around, and we simply adored her. I'm thirty-three now with a career in a male-dominated field, and when times get tough, and I wonder whether enduring the challenges are worth it, I often think of Jean and the barriers she helped break down for me. It helps me have the strength to stick it out in the hope that my work will help break down barriers for the next generation of women."

—Melissa Luu–Van

"Even though we weren't in everyday contact, I felt that I could always call or email and Jean would be right on the other end with a cheery, calm voice. I met Jean in 1975, when I was elected to Cap and Gown, and then went on to be co-president my senior year. Jean was essential in our success that year. She would guide us just enough for my co-president and me to understand what to do next. I always considered her "the wind beneath my wings." I introduced her to my baby daughter (now 34 years old), chatted about what was going on in my life, and got a big hug before leaving her presence. She always had something wonderful to say as I left."

—Jacki Williams-Jones

"Though I didn't know Jean well, I always looked up to her. It brightened my day to come to Cap & Gown events and see her beautiful smile. She just radiated warmth and intelligence in so many good ways, being supportive of other women's aspirations, and she

took such joy in others' success. In this competitive day and age, her generous spirit is one we can all hope to emulate."

—Marli Melton

"I first met Mrs. Jean Coblentz at a Cap and Gown Winter Welcome, my first as a new member. She gave some life advice that I am sure will be familiar to many. She told all of us to take our cookies as they were passed. She warned against trying to find the cookie with the most chocolate chips or the most attractive shape. It's rude and ultimately futile as many times the chips are hidden inside the body of the dough. She was funny. It was a funny image, but she was also right. It's tough advice for young, intelligent and ambitious Stanford students to follow. After all, we only arrived at Stanford after fighting to be the best at just about everything. Were we supposed to turn that drive off? That wasn't her intended message, of course. Even though I heard her, and I listened to her, I really did, it didn't sink all the way into my soul I'm still young, but a few years down the road after Stanford, I think I am just now, maybe beginning to understand. Life, the whole world and al the opportunities and pitfalls in it, will utterly overwhelm you if you focus on "finding biggest or the most chips." The point is to take a cookie when you have the chance. Take a risk and enjoy the sweetness of having a cookie at all, likely a very good one, with an adequate amount of chips.

—Kiah Thorn

"It was an honor to work with Jean while I was a member of Cap & Gown. I remember that we worked on putting together calendars for sale in the Stanford Bookstore. We sold so many that the Stanford Alumni Association took over the project. That did not deter Jean and I am appreciative of her many lessons of grace, flexibility, and leadership!"

—Kathy Welton

"Jean was the glue of Cap and Gown, and we must keep it strong. Jean was one of the few people that encouraged me to forge ahead, and I did take her advice. For example, she was one of the first to *encourage me to run for Treasurer of the State of California when I was Deputy Treasurer. So, let's all mentor others to achieve their potential, and demonstrate that women DO help each other in the "spirit of Jean!"*

—Mary Toman

"I admired Mrs. Coblentz and loved seeing her at Cap & Gown events. What an inspiration! I loved hearing her stories of her time at Stanford, especially because it brought to life for me what campus life would have been like for my great aunt and grandfather, who also attended Stanford in the 1940s."

—Lissa Wilson Filose

"I've known Jean at Cap & Gown forever, since I graduated in '42 and have attended many, many meetings, even last year. What a stalwart Jean was. To many younger members, she epitomized Cap & Gown – a loyal contributor, innovator and stable influence."

—Irma Jean Crouch

"The annual Tapping Tea was a yearly event for me, and each year Jean's animated tales of the early days of Cap and Gown brought so much joy to inductees (and to me.) I loved being a part of that special community of Stanford women who imagined what Stanford must have been like in Jean's day. Younger Stanford women owe a lot to Jean's generation for paving the way for us all to be taken seriously as scholars."

—Sohini Ramachandran

I was involved as a staff member and secretary for the Stanford Associates Board of Governors from 1979 to 2000. Upon retirement, I was voted an honorary member of their board for Life. I graciously accepted this position with one caveat: I told the board that I would serve as long as I felt I was still value added, or until the time when the board itself felt I was no longer value added. At that time, I would step down from those responsibilities. One never knows what the future may hold for us.

There was also lots of volunteer work over the years including Associates of Stanford Libraries: two terms, various committees and Stanford University: Chair of the class of 1947's 65th reunion. Before that: Served on every alumni activities' reunion committee since 1967.

BOARD OF GOVERNORS

STANFORD
ASSOCIATES

I offered suggestions for the Stanford Football game tickets. Nowadays, it is cheaper to buy football tickets for a Stanford vs. Army game than for a Stanford vs. UCLA game. When at one time I looked into buying tickets, I was told the tickets would be $110.00 each and then another time told they would be $35.00. My suggestion is to go for the less expensive, since the wonder of it all, no matter who is playing, is in the game, the tailgate party beforehand and the noise and energy of the crowd.

Paid Employment

A truly unique job happened around 1965 when, due to a degenerating back problem and ensuing surgery, I spent three months in a full body cast in a hospital bed in our living room. Not knowing how long I would be laid up; I was approached by a P.E.O. member who asked if I might consider reading to her husband whose eyes were failing and could not read anymore. He came three times a week with whatever materials he wanted read to him, mostly business stuff and financial publications. He seemed only interested in business, cars and money. I read predominately from "The Economist" to Ken who insisted on paying me. Given the material, for me it became a learning experience. My son Marty took a liking to Ken and rushed home from school to sit at the base of the stairs first to listen and then to chat with him.

I don't think I ever formally taught my teenaged girls to cook, but they had to cook when I ended up in a body cast. We were all very happy though when our family connected with Meals on Wheels and dinner was brought to us. Harry and I were pleased when Kath stepped up to the plate and helped a great deal with many of the household tasks. Thank God she did step in—the spirit of the firstborn again came alive. There was something to be done and she just did it. Kath also prompted Jan to help. It was a matter of all the family pitching in to make sure things went smoothly because Harry was working, and we needed to keep the household running. I was always available for consultation, able to give advice or directions from the bed. Kath was about fifteen; Jan, thirteen; Marty around ten and Scott only seven.

Many years later after I was back to my old self and feeling much better, Ken called Marty who was then living in Elko, Nevada and asked him "Would you like to go to Kansas with your brother and pick up a car for your mother?" I knew it was a *cookie* for both boys, so Harry and I sat down with them to map out how they could get to Kansas in January to pick up the car. Ken knew Marty had a lot of potential and wanted him to have the experience. It turned out to be a wonderful adventure for both of them, and Scott added, "it was quite a fun drive, it being Winter and all, but we were fortunate to make it home with no problems." While still in Kansas with snow everywhere, Scott asked one of Ken's employees, "What do you farmers do in the Winter?" The guy smiled and opened the door to a large barn filled with hotrods and odd, four-wheel drive contraptions. Both boys being mechanically inclined, were impressed. I drove Ken's fuel-efficient diesel VW Rabbit for many years.

Santa Clara County Meals on Wheels

From June 1973 to July 1977, I took a job with the Santa Clara County Meals on Wheels program (then part of United Way) that gave me a wonderful chance to see what it was like working with a government agency. It was during this period that I received the San Jose Mercury News, Women Achievement Award in the creative category and was asked to participate in local politics. This was possibly the only time I turned down a challenging request as I politely replied, "No thanks." Politics didn't interest me at all.

The Death of Noel Eldred

My HP boss, Noel Eldred, and his wife, and Harry and I remained friends for years, following my work at HP. We babysat each other's kids, etc. One day in 1970, I got a phone call telling me of Noel's abrupt death while running the track. I was shocked and bereft, as you can imagine.

The following material about Noel Eldred was taken from the book: <u>Bill & Dave: How Hewlett and Packard Built the World's Greatest Company</u>, By Michael Shawn Malone:

"Thirty years' worth of hard work began to take its toll. On Nov. 30, 1970, Noel Eldred, HPs vice president of marketing, died suddenly of a heart attack at 62, the first death of HP's original management team. He served as Dave Packard's right-hand man when Bill Hewlett left for the army during WWII and perhaps the most capable and versatile of the pack. Aside from Bill and Dave, nobody did more for HP than Noel Eldred. "His death underscored that even success was a poor defense against the stresses of working in a fast-paced electronics company." Those that joined the company in the Redwood Building were no longer young, the two founders being within a decade of legal retirement. "Eldred gave HP both the look and the voice that would define the company ever after."

Following Noel's death in 1970, since I enjoyed keeping busy and challenged, I made a decision to become more involved – just not sure where I wanted to place my energies. I was raising my kids and had been involved with scout troops, P.T.A. and other volunteer endeavors. In early 1973, a group of us heard about a presentation geared toward Sanford graduate women to be held on campus. We attended and listened to the presentation about what women could be doing, if interested or if they knew how to get hold of the information, they needed to start careers. Afterwards, three of us stood outside on the steps where I said, 'You know what's going to happen, don't you? We will get all pumped up say, "Let's do something, let's get so and so involved." We will go home, go to bed and find ourselves once again, doing our everyday things, with no time to follow-up on this.

Can you guess what we did? We pretended to draw blood like blood sisters and began organizing. We brought into our group two more who attended the presentation and showed an interest. Our goal and purpose was to find out what jobs were available out there, what women who were not working might be interested in, and bringing the two together. This was how the Women's Resource Center was formulated. We found a house for rent on a little side street off University Avenue in Palo Alto and began matching women to opportunity. We managed to set up an office where women came and felt good about talking with us and where important papers could be kept on all the jobs out there for women. Even though we heard about it at a lecture at Stanford, it was not a Stanford University run program. We did this all on our own. What a *Cookie* that challenge was.

There were five of us who started this project and from there, it grew by word of mouth. While volunteering one day, a woman came in and began describing a job to me we could recruit for. In the next breath she then said to me, "I've decided to take the job off the market; I'd like to hire you." Her job was to find some help for a position that I took with the Homemakers Service of Santa Clara

County. (Meals on Wheels) I was in the PR/Development end of this business, received wonderful training and learned how to work within the state and county and with all the politics involved therein. I listened intently to what was being discussed and learned from the social workers associated with the program. My horizons were expanded. What a *cookie* that job turned out to be. The plaque on my kitchen wall with my favorite saying, *"Take Your Cookies When They're Passed,"* was given to me by one of the schedulers of Meals on Wheels. This was the perfect part-time job for me since my youngest kids were still in school. The money earned went towards our children's college fund.

Homemakers Service 1973-77

The Homemakers Service used Don Hostetler's printing business. When he and his wife returned from a trip to China, he remarked on how exciting it all was. I told him I had something of interest he might like to see. When I showed him the biography my father wrote of my mother, Don offered to print the entire love affair story at no charge. He felt the story was too important not to be shared. Honestly, I have shared this bio with dozens of people and the response is always the same, "This is an amazing story, Jean. You have to continue the story of your life."

Overview of Professional Experience

5/1942-9/1943: <u>Kaiser Permanente, Stockton California,</u> purchasing agent at the stockyards during the war. I was just sixteen at the time and considered my job to be such an important and good job for the war effort that I held off entering Stanford until I was 17, where I had already received a scholarship.

2/1948-6/1950 <u>Hewlett Packard, Secretary to VP of Marketing,</u> Noel Eldred. Hired, among other things, for my shorthand and 80 wpm typing skills. What a *cookie* that job turned out to be!

6/1973-7/1977: <u>Homemaker Service / Santa Clara County, PR / Development</u>. My springboard into the larger arena of community service- another *cookie*

7/1977 - 8/2000: Stanford University Development Office: Director of Parents Program; Secretary of Stanford Associates and Emeritus member of Stanford Associates Board of Governors. I was involved as a staff member and

Secretary. Upon retirement, I was voted an honorary member of their board for life.

1988-1994: <u>Associates of Stanford Libraries</u>: I served two terms on various committees, often using my successful fundraising experiences from other departments to help organize fundraising activities for the library. Also, I encouraged one of my best and brightest friends from the class of 1947 to volunteer for the library. I offered her a *cookie* that turned out to be life changing for Marnie. We still stay in touch. Marnie Furbush's dedication and involvement was much appreciated and remembered as she went on to edit Imprint: A Journal of the Associates of Stanford University which is sponsored by the Friends of the Stanford Libraries to showcase the library's special collections. Marnie later became the president of the Friends of the Stanford Libraries.

This is how it all began, and I count this long friendship as a huge *cookie* in my life. It was the first day of class of our freshman year at Stanford in 1943 and Margaret "Marnie" McKittrick (Furbush) and I walked into our freshman English class (NOT bonehead) together and have been friends ever since. Throughout the years we have shared the trials and tribulations of rearing children, the community involvement of volunteering, and the continuing love of books. I invited Marnie to join a book club, of which in 1962 I was one of the founding members, and what a wonderful addition she is. She always brings such a scholarly, researcher's approach to every book she reviews for us (and as a fringe benefit, the lunches she serves are exquisite!!)

New directors: Jean Galt
Coblentz, David Weber, and
Marnie Furbush in
Wredenhouse. Spring Edition

The Associates of the

STANFORD UNIVERSITY Libraries

Newsletter

Summer 1995

Volume VII, Number 3

Meyer Library, Stanford University, Stanford, CA 94305-5095

Annual Meeting: Chairman's Report, Elections, Keller on *Internet*, Knuth on Libraries

Two new board members were elected and three incumbents (Jean Coblentz, Margaret Furbush and David Weber) were re-elected to three-year terms at the ASUL Annual Meeting on May 2nd.

The welcomed additions are: Gerald L. Alexanderson, Stanford MS '58, who is a mathematician and the Michael and Elizabeth Valeriote Professor of Science, Santa Clara University. He is a Senator of the Phi Beta Kappa Society and the National Secretary of the Mathematical Association of America. Professor Alexanderson is a book collector of the History of Science and of the works of Lewis Carroll; and the second new board member is:

Claude S. Brinegar, Stanford AB '50, MS '51, PHD '54, who was mentioned briefly in the last ASUL newsletter upon his marriage to Stanford News Service's Karen Bartholomew. Claude, the retired Chief Financial Officer of Unocal Corporation, is currently a Visiting Scholar in Food Research at Stanford. He is a noted, avid book collector of Mark Twain.

Following the Annual Meeting officers were elected for a one-year term: Joe Cusick, Chairman; Alan Nichols, Vice Chairman for Programs; Jean Coblentz, Vice Chairman for Membership; Harry Goff, Treasurer; and Jane Miller Chai, Secretary. David Weber, as Immediate past Chairman, joins the above members of the Executive Committee.

The Annual Meeting featured "INTERNET 101: An Introduction to the Information Superhighway" by University Librarian Michael A. Keller. [See INTERNET on Page 2.]

ASUL Officers for 1995-96, from left: Joe Cusick, David Weber, Alan Nichols, Jean Coblentz, Jane Chai, and Harry Goff

About twenty year ago, a few years after I had gone to work for Stanford, we were lunching one day, and as I listened to her talk about her experience of going back to get a master's degree, and enrolling in a class to learn Greek so she could read original documents, I thought "What a waste that she is 'just a housewife', so put forth a proposal she couldn't refuse. An introduction to Susan Abernethy, at that time the development officer for the library, who did the rest, brought Marnie into the ranks of library volunteers. It wasn't long before she was entrusted with the same kind of project a trained librarian would have been assigned, and she continues to provide this quality of free service.

Later we went on the ASUL board together (she had been editor of Imprint for some time and her scholarship was manifest in the revitalization of that publication.) Always thoughtful and meticulous about dealing both with detail and with volunteer and staff sensibilities (she should give lessons,) she seemed the obvious choice to become president of the organization as chair of the nominating committee, it became clear to me that every other member felt exactly the same. She demurred, arms were twisted, logic triumphed and the rest is history.

Marnie has guided the organization with a steady and thoughtful hand, brought in new blood, maximized talent and in recognition of which, was offered membership in Stanford Associates.

"In 2000, Marnie received the Howell Award, named for Stanford alumnus, bibliophile, and donor Warren R. Howell, which Stanford Libraries grants on an occasional basis to honor an individual who has made an outstanding contribution to the local world of books and libraries. What follows is the slightly modified text of the tribute I wrote for the Howell Award program: The Howell

Award of the year 2000 honors Margaret McKittrick Furbush, whose roster of accomplishments on behalf of Stanford's Library is nearly as long as her commitment is deep. Marnie came to Stanford as a freshman in 1943 keen to study literature. She received her BA (1947) and MA (1949) in English philology, and met her future husband, Malcolm Furbush, a classmate and law student. After considering a career in academia, she chose marriage and family and devoted her considerable energy to raising three children, managing a household, and doing extensive community service work."

—Becky Fischbach, May 24, 2018
Stanford Libraries Blog

It pleases me enormously to note that others view Marnie Furbush accomplishments as I do – she is an example for us all. In 2000, when she received the Stanford Associates Award for continuing exemplary service to Stanford, the telling of her accomplishments includes only the tip of the iceberg of the truly amazing, above and beyond dedication "in sickness and in health" she has brought to her involvement with the libraries, and the stories I haven't told of when she has stepped in to do the task of folks who were "too busy" after having made the commitment, would bring an award by themselves, but would only distress Marnie and embarrass the guilty. Trust me on this one!!!

This above story was a classic "Cob" story. "Cob", from Coblentz, was a nickname given to me by coworkers I worked closely with at Stanford. As "Cob," my M.O. was to easily recognize potential in people and to help offer them connections, shared ideas and enthusiasm to get them involved in way that would showcase their talents. I try to wear red outfits to Stanford events. Hence, many an individual at these events, recognizes me in red, comes up to me to reintroduce themselves. They talk about how I directly inspired them to volunteer for Stanford, which moved them onto a path of greater involvement with the university. They each voice true gratitude, which brings me much pleasure.

Dick Bennett and How I Got to Stanford

The Tally Ho *cookie* to which I volunteered my time, led me right into another *cookie*.

As synchronicity would have it, at some later point in time, I received a call from a Dick Bennett. I knew of him but didn't really know him since it was his wife who had worked with me on the Tally Ho fundraiser. That was about it.

On this call, Dick asked, "Have you ever thought of going to work for me?"

I said, 'Well, no, I have never thought of going to work for you, what do you do?'

He laughed and told me he was the Director of the Annual Fund at Stanford University, which at that time didn't mean a whole lot to me. They had just finished up a very large campaign that I had been involved with as a volunteer. He talked about his idea for restructuring the entire office, and it dealt with having a better representation culturally and otherwise. After listening and fifty-years-old at this time, I laughed telling him, 'So, I'm your token older woman.'

He went on to say, "You must have had 100 people working for this Tally Ho thing a few years back. I received a handwritten note of thanks from you for nothing more than moving a few of the horse jumps." He remembered that and said that was the type of person he wished to work with him.

He asked me to come talk with him about that job. Since Harry and I were soon attending a wedding about two blocks from his home, he said, "That would be great. You can stop in before or after and we'll talk about it." Harry thought it a wonderful offer, so before we left, we shook on it, and I was on my way to joining the Stanford payroll. It was a fulltime job working in fundraising – an area in which at that time had very few women. It was also at a time when women didn't make much money nor ask others for money. It was primarily a "good old boys club." The year was 1977, the beginning of my work at Stanford in a job that led me on an entirely different work path. We wrote thank you notes because it was the thing to do. Who would have thought writing thank you notes would lead me to a job at Stanford University? What a beginning for an amazing chapter in my life. Over time, I had the opportunity to create new programs, travel all throughout the United States and meet amazing people.

I didn't just work *for* Dick Bennett but *with* him on a number of things. We knew each other very well. He was married at the time, and I knew that his wife had left him for a number of reasons (none of which were my business). Every so often, we met for coffee. One time he told me about a new lady in his life and was hopeful. He asked me to follow him into his office where he held up the sign that said, "She took the *cookies* when they were passed," which was his way of telling me that his new lady-friend was going to come and live with him. Dick and Ann Kaye married and were very happy for many years until he passed away. They lived in a house on campus, which they had nicely fixed up. He came in one day and showed me a photo taken of the archway that led from their kitchen to the back door. On the archway were these words, *"Take Your Cookies When They're Passed,"* a saying, of course, introduced to him by me.

"You're better looking when you smile: Even in my 90th year, many people say how happy it makes them to see my smile and what joy it brings the "as she walks through the door with that smile.""

—A Favorite Saying.

Hello Muddah, Hello Faddah
Parents of the Farm

Jean Coblentz has been active with parents' organizations and the Stanford administration for 21 years.

By Chawadee Nunikhair

Stanford parents don't just lend support to their Cardinal children with the occasional care package and monthly cash infusion. Organizations such as the Parents' Club and Parents' Advisory Board are encouraging an increasing number of parents some from places as far off as Bangladesh and Korea, to get involved in admissions events and fundraising activities to enhance life for the Stanford undergraduate.

"It's a really nice feature that a lot of schools don't have," said Nancy Stevens, a parent involved in both the Advisory Board and parents' Club.

Parent-sponsored initiatives such as catalog sales and the Chrysanthemum Champagne party result in scholarship funds for incoming students and extra boosts to the education of the undergrads themselves.

According to Jean Coblentz, director of the Parents' Program sponsored by the Office of Development, every student needs some financial support.: "Last year parents gave over a million dollars in annual gifts which illustrates graphically that most parents understand that every student is subsidized to some extent since tuition only covers about 50 percent of the true costs of a Stanford education – the rest has to come from other sources.

"People think that Stanford is rich because of the really large gifts they read about in the paper, but almost every one

313

of the gifts is restricted and none of the dollars may go to an undergraduates' education," said Coblentz.

An anchor of the Stanford administration for 21 years, Coblentz helps the parents' Program educate parents about the importance of providing support to Stanford. She also helps coordinate the program's Advisory Board with 27 regional committees, head-quartered in 13 states and 11 countries around the globe.

The program boasts approximately 150 people available to volunteer work if asked, as well as 45 families active on the Parents' advisory Board itself.

The Board represents "all the classes and all the regions of the world where there is a critical mass of students," Coblentz said, "Both dads and moms are very active on the board- a change from the days when most volunteering was done by moms." The critical mass of students includes countries where a parent is willing to act as a "Stanford ambassador" in welcoming and sending off parents and students.

While the Parents' Advisory Board was created in 1990, the Parents' Club is celebrating its 75th year of service to Stanford undergraduates. The money raised by the club goes to benefit its own Scholarship Endowment Fund. Known until recently as "the Mothers' Club," this organization is locally based and made up of 75 active volunteers – including faculty wives and parents whose students have already graduated.

"There are quite a few alumni and we also have quite a few alumni and we also have quite a few older members, many faculty wives," said Carol Knowles, vice president of membership. "We have many people whose children have graduated but still want to get involved."

"This is one of the only organizations on campus that directly services the undergrads," said club president Mary Popek. "You're giving them a touch of home."

The Club offers a birthday cake service, which may help parents who cannot be there in person at least be there in spirit for their homesick students. "It's a birthday party on wheels," said Popek.

"We make them feel less than 3,000 miles away" from their parents, said Parents' Club volunteer Carol McKenna. "And these cakes are delivered by Stanford moms."

The Parents' Club is also actively involved in events such as Orientation and Parents' Weekend.

Stanford Associates

The material for this came from an email sent by Jean Coblentz to S. Smith probably around 2000 with a subject line: "Legal Status of Stanford Associates."

The Associates began as a volunteer organization. During the depression, Stanford needed a lot of money. Then President of the University, Ray Lyman Wilbur (1916-1943), met with the head of the Board of Directors and said, "Look, we need money. We've got kids who are going to have to leave Stanford because they can't afford it and kids waiting to come who also can't afford it." He told the board to choose twelve of their richest, most loyal friends and get as much money from them as possible, telling them that this money was for the students and only the students. This was how Stanford Associates got started. In the past, the fundraisers planned an event of some sort and appointed one person to be in charge. All the fundraisers were men who had run out of good ideas when it came to fundraising events.

In February of 1935, the formation of a new organization was reported to the board, approved and a grant to cover their expenses was made. The Stanford Associates' gift procurement program started as a volunteer organization working for the university and reporting to the board, endorsed by the Alumni Association. They declared themselves ready for business in October 1934. In January, the members were introduced to the officers of the University.

Their first report, "Stanford Funds Program of Stanford Associates" was made to the board in August of 1935 and accepted. The Associates efforts continued to be funded by the trustees until 1941 when the Office of the General Secretary was formed to take over fundraising for the university.

At the very beginning, the men really got into it, becoming interested and bringing all kinds of wonderful offerings. But their idea of fundraising was to host really nice parties, which became more and more difficult since the men were from all over the country and couldn't get together that often. When the head of fundraising asked the men to take charge for putting on little parties, they balked and said, "Look, we were hired to be fundraisers, not party givers." It seemed they were operating more as a social group whose activities kept the university in the eyes of alumni. Individual donors continued to give but did not solicit. The group continued to act in an informal advisory way, and many of their ideas became integrated into the formal structure.

Not being a 501(C3) organization in those early years, dues and gifts were not deductible. It was not until 1992 when a decision was made to work toward coming under the umbrella of the Office of Development, where dues would be allowed to come into the university stream and be counted as gifts.

Stanford Associates Report

301 Encina Hall Stanford, California 94305 — Summer 1981

New Officers
Elected in May 1981

Bill Clebsch

John K Pike '57; William A Clebsch; Jean Coblentz '47; Vernon R Anderson, '53 MBA '57; Franklin P. Johnson Jr. '50

Jean Coblentz

The Board of Governors elected a new slate of officers at its meeting on May 8, 1981, following the recommendations submitted by a nominating committee headed by Stanford Associates' past president Stuart Morshead. Two new officers have had previous service on the Board: President Jake Pike served from 1968 to 1974 and second Vice President Bill Clebsch is completing his first term as a governor. Vern Anderson is the newly elected first vice president and Pitch Johnson is treasurer. Jean Coblentz of the Development Office staff has been named the new secretary, replacing David Fulton.

Vern Anderson

Pitch Johnson

We have never been audited nor instructed to make reports to a government agency of any kind, which would suggest that Stanford Associates was a volunteer organization providing a service to the university, with their by-laws simply being guidelines for doing business. That was how Stanford Associates got started.

Purpose of Stanford Associates

The purpose of the Stanford Associates is to cooperate with the University authorities and members of the Stanford Family in promoting the welfare of the University, primarily in support of the gift procurement programs.

Article II, Stanford Associates By-Laws

• To provide recognition for exceptional service to the university.

• To encourage individual members with special capabilities or interests to serve the University as needed.

• To encourage alumni and friends of the University to participate actively in Stanford fund raising.

• To keep members currently involved in the gift procurement programs.

• To aid the Office of Development in identifying and developing future volunteer fund raising leadership and prospects.

• To foster "esprit de corps" among members.

Approved by the Board of Governors January 25, 1980.

The director of fundraising, Dick Bennett, listened very carefully to the rumblings of those twelve who did not wish to be party givers. He realized someone was needed to run the Stanford Associates – run the fundraising ideas the men, who were volunteers, came up with. The head guy in New York City wished to put on a big Whoop-T'-Do fundraiser. That was when the Dick Bennett came to me and said, "Have I got a nice job for you!" You have to do me a favor." I stopped in my tracks. He went on, "I have run out of people who will do what needs to be done for the Stanford Associates." I said, "We can't afford to lose them." He then told me, "I'd like you to take this on." I said I could not do it alone and needed help, which he was more than willing to give me. That led me off on an adventure that is still going strong. I also was not a party-giver but could talk to people who put on parties! That was in 1977, and

Jean Galt Coblentz, '47, the new secretary to Stanford Associates is director of the Special Gifts Program and Field Staff Manager of the Annual Fund. She joined the Development Office in 1977 and has held a succession of increasingly responsible positions. She has served several terms, both as member and President, of the Board of Directors of Cap & Gown. Jean was born in China and received her early education there (via tutoring from the Calvert School of Baltimore) while her parents were medical missionaries in Yunnan Province. During her undergraduate years at Stanford, she received a unique exposure to the University's history as a part-time chauffeur for Mrs. David Starr Jordan. She and her husband Harry have four children and two grandchildren and live in Sunnyvale.

how I initially became involved with Stanford Associates, a paid job as Development Officer. My intention was to begin to develop ideas and report to "the powers that be" what could be done. Hopefully, they would listen and provide what was needed to carry on.

Following my retirement from Stanford Associates a young woman, Charlotte Glasser, asked to interview me about the story of the Stanford Associates. That interview was for the Stanford Historical Society; it is also housed in the library archives. I once gave a public talk on this topic to the Stanford Historical Society. Kath and Harry were able to attend.

As far as Stanford Associates goes, it once consisted of all men, highball guys who sat in a room, drank cognac and smoked cigars as they brainstormed about fundraising. I came along with a different approach. I think it was just luck that my ideas were considered. There were no more male fundraisers, those who used to gather and plan an event of some kind, to pull from. No vice-president of development position existed until just before I began working there. There was no structure to a plan that really didn't exist. Up until that position came into view, it worked on a very personal basis between the President of the University and his friends.

It was necessary to produce a transition. The Development office didn't even have a name. It was time to focus in a different way. The existing men didn't want to carry the ball, so I came along and offered to help out, but only if someone worked with me, and over time, many great people did. Early on, I needed a person who had really nice handwriting to address the envelopes to the Gold Spike Dinner. It started like that. The person I hired was my daughter-in-law Alma, who I knew had beautiful handwriting. After that, Hershey, one of my colleagues, said, "Oh, she can help me do this....and that" Pretty soon she had a fulltime job. I knew she would put a good stamp on whatever she did. Alma was there for 29 years.

I basically had to put together an entire infrastructure. The idea existed, but no infrastructure. They were happy I was willing to take it over. From what I know, I don't think they were disappointed with their choice to have me do so.

I was handed a vision, the initial foundation, but not a recipe; it blossomed from there. I know there were many tries, many revisions. I started with only twelve names and was basically a hero for just taking the time. With nothing else to base it on, it was figured out by trial and error. I attended many parties, and nobody ever turned down an opportunity to have me sit with them and ask questions. The phone became my friend and tool. Most people were flattered that I called to get their expertise about this or that, once I explained what I was trying to do.

We worked out of an open office with desks all around on the third floor of Encina on the Stanford campus. I sat at one desk and my secretary at another. I did not have a secretary when I first worked there; but before long, it was obvious I needed somebody to help me.

Throughout my time there, I had many personal assistants who offered ideas. It was a great adventure. Although I do still have my finger in the pot, I do not hold the responsibility I once had. I recall many times waking up in the middle of the night to brainstorm ideas. I'd write down the ideas then go back to sleep.

I feel there is something about the academic world, Stanford and elsewhere, that displays a vibrancy and emphasis on the development of each student in attendance, on what they can become, and how they can emerge as a winner from this maelstrom of people. All makes me so very proud to have been part of the process of this outstanding and distinguished Stanford University. My comment to some people wanting to form a "Jean, wanna-be" club? To paraphrase the famous Abraham Lincoln quote, 'Well, you can fool some of the people some of the time, but not all of the people all of the time.'

The term of office for most board members is three years. The board is a wonderful combination of people of all ages, from all over the U. S. I didn't want to miss meetings because one year someone may be there and not the next, due to the expired term of office rule. I felt one of those board members had a crush on me, always commenting on how I always wore red to the meetings and that he would be very upset if I wore something else.

Jean with Presidents Hennessy and Casper.

The following is a brief note of gratitude to the 2010 Stanford Associates Board of Governors and their fabulous staff.

YOU GUYS!!! (AND DOLLS***)

You got me right behind the knees
With that great surprise, which did me please
The sandstone reminds me of long ago days
And the mission we still further in our myriad ways

The Associates history is a source of great pride
Raising dollars so students could keep studying in stride
Now thousands of vols have followed our leads
And we encourage, recognize and reward their good deeds

So why did y'all give those great gifts to me
When for 30 years I've had the pleasure of "your" company
Ever changing to keep up with the needs of the day
You did the work while I got to play   (yeah!)

The staff whiom I had are still my dear friends
In a tie which binds and never ends
That having been said, give logic its due
I shoiuld send gifts to the whole lot of you.

Now that's off my mind, let's start to get real
Here is a message with a kiss I do seal
It's an honor to serve and be a partner so true
THANK YOU THANK YOU AND ESPECAILLY THANK YOU!

STANFORD ASSOCIATES
Celebrating 75 Years!

For her continuous dedicated service to
the Stanford Associates, both as a former staff member
and now as an honorary board member

For her invaluable role as a resource to staff and fellow
board members and her willingness to share her deep understanding
of the organization and how it has evolved over the years

For her stylish red suits, incomparable Stanford spirit,
and her ability to always keep the big picture in mind.

For her warmth and friendship and broad sense of the
meaning of Stanford volunteerism through her own involvement
with Cap & Gown and the great class of '47

For her energy, her humor, her support and appreciation
of staff and her fellow volunteers

We are pleased to present

Jean Coblentz, '47

this special commendation by the Board of Governors.

Presented by the Stanford Alumni Association
October 21, 2010

Farewell Party

My farewell party at Stanford was a complete surprise to me. I had been at a meeting and came around the courtyard of Bakewell where my office was located, to a scene of tables with umbrellas and chairs. I noticed a couple of chairs up front. Being the naturally shy person that I am, I went right up to Presidents Hennessy and Casper and said, 'May I join you gentlemen?' They both said, "Oh yeah." So, I sat down and listened to them go on about the successful year they had had, number wise.

Donna Robertson, events coordinator par excellence, then got up and announced that this gathering was also chronicling another important event no-one had heard about—my retirement! This was a farewell party for me! Lordy, I couldn't get out of it now! I can't remember all that was said and probably a lot was not all true. I was 74 years old at the time, and during the few words I spoke I said, 'The reason it has been so easy to work here is that I've always carried these two notes—one in each pocket. One says, "So Fire Me," and the other says, "I Quit." Everyone laughed.

When I retired as a staff member of Stanford Associates, someone stood up and made a motion that I be given Life Member status on the board. Although immensely flattered, I was not stupid and said, 'I'm moved practically to tears for this motion because I love this very interesting group. However, we all age and become different. I have to ask that when the day comes where I feel I am no longer of any value to the group you will let me go and not argue with me.' I also said, 'On the same line, if you conclude I have become a babbling idiot and don't notice, I hope you will have the guts enough to come and tell me in a very nice way that I had served long and well. I suggested that if they need to tell me I am no longer giving any added value, they do it over a glass of wine. I insisted that all the restrictions be entered into the minutes since when things are sometimes said and done in a moment of high emotion, the follow through doesn't materialize. The party ended with all the thanks for the memories and so forth. My response to that? 'It goes the other way, too.'

As I write this book, I am still an honorary member of the board and have never said, 'This is the way I did it.' Instead, I offer this: 'You might be interested to know; this is how this got started.' They don't have to do what was done at the beginning but need to know what the thinking was at the time, which might help figure things out. Some things that happened in the past are kind of interesting, giving a different perspective. A reply to that might be, "Oh, I didn't realize they did it that way."

A Fundraising Story

I remember the day Chris Ponce, another fundraiser, brought his newly adopted baby girl to the office, introducing her to the entire staff. Proud papa. Now when I talk to Chris and Lisa, I ask about their daughter Avery's university experience. Day by day, time passes for all of us.

At another time, a new staff member was being introduced around and in walked my husband Harry to pick me up for something. There were a number of people who had never met Harry and I said, "Oh, I'd like you to meet my current lover, Harry." Since that just came out of my mouth, not planned, the look on everyone's face, including Harry's, was priceless! We all had a good laugh. From then on, the phrase was coined.

"What a spark she was! In the true sense of the word, any meeting lit up when Jean participated. Always positive (the glass is nearly always full,) she had a way of keeping everyone on point with a combination of humor and good judgment (like when to skewer someone in a polite way). And, her ability to ask the right question at the right time was second to none. Wow! She was a treasure to know and be associated with for so many years."

—Dave Glen

"When a wise person comes into your life and shares her time and friendship with you, and you are fortunate enough to recognize this sage and old soul as a gift from the Gods, you are blessed beyond measure.

I met Jean when I was hired as an Associate Director in Stanford's Office of Development in 1979. Jean served as my immediate boss for a while and her warm welcome and willingness to offer guidance and true mentoring helped me understand my responsibilities and to frame expectations. Since this was my first professional fund-raising job, you can imagine my sense of relief and grateful heart. I spent years simply watching her in any setting: her style, sense of balance and fairness, nothing wasted, on target and purposeful.

That twinkle in her eyes, gentle good humor, and wit, offered inspiration and centeredness. I knew she understood my intentions, decisions, and the needs of another creative spirit. Never judgmental, always open to new ideas and inclusive. Jean was the heart of any organization graced by her elegant presence and grounded integrity.

Life is about stories and the sharing of memories, experiences and wisdom and Jean's life is rich with and framed by them. To re-capture life with our darling Jean, is to tap into the treasury of moments that helped you define and refine who you are, using her as a yardstick, as a model of all that is good and holy and true."

—Judy Donnelly Stearns

"I thought it was sheer luck that my office was next to hers. It turned out to be by Jean's design. So that I, a new hire, could be nearby for her coaching. This arrangement of hers was not revealed to me until my retirement. Many of you may have had similar experiences like this with Jean, who invested in people selflessly, tirelessly, and tactfully unknowingly to the benefactors. She became my American Auntie after I learned about her family's connection to China. Now, coaching runs in the family since I have been trying to follow Jean's bold and big footsteps in coaching others thoughtfully. Jean lives on..."

—Irene Yeh

"When Jean would bring her husband to the office at The Stanford Fund, she would introduce him a "her current lover." Still love that. We all loved it when she would say that. She also referred to Mr. Coblentz as "Handsome Harry," and it was always fun when he visited the office. She also used to joke that she never put anything in writing, saying, "I even signed my marriage license in pencil."

Jean was an incredible mentor to so many of us at Stanford, and she was very supportive of young people advancing and having significant roles in the office. She also exemplified the point that if you enjoy what you are doing, you can do it forever and it will never feel like work. I always called Jean 'Jeanius' and she was. She was a social genius and a genius at making relationships and connections with people. I always loved getting her season's greetings cards – at whatever season she felt like sending them. Doing this showed her spark, her humor, her individualism, and her creativity. Of course, her letters were always so fun to read with a dose of humor, a dose of realism, and incredible pride in her children and grandchildren. Jean knew that you just have to take your cookies as they are passed. Her using this expression widely made us all realize that truer words have never been spoken. Learning that at a relatively young age has been important to me, as difficult and sad times hit everyone. No one escapes unscathed and having her wisdom at hand helped us all more than she could ever know. Jean is a wonderful friend—always so upbeat, positive, and optimistic—one loves her friends dearly. She offered when I left, to host a party when I came back for a visit and very significant to me she was a shoulder to lean on when my younger sister died tragically in 1999. She was there for me, as I know she was there for countless friends at their times of need.

—Joel Getz

"I joined the Stanford Fund in August of 1994, as it was being launched, and that was when we became colleagues. We had such fun building this new program and we all benefitted from Jean's wisdom, "take your cookies when they're passed." Jean offered so much every day by her mere presence, that it is impossible to say what she meant to countess Stanford staff and volunteers."

—Julia Hartung

"Jean was very special to me, and I miss the many fun times we had together when I was on the Stanford Associates Board and worked in the Development Office. She will always be in my heart."

—Stephen Player

"Her smile and the twinkle in her eyes are remembered by the many whose lives she touched. What a huge influence she was in my life. Jean was basically responsible for my commitment to raise funds for Stanford for the past 40+ years. She was my Stanford Development Office contact early on, and with her encouragement and enthusiasm, I just kept agreeing to volunteer year after year. I was on the Stanford Associates Board of Directors with her, and we all appreciated her wise counsel, as well as her sense of humor. More recently, I admired her cleverness in creating the sash to hold all the Stanford pins she had acquired and received, (a la the Girl Scout sash). She was definitely an institution in the Development Office. Who knows how many other volunteers she inspired?"

—Barbara Hart

"Jean hired me for my first real job back in 1997. I had zero work experience and she was wonderful. She interviewed me and said," when can you start?" What a confidence booster! I was Jean's

assistant at the Stanford Fund for almost two years, and my job was to help her increase donations from grandparents.

She was an incredible example of tenaciousness, intelligence, and enthusiasm. How fortunate for me to start out my career with a boss like Jean! All others I compared to her and truly, none came close to her commitment and kindness. I count myself very lucky to know the famous, Jean Coblentz."

—Laney Pitstick

"I first met Jean when I joined the Associates Board of Governors in the early 90's and was truly lucky to have known her for so long (and benefitted from her sage advice and kind spirit.) Stanford won't be the same without her, though they are so much better because of her."

—Christina Dickerson

"I had the good fortune of working for five years with Jean on the Board of the Stanford Associates. As you might know, Jean was (and I think always will be) the only permanent member of the board. Everyone else served on the board for four to five years. Jean was an incredible resource and a treasured colleague. She was always wonderfully upbeat, and her enthusiasm was infectious.

When I became chair of the Associates Board and had questions about how things should be done, I knew that Jean would always have insightful answers. I have no doubt that Jean impacted everyone with whom she came in contact in a profoundly positive way."

—Peter Boutin

"Jean has always been the "Lady in Red" to so many of us, the very embodiment of Stanford spirit – always upbeat, measured and always the adult in the room. Jean's commitment to Stanford was especially notable as a member of the class of 1947, a class loaded with crusty WWII vets who were notoriously tough nuts to crack for fundraising.

—Doug Brown

"Whether it was as a Stanford undergraduate or later when I began my professional career at Stanford, I could count on Jean to provide good guidance. Sometimes, her questions weren't the easiest ones, but she could slice through a muddled discussion with one zinger comment that would bring everyone back to clarity. Her questions, consistently relevant, always set me to thinking

Always the consummate lady, dressed elegantly and in Stanford red more often than not. She could quietly make sure that work got done, but never seemed to over manage. She loved Stanford and everything about it, but also recognized the institution and people who worked for that institution weren't perfect. She was gracious, funny, humble, forgiving, exacting, a reservoir of energy and she was a terrific role model.

"Here's to a great lady. Petite she might have been, but her stature in the world was large. Thanks for being a part of my life, Jean."

—Margaret Kimball

"I remember Jean for her enthusiasm, her constant good cheer, her devotion to Stanford and to serving the broader community. I remember her generosity of spirit, her wonderful stories and, most of all, her kindness and encouragement to me. She was one of a kind. I feel lucky to have known her."

—Betsy Collard

Jean's Tenure on the Parents' Advisory Board

When I first came on the Stanford Associates Board, the Board VP said, "You know, we really think that we need a parents' program." That became the Parents' Advisory Board, which I ran until I retired.

Getting "the parents," as it was referred to, established was a busy time with lots of traveling around the United

States. One could liken it a little to cooking, which can be a chore. After you've done it 100 times, it is not quite as difficult as it was the first time around. I thoroughly enjoyed the traveling, which happened way before Google Maps came into existence.

The funding for the Parent's Advisory Board, however, was a juggling act, because you borrowed from Peter to pay Paul. Permission had to be given if monies had already been donated for a specific item. Pat Engasser, MD, was the first chairman of the Parents' Advisory Board and had previous experience with Stanford fundraising. It was important to have a person on our side with a name and some clout at Stanford. Pat gave outstanding service to her commitments and was later nominated for and received the Gold Spike Award, Stanford's highest medal of recognition for volunteer service to the University.

The board members for the Parents' Advisory Board were not necessarily Stanford alumnae. They were parents of present students at Stanford. The first board member was the mother of a freshman girl who had been in a bicycling accident where her tooth was broken. Parents came from all over the world, their passion for their children bonded them. It felt good to establish this board because it gave parents a connection to the university.

One time we were visiting the house of a parent who was a bit flustered when she got off the phone with her daughter. She said, "Oh, my God, that was my daughter, and she has just been elected to be the tree." I said, "Nooo," not knowing whether to be happy for her or not. I later learned being elected to be the tree means you are the Stanford mascot and extremely visible, since the mascot marches with the eclectic Stanford marching band during football season.

Wonderful friendships were made among the special parents on my advisory board and among the volunteers who helped make our events a success. Two parents share their stories before the story continues.

"We first had contact with Jean in the Fall of 1995, when we got a notice that there was a Stanford Parents Association. There was no District of Columbia contact, and when we inquired about that, we found we were it! Jean gently and quickly nudged us to represent DC. And that was Jean: gently—that is diplomatically, graciously encouraging—that is nudging and tapping—people to carry out tasks for Stanford. She was so lovey, so enthusiastic, and so passionate about her causes that one could not help but join in whatever task she asked. Jean was also a very caring person. She knew each of our children by name and always remembered so many details of our lives. Besides Stanford and Allied Arts (another of her interests), she was passionate about her family. She talked often and enthusiastically of her children – where they were and what they were doing. We heard every Christmas from Jean, even years after our daughters had graduated from Stanford."

—Marguerite Sullivan

The Stanford Parents Program Honors Jean

"This box weighs more than I do! What could it be?"

In a lovely silver Tiffany's Frame inscribed is a picture with Jean flanked by past chairs: Susan and Phil Bergan.

"My friendship with Jean goes back to 1995, when our son Nick began his freshman year at Stanford. I visited Stanford often and, early on, had the opportunity to meet Jean. Jean was instrumental in my involvement with the Stanford Parents' Club, which I have continued in many ways over the years. During those years, Jean would introduce me to her Stanford friends who visited Thailand, and I had the pleasure of meeting them and offering help and advice during their visits. Jean also offered her kind support and friendship to Nick during and after his time at Stanford. To this day, Nick has fond memories of lunches at the Stanford Faculty Club that Jean hosted for our family—an opportunity for good fellowship enjoyed over good food. My friendship with Jean was a basis to strengthen Stanford's ties with Thailand. I began to reach out to former Stanford parents in Thailand to get to know them. I had the opportunity to help the Stanford Club of Thailand organize the welcome reception for President Casper's visit to Thailand in 1998.*

Jean has showed me the way to get involved with Stanford and I took the opportunity enthusiastically with her as a friend and supporter. She is a true friend, personable, and always with a big warm smile. I often think of her and how we used to work together. Jean is a true treasure to the Stanford community around the world.

—Nirund Jivasantikarn

Philosophy

Words I've Tried to Live By: Golden Rule–Though usually associated with Christianity, every world religion has its version of this universal code of behavior. *"Do unto others as you would have others do unto you."*

The Universality of the Golden Rule in the World Religions

Christianity: All things whatsoever ye would that men should do to you, do ye so to them: for this is the law and the prophets.   Matthew 7:1

Confucianism: Do not do to others what you would not like yourself Then there will be no resentment against you, either in the family or in the state.
Analects 12:2

Buddhism: Hurt not others in ways that you yourself would find hurtful. Udana-Varga 5,1

Hinduism: This is the sum of duty; do naught onto others what you would not have them do to you.
Mahabharata 5, 1517

Islam: No one of you is a believer until he desires for his brother that which he desires for himself.
Sunnah

Judaism: What is hateful to you, do not do to your fellowman. This is the entire law; all the rest is commentary. Talmud, Shabbat 3 id

Taoism: Regard your neighbor's gain as your gain, and your neighbor's loss as your own loss.

Tai Shang Kan Uin P'ien

My Wish for The World:

I wish everyone would live by the golden rule.

I Wish My Parents Had Told Me
There is nothing they didn't tell me or show me.

Cookies

Almost everything I have ever done has come through somebody asking me to become involved. I performed the task or job and gave it my own special twist. My life has been full of *cookies*. My past *cookies* were the opportunities and challenges, I never dreamed of until they were presented to me. My glass was always half full, which allowed me to take advantage of those many *cookies* offered throughout my life. Just be honest with yourself. If you take a *cookie* and not care for it by giving it energy and enthusiasm, that *cookie* may not have been right for you.

Thoughts on Growing Older

If finishing a book, you are reading becomes too stressful, should you finish reading it? 'NO!' I have been an avid reader all my life and, actually I don't think there are many books I didn't bother to finish. I think I was giving the author the benefit of the doubt, by seeing it to the end. In my later years, however, as my eyes worsened, I "read" audio books just as voraciously. However, there came a time when it became harder to follow the storyline, leaving me inclined to stop "reading" that book and start another. Kath was always on the lookout for books on CD's she thought might interest me. My poor eyesight kept me from using a Kindle or any audible app on a smart device. Hence, our audio CD library at home is extensive at this time. I also had a subscription to the Library of Congress for "Talking Books" for the visually impaired.

My experience shows me that I get back more than I feel that I give to Stanford. By keeping me involved as a volunteer, Stanford has helped me stay busy and current to this day. Stanford has not let go of me, and I haven't let go of Stanford.

It is often more important to figure out what you learned from something you did or didn't do than how well the project turned out. If I can't have fun with the activities I do, I'm not going to bother. Fortunately, even this late in life and with my personality I'm still having fun and enjoying my days.

TV/Radio

Kath and I sometimes listened to a program that was pretty good, funny and poignant. It was called, Selected Shorts. It made me think of how many things in this world either interest us or don't. Radio has continued to be a source of entertainment and information me. My weekend almost always included time in my reading chair listening to Garrison Keillor's <u>Prairie Home Companion</u> radio show. Never a TV watcher, I did find it a novelty during the early days of our marriage when our TV was new and enjoyed seeing all four of my kids in the family room watching the Mickey Mouse Club. In my later years, when Kath and I watched reruns of The Lawrence Welk show, it was a real treat.

Because I was such a Prairie Home Companion fan, and had been for at least

Jean Galt Coblentz has a radiant smile. She is traveling with her daughter Kathy and her granddaughter Milena, and has listened to Prarie Home Show since it began. "A missionary family knows those songs," she says. Jean was born in Kinhungkiang, in the the Yunan Province of China where her parents, Curtis and Mabel Galt, were medical missionaries - he a doctor, she a dietician - at a Presbyterian mission. To get there, they landed in Siam and took, on unpaged roads, an 8 day trip by horse. Her father founded a leper colony where, as soon as she was old enough for her toes to reach the pedals, Jean learned from the minister's wife how to play the organ.

Jean and her borther and two sisters were educated by their mother. There was a victrola, and music, and laughter. When Jean was twelve, they moved to the US and eventually settled in Manteca, California, where Jen was valedictorian at sixteen. She attended Stanford on scholarship, where she majored in psychology and met Maurice Henry Coblentz, Jr. who was attending Stanford on the G.I. Bill after flying B29s in WWII.

Jean had some lessons in shorthand nd typing along the way, and peering into the window at Hewlett Packard led to a job in industrial psychology. Maurice became a businessman and Jean volunteered for the Scouts and at the Stanford Children's Hospital where, after their two boys and two girls went off th school, she wen to work for the director of fundraising. For 23 years.

Jean comes from a writing family. To celebrate their twenty-fifth wedding anniversary, her father worte and had printed a biography of her mother's life. The couple wasn't able to be together thtat day, so her father sent the manuscript to Jean, who - with her brother - delivered it to her mother. And now Jean is writing s memoir that begins where her father's left off. The questions she asks? "What is important? How do you show it? Whom do you include?" In teh span of three years, this woman lost her husband, a child and a grandchild. "I have suffered but it made life beautiful," she says. "From the mud grows the lotus."

25 years, when Kath found out they sponsored cruises, we talked about joining the group. But they had sold out. So, the following year in 2015, the minute Kath heard they were going to the Eastern Caribbean, she said, "Mom, we're going." I replied, 'maybe we should think about it' and she said, "if we think about it too long, it will just sell out again, Let's just do it." Her rationale and decision were based on the desire I had expressed a couple years prior about wanting to go on a cruise, She thought about it and realized that with my failing eyesight, there would be no point in floating down the Rhine River with me not being able to see the scenery. But a Prairie Home Companion cruise where Garrison Keillor would put on two shows a day and poet laureate, Billy Elliot was a guest on the cruise, would be just fine. Along with Garrison's entire cast and crew, it would make for a perfect venue even for me with my failing eyesight.

Three generations in red.

Once she started the reservation process, we had decided it would be even more fun if Milena flew to Florida from Italy to meet us and the three of us would travel together. I must say that with the three of us, three generations of strong women who clearly cared deeply about each other, touched many hearts. I was interviewed for the person of interest column in the daily, "Cruise News." I got to meet many of Keillor's staff and, of course, Garrison himself, as well as the poet laureate. Kath's bucket list included riding in a helicopter, so I figured I might as well go along. I sat next to the pilot and flirted the whole time! Our Catamaran outing was just as fun, as most of the staff on the boat were handsome young men, all wanting to take care of me, while the rest of the passengers jumped into the sea and swim to the shore. It was an experience not to be forgotten and strengthened, even more, my close bonds with Kath and Milena, my oldest child and oldest grandchild.

Life's Question

I gave up a long time ago trying to figure out how genes are distributed and how or why some people have one very healthy, normal child and another child with all kinds of problems. I don't think we are meant to know the answers to all those questions.

No need for us to roll over and play dead for everything negative that comes down the pike. We don't have to play the "poor me" card and buckle under adversity. An attitude of gratitude is a wonderful thing to have. Be a participant. I have been able to guide a lot of what happened and, as time went by, to also accept and be realistic about what my capabilities were. I cannot do now what I did ten or fifteen years ago—don't even wish to. I realize how important it is to stay healthy. More sleep is necessary now than it was ten or fifteen years ago. If I live a lifetime without learning anything, then that is a tragedy. That doesn't mean that I can always have control over what's coming up. One must be flexible and willing to always look for the good in something, the bright side. If I throw up my hands without waiting to see what the other side has to offer, I might miss an opportunity – a *cookie.*

My Greatest Accomplishments

It would be difficult to say what my greatest accomplishment is since life was so full and varied. I would like to be remembered for my sense of humor. No matter what the situation, there is always humor somewhere in it. I got that from my parents. They were both really funny, especially mother. I often say to Kath when we are leaving a function, 'Did you see that? I left them laughing!' I love to do that!

In a conversation where someone gives out a straight line, I love to immediately respond with a play on words or something on the witty side producing laughter. An example of this happened when we recently went to the bank. One of the people there loves to hug so I always get a great big hug when I go there. Somebody saw that and said, "Are you passing those out?" I quickly said, 'No, but they're on sale today."

I don't like to just sit there and not respond. Recently, I also spent an hour with my attorney. We "battled" back and forth in that manner and had such a good time. It is fun to do, and nobody gets hurt. Just make it relevant.

Getting Older

I look at some of my younger pictures and say, 'Wow, I got old.' I don't care; what are you going to do? If I step back from the mirror, I look just fine. And as I like to say, it's all in the eyes of the beholder anyway.

I have made it clear that I am not interested in living when I can no longer enjoy my life or have become a burden. My family knows what I mean by this.

I'd like to die in a way that will cause the least nuisance. I have lived a long life and have watched many things happen, including death. I have been able to have the kind of life I wanted. If I were to go "bump," then I would feel perfectly good about dying because my life has been good. I have done and tried the things I wanted to do and try. Death does not frighten me. Do you like to go to bed and cuddle up and sleep? Well, that is what I think death is – no more turning over at night in bed because you are getting cold. All my children are good, and they love each other. That makes me very happy.

I believe it important to have my "house in order" before I die, because that means that when I die, my attitude about it brushes off on these people. If I don't make a big deal with it, they won't or won't have to. I have done everything possible to have a plan to distribute my estate fairly to avoid family strife. I don't believe in "another life," but I love going to sleep, so all should be well.

Grief and Mourning

Grief hits you when you least expect it. It comes from outer field and is a huge surprise. It can affect you in the moment before you have time to put up defenses. I don't think I did grieve much over anything except when my daughter Jan died of cancer at age 58. When my Mother died, we sat around and told stories and commented on how it was such a "mother" thing.

When my Father, Curtis Martin Galt died, we had a funeral service in the Presbyterian Church where he had contributed so much. One of the last things he did in public at that church was walk my youngest sister Corny down the aisle when she married Jack Leach in Manteca. He had already begun to exhibit signs of dementia, and my mother Mabel became his caretaker. He was kept at home until he passed away peacefully in his sleep. When he left this earth, all his affairs were cleared up.

Most of my grieving was done in private or in the company of another family member where more talking rather than weeping or anything else took place. We mostly tried to find funny stories to reminisce about. That is what I hope people will do when I die.

Management Skills

I certainly learned management skills early by being a dorm manager while I was a Stanford student. I also learned that it doesn't matter who you are or what level of strata you have reached. In the end, you are just a human being. I was taught to do unto others as you would have them do unto you. It works, it really works. I absolutely do not judge people by their status or lack thereof. In this day and age especially, you might be fired more than once if you are not realistic about how you deal with that.

Corney's Wedding Manteca, California 1957. Mabel's Kitchen.
Grandma Moore (front left), Mabel Galt (front right), Rear (l-r)
Alice Crowell, Curtis Galt, Jean Coblentz, Alan Galt, Cornelia
Leach.

Christmas in Manteca 1950

More About Hobbies

Until my senior year in college, I made all my own clothes. Mother and I sewed together. I am sure that contributed to our great friendship. Mother made my wedding dress that still hangs in my closet. I had hoped one of my daughters would want or be able to wear it, but neither of them had "traditional weddings." I did later, however, offer it to a Stanford colleague of mine who was thrilled that it fit her perfectly. It was a *cookie* for her, and my great pleasure to lend it to her for her wedding. She was also a book club (Book Tasters) friend of mine, and the shared wedding dress created a special bond between us. I loved telling people about my wedding dress and often took them upstairs to show them my mother's handiwork.

Book Club/Book Tasters

When I was a young mom raising four kids, Harry took the train to the city (San Francisco) for work every day. I had a schedule with a friend, Sally Holland, whose husband also commuted. We began trading off driving the husbands to the train, and over time, we noticed that we were always talking about which books we were reading. In 1961, we started a book club together. There were only three of us: Sally, one other friend and myself. We had such an interesting time, and we spent so much time reading, discussing, and trading off whose home would host each meeting.

The book club was started in 1961 and is still active. The only rule we have about admitting new members is that they must attend two of our meetings to make sure it is the right group for them.

The concept back in 1961 was that we wanted to share our literary discoveries and have time for discussion and socialization. So, three of us who were close friends, (two have passed away) decided on an unusual format and called our group, "Book Tasters." Each month, one member would do a review of a book of their choice – we rarely knew before the meeting what the book would be. Each month we got to sample someone else's taste for books. Sometimes the book was inspiring and sometimes you knew it was not for you. After the review, the hostess would serve lunch. So, we not only got a taste of books, but also a taste of someone else's cuisine. Each member hosted once a year and reviewed once a year and, of course, did not have both responsibilities in the same month. Over the years, members have come and gone, but 53 years later, I'm still with the group – the longest sustaining member, although no longer reviewing books due to my poor vision (AMD.)

After I stopped driving, my dear friend, Toni Bennett, swung by the house to take me to our book club monthly meetings – usually in the Palo Alto/Los Altos area.

I also did book reviews, twice a year at Channing House in Palo Alto, one of the first serious senior communities in this part of the bay area. Over the 50 years that I was on their calendar, I got to know many of the residents, some were people I had known from Stanford.

Accomplishments

No one ever gave me a bad time about what I accomplished or how I accomplished it. I don't think I came across as a threat to anyone. I have tried never to flaunt what I did and often would stop mid-sentence to think about how something I was going to say might sound. I never wanted to hurt or be misunderstood. I never wanted to run for office either, although I was asked to become active in local Santa Clara County politics when recognized for some of my volunteer accomplishments. I could not have played that political game and am forever grateful I trusted my instincts. Soon after that offer, I started working at Stanford.

Holidays

Take your *cookies* when they are passed. If there is an opportunity to celebrate, you can always shift things around so that it fits you, rather than you fitting it. An example of that was when Kath, Renato and Milena were coming from Italy to California for Christmas. Their flight was delayed, which kept them from arriving on Christmas day. NO MATTER! We made Christmas on the 26th and people stayed to celebrate my birthday on the next day, the 27th of December.

During Christmas time in China, we had a tree but not what is now considered a Christmas tree. It was sparsely decorated and NOT a pine. Santa Claus, also not part of the celebration, was too confusing a concept for the local people to grasp onto. Since Dr. Goodenberger was there at the mission to teach the local population about Christianity, it was more befitting to stick to the original story of Jesus' birth.

Regrets vs. *Cookies*

I think it a regret that I never took the time to learn a stringed instrument. I have lived in several places and remember my college years at Stanford where girls individually played a ukulele or guitar. I felt that a great way to bring people together after supper or at other "gathering" times. I was grateful, however, for my opportunity to learn a keyboard instrument in China as a young girl. In Manteca, where I continued my music training, my parents had a Steinway baby grand piano. After I married, we always had an upright piano in our home.

New opportunities to try something presented themselves at almost every turn I took. Those were the *cookies*.

When something brings you to an area you hadn't thought of before, you find yourself saying, 'Goodness gracious, let's try that.'

Most of the memorable events of my life have been where an opportunity was presented, and I took it. With that kind of belief, my glass usually started out half full!

When you are offered *cookies*, how do you decide which ones to take? You consider all the details. How soon is this decision needed? What are the specifics? Maintain relationships. Keep your ears open. If this specific invitation doesn't work, say "I am interested, but this particular opportunity doesn't work for me. Please keep me in mind next time." Keep your bridges strong. You never know what these relationships and opportunities may lead to down the road.

Greatest Contribution to Volunteer Work

This happened in 2002 at about the time when Allied Arts, founded in 1932, celebrated its 70th Anniversary. I was asked if I would head the fundraising to completely renovate the entire guild. There were about 12 people on the committee that raised 10 million dollars, which was a lot of money back in the early 2000's. The money came from people who loved the guild and wanted to preserve and protect the historic Spanish architecture and beautiful gardens. Renovation was necessary to bring it up to earthquake standards in order to continue to be a source of inspiration and beauty to all its visitors. It is also home to the Allied Arts Auxiliary that operates the entire property for the benefit of the Lucille Packard Children's Hospital at Stanford. It may only takes two or three people who really love the guild and have a lot of money to donate, for a funding campaign that large to be successful. Part of my job was teaching others to not be afraid to ask for the "big bucks." In the fundraising world, you can always come down, but you can never go up! Many of my Stanford *cookies* came from opportunities other people didn't want to take. I had been volunteering at Stanford for many years before I actually started working there for pay in 1977. Some of my best experiences, memories and friends came from those unexpected developments offered as *cookies*.

The Stanford license plate on my car said, **Fundraiser.** People stopped me more than once at traffic lights that wanted my phone number to have me help them with their fundraising causes!

Notes from Jean's Allied Arts Friends

"Jean has been my mentor almost since the time I met her in 1967 when I joined the Woodside Atherton Auxiliary to the Children's Hospital at Stanford. I very much admired how Jean was always in the moment; always thinking creatively and in a positive mode.

When I needed back surgery in the 80s and was hesitant due to unfounded fears, I called Jean from the hospital and she visited me and told me what I might face if I didn't have it done. She dispelled fears that somehow my doctors had failed to do. I had the surgery, did well and Jean and I keep in touch.

For me, Jean is so valuable because whenever I've asked her for advice, she has listened, gotten me to think and to talk to her, asked a few questions and somehow led me to my own conclusions without ever making the decision or solving the problem for me. She does it every time. Jean doesn't gossip. Jean ALWAYS has a smile on her face. My cookie was: meeting the love of my life at an inconvenient time for me and dropping everything temporarily to go with the flow. A second cookie was being offered a part-time professional position in PR volunteering for the WAACHS and taking it...just to see. Yep, cookies work. It's being open and taking a chance."

—Robin Liston

"Jean was an incredible woman, full of life and wit! She and I became close when she followed me as President of the Allied Arts Auxiliary. This would be her second term. We worked closely together during the transition.

I admired Jean's honesty and straightforwardness. She shared many stories of her life. She was a great leader who could be relied upon to do the job well. The auxiliary benefitted from her presidency."

—Libby Russo

"At my very first meeting of the Woodside-Atherton Auxiliary to the Children's Hospital at Stanford in 1975, Jean was the president. I was immediately in awe of her poise and warmth as she chaired the meeting. I knew I had made a wise and wonderful choice to join this organization.

Jean always had such a wonderful smile and, indeed, a twinkle in her eye. She was always so positive and engaging, and I felt that we had become instant friends.

And it was not just a feeling, but a true friendship that developed over all the 25 plus years. I could always count on her.

—Veronica Arthur

"You Cob, will always be on my mentor's shoulder, urging me to keep thinking, trying, and laughing. You are high on my list of mentors who deserve credit for my accomplishments in various roles within the Auxiliaries and Lucile Packard Children's Hospital. I took the opportunities that presented themselves and relished engaging with them. Along the way, the best cookies came with new friends and greater peace."

—Anna Henderson

"I served on the AAG Board of Directors with Jean when I was a relatively new member. I remember her as smart, practical, straightforward with a kind heart and wicked wit. She became a mentor to me. But my fondest memories are of the times I visited her home to bring her lunch when she was recovering from an illness. We sat on the patio and talked for hours about her family history and other topics. Jean was a very special person, and I will not forget her.

—Kay Bates

Pamper Myself

Do I pamper myself? I don't know ... having a piece of chocolate every day I don't consider pampering. If I wanted a piece of chocolate, I would eat it because it tasted good. It would just be my acting on something I want. I consider pampering to be a little on the naughty side.

Exercise

I used to get up at 5:00 a.m. and swim for an hour in a nearby pool at the middle school. I swam up and down doing all the strokes. Now when I go to a pool with Kath, I cannot swim and can't, for the life of me, figure out why. Water gets up my nose and there are so many people that I have to be careful of not running into any of them. Some

351

things at 90 are just not what they were at 50. To tell you the truth, swimming was always a nuisance. Since I wanted to look nice when I got to work, I'd have to spend too much time fixing my hair. It was never a passion but rather, only a way to be active and more importantly, a way to keep my back pain from rearing up.

After I stopped swimming, I had no exercise routine other than the significant amount of walking I did on the Stanford campus. Although Harry would have loved it, I was not interested in learning to play golf. I was happy he enjoyed the game, which he played twice a week until about six months before his passing. When Kath came to live with me in 2011, she brought a recumbent bicycle that I started riding to keep my legs strong. I enjoyed riding it 15 to 20 minutes every morning as I listened to music and enjoyed many a chat with her.

One of My Proudest Moments

I don't know that I have one single moment of which I am most proud. No awards as a child. Life was just part of the ladder I climbed. Proud moments happened when my children did something. I have received all kinds of awards and recognition as an adult. I don't consider the "prizes" something I have done but rather a conglomeration of opportunities. *Cookies*, I took advantage of, made me into who I am. It is not the action I feel that is awarded but what that action did for the person – how it changed them into a better person.

I am very, very proud that Marty has turned into the kind of person he is, that he was able to hang in there when being tested. His dad and I agreed, thank goodness, that he didn't have to complete high school in the "status-quo" way. To watch him, way back then, climb out of that hole he was in and from there to where he is today is a miracle. It was so awful to watch our very bright kid with so much potential, struggle. Harry and I went on a hope and a prayer when we let him go to welding school.

Book Dream

I've accomplished my dream ... when this book is completed.

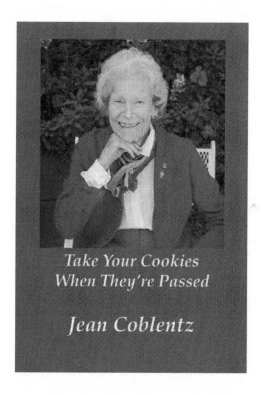

Take Your Cookies When They're Passed

Jean Coblentz

From the Stanford Daily Newspaper while Jean Coblentz was working at Stanford in the 1990's.

Activity

Although I am still very active, I am still trying to clear the decks so I can write my book. Somehow time just creeps up on you while whizzing by. In my 90th year, things are finally coming together for the book with the help of family and friends.

Birthday Celebrations

Throughout my life we didn't make a big hullaballoo about birthdays except there was always a birthday cake and a few candles for the birthday person.

I am not the surprise party type, but I insisted on surprising Harry on his 70th birthday, as mentioned before. Ten years later, my four kids planned an early surprise party for my 80th birthday.

They figured if it were held a month early on November 27, which happened to be Thanksgiving, with all the family gathered, I wouldn't suspect anything. It was a grand affair, and in retrospect, perfect timing to have so many friends and family present.

A few days later, Harry was hospitalized and unable to return home. Our family and closest friends were with him every day in the hospital. He passed away on December 13, 2005. Unbeknownst to all, my surprise party was also a farewell party for Harry. He absolutely loved being surrounded by all his family as he sat quietly on the couch, the best seat in the house, to observe all the festivities

Birthday Wishes

The boys volunteered thoughts and remembrances for Mom's 83rd Birthday.

Scott's Birthday Remembrances:
"I think Mom's favorite color is red because of the fire she has burning inside of her. Red is the color of heart and we all know what a warm heart she has. Red is the color of flames and when she lights a fire under your butt, you had better do it!

I am glad to be a part of this clan because I think we represent what is good and inspiring when it comes to family unity. I am also

glad to be a part of this clan because whenever we all get together, there is always a wonderful experience awaiting all of us. And finally, I know that when we plan events like this, everybody in our family looks forward to it, and that is why I am proud to be a part of the clan.

When I think about my mother, the mental image I conjure up is one of a person, despite the circumstances, as someone who always has a positive attitude. She is a person who has oceans of good advice and will never hesitate to wave her crooked finger at you with those words of wisdom. She spends most of her time helping other people directly or indirectly.

My mother is small in size but big in stature...
Long live the matriarch of Nome Court.
Applause!"

—Scott Coblentz

From Marty at Jean's 83rd Birthday Celebration:

"As today is an auspicious occasion (your 83rd birthday,) I thought I'd jot down a few thoughts I can remember since we have been together. Some of the very early memories have been lost to age, but I do remember:

"Mama's Tick Tock" clock and the valiant effort by Mr. Harmon to recover the lost treasure, and the subsequent replacement, some years later, with a replica.

Walking on the brick patio in our Hedge Road yard, holding Grandpa Galt's hand, leading him to some point of interest in the back yard. It must have been the rose bushes with the special grade of mud!

Learning to ride the hand-me-down bike in front of our house and getting it right the first time and then promptly running into the pole at the entrance to James Flood School.

Having the honor to be on the Milk Monitor squad and responsible for fetching the tray of little milk cartons for the class (and for some unknown reason, poking holes in them with a pin).

Eating a wonderfully prepared lunch in my second-grade class after carefully removing my retainer and placing it in my lunch bag before promptly throwing the bag in the all-consuming incinerator. Teeth turned out OK in spite of this.

Playing "gas station" in the driveway...topping off the tank with water and seeing if nails would really pop all four tires.

Breaking the glass milk bottles on the Landrith's porch. I thought I was breaking the ice with the new neighbors and I guess I was.

Building the go-kart in the garage with Dad and then, after a few wonderful rides, failing to put it away. It disappeared during the night. Michael Durr was, and still is, a "Person of Interest" in this unsolved case.

Having a genuine hero, in my eyes anyway, Paul Cross, who lived almost directly across the street. Can't remember why he was a hero figure, but he was. I remember how he used to look at Kath too. I'm sure there is an untold story out there related to "the look." I believe he was trying to rekindle something when he showed up at Nome Ct. in his Austin Healy and gave me a ride! It probably wasn't our friendship.

Being disgruntled over some real or perceived event and deciding that I would be better off on my own. Packing all the necessities for a long road trip and climbing over the fence next to the freeway, only to discover that the grass appeared to be brown there too. I don't remember the joyous homecoming....

Being teased incessantly by Lenny DeAndre and eventually learning how to deal with it.

Getting permission for the civil work to construct what was to be the swimming pool we would all enjoy. Donny DeAndre graciously assisting in his spare time. Me being the only one to enjoy the partially finished project. I have since learned to finish what I start .... for the most part."

Riding on Dad's shoulders and being launched through the air in the big pool at Ladera Oaks Country Club.

Scott jumping on my head in the wading pool at the above location and getting my first stitches. Scott contends to this day, that I veered off course, hence causing the subsequent contact.

Focusing on the little bird in our dentist's office (his name, the dentist, not the bird, has escaped me) that would dip down and appear to be drinking while said dentist merrily drilled holes in my teeth.

Hiding behind the couch with Scott in a failed attempt to surprise Santa and being amazed at the disappearance of the milk and cookies (no holes in the milk carton for Santa as this was expressly forbidden.)

The joy that snow brought all of us on Hedge Road.

Walking through our house on Nome Court when it was in the rough framing stage and having a picnic on the floor where now the famous pool table resides.

Sitting in Mr. Daughlin's class and being embarrassed at not completing my homework. Oddly enough, this trend would continue even though the negative attention was excruciating. I believe this was part of what eventually taught me to "Just Do It!" along with many other good examples offered me throughout the years.

Standing on the playground at Serra School near the east basketball backboard pole and receiving the news that President Kennedy had been shot.

Wanting a pair of Beatle Boots so bad (and not being able to convince the powers that be that these were essential) that I bought Todd Tomek's and would put them on after leaving for school. They were two sizes too small, but that seemed a small price to pay.

Playing little league on Fawny Ho's team and being sent all the way home from Cupertino Jr. High to get my forgotten belt. Being a pretty good catcher and making the All-star team and throwing a couple of guys out who were trying to steal second base.

Waiting seemingly forever for the big 7th grade ski trip day to arrive. Spending the night at Clay Smith's house and sleeping through the alarm and missing the trip.

Riding Minibikes at Lester's Hill with Harry Bright.

Convincing Dad that it would be OK for me to buy the old Renault on my paper route because the owner said I would never get it running. Subsequently, getting it running and having Dad catch me driving it.

Teasing my siblings incessantly with skills acquired from Lenny.

Invading Kath and Jan's dance parties in the pool room.

"Double cutting" the grass. Only after I had my own lawn did I appreciate the value in this.

Going to get Dad at the train station and putting pennies on the track.

Mom and Dad finally acquiescing to the purchase of the Hodaka brand motorcycle and learning to ride the big bike.

Dad renting a trailer and taking Scott and me to the redwoods for a day of riding.

Mom renting a trailer and taking John Brandt and me to the motocross races in Livermore.

Working at the Engine House for Easy Schwafel for 75 cents an hour and getting reprimanded for not sifting through the floor sweepings for small locomotive parts.

Working for Jerry Henry at the Chevron station (for a substantial increase in pay) and providing the consummate service to motorists that was the norm in those days. Speaking of Norm, Jerry's mechanic, I remember emptying the trash in the men's room and always finding empty pint bottles of whiskey. Norm's cars were running on all cylinders, even if Norm wasn't.

Working for Mike Kalochie at the repair shop down the road and him always calling me "molly."

Scott and my teaching Rennie (Kath's Italian husband) all the pertinent English words he needed to know.

The look of joy on Dad's face when he discovered the now famous pool/laundry folding table in the playroom.

Seeing if a Cherry Bomb would still go off if it had been lit once. Jan's hasty exit from the garage on the way to the emergency room and the scrape on the garage door jamb from the passenger side door handle.

Driving home from Dodge Ridge ski resort at the ripe old age of 15 while Kath nursed a broken wrist. The fact that Ford did not build a sun visor capable of shielding a short driver's eyes while traveling west at dusk. Wearing ski goggles to combat the setting sun.

Cruising San Francisco Bay with Dad in our boat, the Kittiwake and learning the seamanship skills still practiced today.

Moving out of Nome Court and moving in with Jim and Dave Lewis and shortly thereafter, moving back to Nome. Dave, repeatedly leaving his cold, untouched bowl of Cream of Wheat in the sink on my days to do the dishes was the deciding factor in this decision.

Convincing Landlord Louie that he should rent me the house on Lomita Ave. for $225.00 a month.

A whole new chapter of memories began with this permanent departure from the "nest," but as Paul Harvey says, you'll have to wait until your next birthday to hear, "The Rest of the Story."

Your never giving up on me (Dad too, but sometimes I think he wanted to) has allowed me to continue amassing memories that I will cherish (well, most of them anyway) forever. Thanks, and Happy Birthday."

—Marty Coblentz'
Thoughts on Mom's 83rd Birthday

Jean and Marty

Marty's Tender Words for Mom's 90th Birthday

Happy Birthday Mom!

My original intent was to write you a poem but, as I'm sure you know, it can sometimes be difficult to express all of your feelings with words that rhyme. Not that I mind difficult, but this birthday is special, and I didn't want to exchange my feelings for an attempt at poetic prowess (hope you're not too disappointed!)

The two of us have never been shy about communicating our love for one another and I won't end that tradition here. You have inspired me in ways that no one else could and for those gifts, I will always be grateful. The examples you have set for me and your other children will live on long after all of us have moved to the next phase of life.

I often mention how blessed we (your family and countless others!) are that you are a part of our lives. You continue to display the personal qualities that have endeared so many to you, even if you can't always remember who they are! We'll cut you some slack for that because after all, it is your ninetieth birthday!

As I watch you deal with the things that beset most people who have been around for ninety years, it makes me proud that you are my mom and reminds me how I must behave when I get to where you are (never too early to start practicing!) You are the embodiment of the Serenity Prayer (for those who don't know this particular prayer, look it up!) as you display the courage, acceptance (well, sometimes) and wisdom in dealing with the challenges of being ninety. This is a badge of honor that befits you.

I would be remiss if I did not mention your parents in this letter. Without them, none of the many lives you have touched would be as enriched as they are today and, not to mention, some of us wouldn't be here! Curtis and Mabel have been watching their special daughter for all her years and it is safe to say, are as proud as we are.

I love you Mom."

—Marty Coblentz

Friends

Who Was Your Best Female Friend for Life?

I guess there wasn't one. I am still in contact with people from my Stanford freshman class but there was never a #1 friend. Most of my friends were men, boys. I grew up with, boy cousins interested in playing football in the potato patch. I played with them since they were a lot more interesting than girls. I never played with dolls, although I did bring one home from China.

As an adult, Dee Ellis is my best friend now. We first met through the Packard Children's Hospital Auxiliary. We realized we lived fairly close to one another and did a lot of sharing rides back and forth. She is originally from Texas. Her workplace was near the VA hospital. They also had four children. However, her marriage didn't last due to bad choices her husband made. After they separated, she surprised me by doing the following: She had a friend take her children for a long weekend and gave herself 24 hours only to do whatever she needed to get the anger and angst out of her system. She then was going to get a job, which she did. I admired that part of her immensely. The two of us are alike in several ways. She is very pleasant and not a moody person at all. Early on, she decided it was okay to reveal to me stories about the people in her family and everything.

When I stopped driving three years ago and still very active in the community, she said, "Anytime I am going in your direction, I'd be happy to take you." Now that is a friend. And to everyone else I said, 'If you want my brains, come get my body."

Clay Play Group 2015

During my later years with the Allied Arts Guild Auxiliary, (2000-2017), I worked closely with many exceptional women, and they became good friends and a major part of my social life. I'm so grateful to have been able to serve with them for a greater cause.

Another way we AAG ladies came together was in a group we called, "Clay Play,"

Jean creating at Clay Play

hosted by Louise Scott, a professional artist / ceramist. She has recently completed a ceramics project for the new Lucille Packard Children's Hospital, and we all were able to contribute – even with our varying levels of skill with clay.

"Please know that I was a huge fan of Jean's. I told her so many times, and that I wanted to be just like her when I grew up. I'm sorry she isn't here to continue teaching me. I dearly loved her.
—Louise Scott

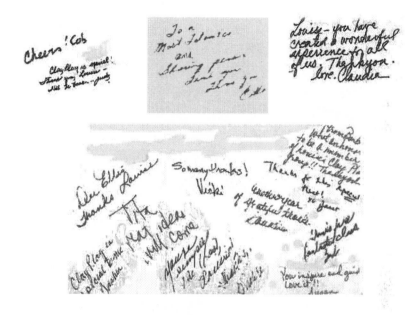

Clay Players Speak

"The kiln is MY responsibility,"
sayeth our dear Louise.
How about clay and glaze, brushes, and the etcetera's galore? Not to mention cleaning up the garage??? Norman's job??? Ha!!!
Let's put our heads together and come up with THANKS ideas.
We're great with "clays", let's go farther afield than that!
So, by our first "forget me not" lunch, we'll have something from the heart created by, this "committee of all" as each of us is smart. In the meantime:

THANK YOU LOUISE.
From Us!

One in particular, I would like to highlight, while having a little fun. She was a major player during my leadership years with Allied Arts and, as you will gather an extremely talented artisan who initiated our Clay Play group. Read on ... to the end and it will be revealed!

Jean Sets A Test: Who Is This?

She is way cool. Seems always in control (even when she isn't)

Smarter than most of us. Takes on big jobs and makes them look simple.

Says "YES" to requests where she feels she can make a difference and then moves.

When we were putting together the Renovation Committee, she was name #1 and took great minutes.

And, became a friend.

She does Haute Courtier sewing and always looks, "Model Sharp!!" (wonder if she does alterations?)

She is a fabulous hostess and invitations to her "DO's" are cherished.

She has friends all over the world and each knows he/she is a favorite!

Want a professional potter for a special something? Call _____ .

Who is the generous soul who shares her expertise with clay to teach a group of neophytes who gather for clay play and to get the new year off to an artistic start...and an invitation to join!!! More coveted than tickets to the Oscars!

Ask the "Decorating Committee at Packard Children's Hospital who creates the one-of-a-kind tiles for pillars or tiles for sick children to work on and make personal.

Ask the Association of Auxiliaries and the Packard board about her leadership qualities, and work behind the scenes to get the endowment created...now in the millions!

Who has said YES when we tried oversight, and who is doing exactly what she should, and no one has to wonder if she's done it — she has!

Who has had more than her share of physical imperfections and complaineth not?

Who is always there when someone is having physical imperfections and needs a helping hand?

She manages to look elegant always in every setting

Who had a special, handsome husband and together they set the standard?

Please take the test and sign the honor code.

Hint: There is only one answer to every question and spelled backwards, it is: esiuoL ttocS

And I would be leaving out a very important, long lasting, "Dear Friend" relationship if I didn't mention how precious my friendship with Marnie Furbush was. We met in our freshman English class at Stanford and quickly recognized each other's kindred spirit. She married after college and stayed in the bay area, which made it easy for us to stay in touch. She became a member of our book group early on. Our literary connection was always strong. I knew she was brilliant and imagined what an asset she'd be for the Stanford libraries. She was not looking for paid work, but I interested her in volunteering, which was exactly what she needed in order to blossom and thrive while sharing her talents in that intellectual environment.

Through our friendship, we worked together for the Stanford Library and doors opened for each of us, which Marnie also saw as *cookies.* Even in our senior years, well into our 80s, we had long and thoughtful phone conversations, as she had moved to Placerville, California and later to Reno, Nevada to be closer to her daughter.

She hired a driver to bring her to Sunnyvale for my 85th birthday. Kathy understood our friendship and would dial the phone for me when my eyes were too bad to see, and she saw to it that I was able to visit Marnie up in Placerville. Kath later took me up to visit her in Reno in her assisted living community. Even then, in her early 90s she was editor of the local newsletter and her room was filled with books. A dear friend indeed with such a kind and gentle soul.

Marnie at Jean's 85th birthday.

Chores

When Harry and I married, the chores were divided up by what made the most sense. For example, he might do the shopping and cooking after a new baby had arrived. Or when Harry went out of town, then the chores were all mine and maybe if the kids behaved themselves, they could help me. I was fortunate to have men in my life that didn't say, "You will do this or that."

I would say we always found ways to help each other through the years of our marriage. While I was working at Stanford, Harry at age 64, retired. It was understood that he would become the househusband and was I ever thrilled that I no longer had to cook or do the grocery shopping, a role which Harry really enjoyed as he won the hearts of the women at Safeway's checkout counters. This all meant that when I got home from my 12-hour workday, dinner was on the stove and Harry already had a glass of wine poured for me. I couldn't have asked for more. A great number of my colleagues professed their envy of my support at home. Harry's reputation as a sweetheart flourished.

People I Respected and Admired

The Woodside Atherton Auxiliary was a group I learned a lot from. Watching individuals with leadership skills and how they maneuvered was fascinating. Although not just one person can be named, the dynamics of the group as a whole worked well. They welcomed me into the "governing roles" where I contributed, serving two consecutive terms as President, well into my late 80s.

I give thanks to a variety of people who "took a chance" on me. Every one of them was a winner and a role model for me.

Stanley Hawkins, my high school science teacher, offered me the chance to learn life-long, work-related skills. These skills impressed Noel Eldred at HP in 1947, who hired me on the spot. Years later, Dick Bennett gave me my first opportunity at Stanford, a place where I transferred all I had learned in the real world and started raising money for Stanford. As the years went by, I was given many opportunities to try new ways for raising money at Stanford, to show what I could do. It made for a wonderful variety.

Everyone I've worked with at Stanford or had the chance to interact with, remains somehow connected to me in this wonderful web of life.

The skills I learned and developed at Stanford prepared me perfectly to step into the fundraising role for the Allied Arts Guild renovation project. I was very dedicated to the guild's mission to raise money for the children's hospital. I was instrumental in changing not only the name of the auxiliary, but it's outdated business model, as well. Kath had recently moved back from Europe and had a close-up view of my drive and determination and work ethic – she called me a visionary while I introduced and implemented new business strategies. There were objections from the neighbors near the guild, and we had to present our plans to the city council. Kath remained forever impressed when I told her I had spent a good 50 hours preparing for a one-hour meeting with our lawyers and the city council. I wanted to be thoroughly prepared for any and all arguments. We all learned so much from our renovation committee work together, and it too, was a *cookie* in disguise, because out of those fundraising and renovation efforts, grew many important friendships.

Accepting Aging

I think one of the turning points was when I decided I would not drive anymore. It was not an awful decision –

just a necessity that arose out of the fact that my eyesight was getting worse. It was not the worst day of my life, as it is with many older people, but it did force me to change how I looked at the things I agreed to do. Planning is paramount as I asked the question: How am I going to get there and back? I have good friends who say, "Tell Jean, I'll pick her up."

I remember attending a wonderful Cap and Gown event where the board meeting preceded the social for graduating seniors and parents. It was held in a beautiful home in Los Altos. A dear friend from Cap and Gown called Kath and told her she would pick me up and bring me back because, as she expressed, "With your mother as company I will expect to learn something from her life experience either coming or going." I never would have thought of that as any kind of training session, but she certainly did. You never know how people are viewing you. Being on the board for Cap and Gown as long as I have shows me what changes have taken place and how focus can change, which is good. If everything just stood still, never moved, dry rot begins.

I once came across a greeting card after my memory began to decline that said, "I have many hidden talents. I just wish I could remember where I hid them." I laughed so hard I had to buy the card. I've shared it with many, and it always gets a good laugh - I think because many of my friends are also having senior moments.

Isn't that funny we all have the same words regardless of what nationality or spelling is used. Interesting how words can either cut people down or raise them up. I like concentrating on the latter.

A Last Tribute

Jean's family would like to share the following tributes to her, written by friends and relatives soon after her passing in December 2017. Their thoughts and anecdotes give additional depth to Jean's "self-portrait."

"My remembrances include being made to feel like, "Queen for a Day," whenever I came to Jean's home. She was always attentive and asked many questions about my life. She laughed heartily and made me feel at ease. She even made a recommendation for me with a Stanford faculty member when I was between jobs. Jean was a mighty force and an incredible role model for us all. It's no wonder she has such an exemplary family."

—Barbara Norman

"What a truly lovely human being, a joy to know and to be around in every way. Jean was involved with Stanford in so many ways, and years ago, she got me briefly involved with Cap and Gown. Jean and I corresponded for years afterwards, sending long emails regarding all sorts of subjects, usually Stanford related. My dad was in the class behind her (1948), which was always a source of topics for her. And, her Christmas family photo extravaganza was an annual treat for us to receive; we sent her our Christmas card, so she could see our growing sons each year. I will remember Jean as a wonderful lady, so encouraging, so moral, and so supportive of me during the years that we were pen pals. When I got the chance to meet her face to face, she only grew in my esteem, for I realized that, in addition, she was just plain fun to be around. She will live on in my wonderful memories of her.

—Tracy Mezzatesta

"As the eldest Galt child from that generation, Jean had, I think, received from Curtis and Mabel something like a mandate to keep the

memory of their achievement alive. Her being a writer was an aspect of that since Mabel herself was an inveterate letter-writer, practically until the day she died. I have a great many of the letters, and when reading Jean's letters to me I could almost imagine Mabel looking over her shoulder. Jean's letters had a reflective, ruminative character. And in the end, they all said the same thing: we're rooting for you, you are a fine member of a great family and you can do it!"

—Steven Crowell (Jean's nephew)

"In true Jean spirit, during a meeting between the two of us, she looked me in the eye and said, "Is that what you really need?" I hesitated and tried to back pedal, so she asked me again. I finally admitted that I needed her to organize the volunteers and give them jobs. She said, "Great, I'm happy to help!" Your mom was a natural leader and organizer, and she did all this with grace and style, never taking herself too seriously

—Mary Hohensee

"Jean Coblentz was one classy lady who taught by example, working a room in her trademark red outfits, often with Harry in his red sweater; a few words to each person made him or her feel energized, special, inspired. She instilled the fine points of development, magically turning me from a paleontologist into a fundraiser who LOVED her new career for 11 years. I did go back to fossils eventually, but thanks to Jean, I will always also be a fundraiser. After we moved East, she was still my mentor friend and pen pal. I treasure visits to Nome Court, chats at the kitchen table and walks in the garden to pay respects to Harry. Jean taught, inspired and won over everyone; she always made donors, working committee members, University presidents and staff have a wonderful time."

—Judith Smith

"Jean was often the poet, so to speak, at send-offs for colleagues moving on. One occasion stands out for her ability to pen a story via rhyme ostensibly describing the guy headed to greener pastures in

positive tones, pleasing to the Adonis that he was, all the while employing extended double entendre, which those of us less enamored of him appreciated for sharply drawing his many self-centered shortfalls. Jean was a friend, a role model, a kind and wise human we should all emulate. The world would be a better place if we followed her lead."

—Linda Worcel

"Dwight always described her as a woman of principle, of quick wit and always charming, along with her sense of humor and the twinkle in the eye."

—Rosi and Dwight Edwards

"For a small woman, she could sure light up a room. Jean was so confident, positive, and well spoken. You know she valued and lived her education."

—Colleen Mastor

"We first met in 1989 over a sink of dirty dishes after a Cap and Gown event. As we chatted, she asked me about my future plans, my experience at Stanford and my friends. I was so grateful to have an older and wiser person to talk to as I made plans for post-Stanford.

After that day, Jean always seemed to know when to check in with me…she was magical in her ability to connect with young people. After I got married, she sent me the most wonderful note. She took the opportunity to share a little wisdom about marriage and being a grownup. Every young person should have someone as kind and engaging as Jean in her life. I hope I might pay it forward one day."

—Shannon Robertson

"In my mind, Jean was a person who lived her life with grace. She was positive and stylish, with a good sense of humor and a kind word for all, but still a formidable woman."

—Janet Galt Sherwood

"There was a young lady named Jean
We often would see her careen
From meeting to meeting—always upright'
With her beautiful smile—serene!"

—Mary Goerz (Mary paid a tribute
to Jean in Jean's style)

"My memories of Jean span several decades. Beginning in 1982 with the various and elegant Stanford events we attended in those years, Jean was always smiling and greeting guests graciously, making sure the parties were running smoothly. Later, when I became involved in the Alumni Association, Jean was a bright red punctuation mark at conferences and events. Most recently, our paths crossed at Vista Center, where I spend most of my time – and look forward to seeing her sparkling presence."

—Pam Brandin

"Jean always took time to hold my hand and focus on me, asking how I was doing and how my family was. At the time, with 6, 4, and 1-year-old kids, her care for me, someone she barely knew, touched me. I know I wasn't alone in being focused on and cared for in this way, but in those moments, I felt so honored to be someone Jean took a moment to fuss over. I loved it each and every time!"

—Roopal Mehta Saran

"Jean and I were in the same class at Stanford, 1947. She became my sister's friend, Sally Holland, and when I was in Palo Alto for brief periods, I got to know Jean. I remember visiting Jean when we were all young matrons with young families. She was suffering from severe back problems. This might have been in the '50s. When my sister and I saw her then, she was flat on her back on a hospital bed, and goodness knows what the prognosis was. She recovered wonderfully. Jean was a creative, determined, courageous woman."

—Anne Jacques

"I always liked any family gatherings with the Coblentzes. One specific thing is how much I loved and envied Kath and Jan's beautiful, long, blonde braids. Now when I braid my own hair 55 years later, I think fondly of Jean. Jean was a classy dresser. I appreciated that she would come visit my homebound mother, Lucy Smith, when I was in town so we could talk. She is so intelligent, interesting, practical, and optimistic. I remember when she was in severe pain with her back problems and how I felt so bad for her to have to endure what sounded like something close to agony. I respected her deeply as she maintained a positive attitude toward life and continued her outstanding work wherever she was."

—Catherine Calbreath

My Mother-In-Law Jean Coblentz, Thoughts from Laurie Coblentz

"Marty and I just celebrated our 30th wedding anniversary, so that's how long I have been a part of the Coblentz clan. We lived in Elko, Nevada for the first 11 years of our marriage then started the long journey of moving all over the world for the next 19 years. Living so far away from Jean most of our married life, I haven't spent the time with her that I would have liked. But I can say the times we have been together were, and continue to be, filled with love and generosity. I have to say Jean is one of the most patient, caring, loving, intelligent and wise individual's I have ever met ... and I have met a lot of people in my lifetime – worldwide! If a person was able to go to the store and pick whom their mother-in-law was to be, I would have definitely picked Jean. As the saying goes – I hit the jackpot in that department.

Even though it was, and always will be a very sad connection, I think the event that brought Jean and me as close as we could ever be, was both of us losing a daughter to cancer. Jan passed away the beginning of 2010 and my daughter Trina in October of the same year, so only months apart. Unless as a parent you have lost a child or a grandchild (as Jean lost both), you can only imagine how devastating it is. Jean and I don't dwell on this loss, but instead talk about and share the wonderful moments we had with Jan and Trina. We will always have that special connection, a special place in each other's hearts that only we can relate to.

I would say the "cookies passed my way" have been the great advice and guidance through the years from Jean, something I have tried to live up to and pass along to my children and grandchildren. To have someone like Jean in your life is priceless; not only from a learning perspective, but for all the love she gives so freely and unconditionally. She has a knack for making each and every person feel special and an important part of her life. She has always gone out of her way to be sure and attend or be a part of any special events going on in our lives with children and grandchildren. In addition to all her other thoughtful ways, I can never recall not getting a handwritten thank you note from Jean for anything that was done for or given in return.

I love you Jean Coblentz – not only as my mother-in-law, but as a VIP in my life! Thank you for all the "cookies" passed my way."

—Laurie Coblentz

Our beautiful daughters: Jan and Trina

Thoughts from Jess

"Picture this: a cozy den, a worn old corduroy reading chair with a heating pad, and a grandmother with her granddaughter upon her lap. The room is lit by a lamp in the corner that casts a warm glow over the den and the written words of Hugh Lofting float in the air... I am curled up tight on my Grandmas lap in my favorite spot in the house while she reads aloud to me, my favorite book, The Story of Doctor Dolittle.

Even now as an adult, this memory of my Grandma and me is as vibrant as ever, probably because this was not a one-time event, but rather, a pattern that repeated itself every time I visited Nome Court. I have not read Dr. Dolittle since I was a child, but I could most likely recite the book from memory, if necessary. I am sure we read other books, but this one stands out in my mind. My Grandma would change the tone and pitch in her voice to keep me intrigued. Looking back, I can pinpoint my love (obsession) of reading to this time in my life – curled up on a comfy chair in a comfy lap, feeling loved and surrounded by the wonder of imagination. Most of you, if not all, know that Jean has been in the same book club for what, I think, is close to 50 years. What you might not know, is that when I joined my first Book Club in Morenci, AZ in 2013, I felt the deepest sense of pride! I remember thinking that my Grandma was going to be so proud when she learned that I too was in a book club.

Wanting your loved ones to be proud of you is nothing new – everyone craves praise and acceptance and wants to know that what they are doing is making their loved ones happy. Growing up with two Grandparents that were Stanford graduates and who believed that education was one of the most important things, can add a little pressure. I never had the best grades in school and didn't apply myself as much as I could have. With that came disappointment in me and in my grandparents. I never felt like I was who they wanted me to be, but those were my feelings and even if Grandpa Harry and Grandma Jean did feel less impressed with my academic gaffes, they never said it and never made me feel anything but loved. After moving to the mountains to be a ski bum at age 18, I would chat with them and would be asked if I was making friends, how the snow was and if I was liking my "new" life. We would just chat about the day-to-day ins and outs of normal everyday life. It was then that I realized that they never wanted me to become a doctor or lawyer and certainly didn't need me to graduate from Stanford or Yale. What they wanted was for me to become a passionate, happy contributing member of society. When I completed a course in Aesthetics, Grandma attended my graduation. I could see the pride in her eyes, not that her Granddaughter was now going to be an esthetician, but that I had found my passion. I think we both were proud that day.

I know that I am lucky to have Jean and Harry in my life. They were extraordinary examples on how to be good people, how to provide a meaningful contribution to society and how-to live life with passion. That is what I intend to do with the cookies I have been passed."

—Jess Coblentz Katavich

Jean dancing at Jess' wedding

"The biggest thing that always struck me was her smile and also how she was interested in what you were doing, no matter how trivial. My daughter Alice has a particularly great memory of dancing with her at Jess and Nick's wedding in Murphy. Even though she was using a cane at the time, she really let her hair down with Alice. I took pictures of them both, which we can still enjoy. Wishing The Coblentz family all our very best and hope you have a wonderful time at the celebration."

—Anne Diehl

"I am honored to be Jean's granddaughter and grateful to have been blessed with 34 years of such a radiant example of what I aspire to become. From a very young age, my sister, cousin and I looked forward to playing "dress-up" at Nome Court, which meant having access to the very sought after, trunk upstairs that housed treasures Jean collected from her lifetime and travels around the world. We would select our ensemble and then be granted access to Jean's lipstick drawer, where she ever so generously let us gussy ourselves to our heart's desire, never flinching at the likely disarray we left her fine cosmetics afterward. On several occasions, we even had free reign of her closet and treated the entire family to a fashion show, coming down the stairs in Jean's finest business wear. I still remember that day and how it felt to literally live in her shoes, even if it was just make-believe.

One of the greatest cookies Jean passed to the Coblentz Clan was in the family letter she wrote each month. We always looked forward to it arriving in the mail and would be equally as excited to hear the news about what our cousins, aunts, uncles, and grandparents were up to, as we were to see our own names and discover what she chose to share about us. She was an incredible writer, and would inspire her readers with tales of her world travels, updates about Stanford and the countless boards and auxiliaries she supported, along with silly anecdotes about life at Nome Ct. Grandpa would always close the letter with a funny story about outsmarting the gophers in his backyard lawn or a boast about his latest golf score. His part was always done on the typewriter, being the man of tradition that he was. In the days before Facebook and text messaging, our family that reached far and wide, could have easily been disconnected. But being the matriarch, she was, Jean knew the impact it could have to keep everyone invested in each other's updates and accomplishments, and I believe this is what held us so tightly together regardless of how often we all gathered in person.

I have loved writing ever since I was in elementary school, and I attribute the cookie to Grandma Jean and her literary example. She wrote the best poems to make anyone cry and laugh at the same time. She could type faster than anyone I had ever seen, and she could captivate a reader regardless of topic, just by using her friendly and approachable, yet poised and articulate word choices. In fifth grade, I won a contest of young writers and had my own poem published in an anthology. Grandma was so proud and wanted to celebrate my excitement, so she planned a "book signing" party at Nome Ct. where I sat, (dressed in one of her gowns and jewels, of course,) in the fancy throne chair she had in her living room, and signed autographs for family members. I can still to this day remember the way it felt to be a published author and firmly believe that her overzealous celebration of my 10-year-old self, created a confidence and passion in my writing that has inspired me to take on many more writing projects over the years.

Jean was always eager to help inspire and launch the careers and ideas of other people around her. Education was her first passion, and she instilled in me and the rest of her grandchildren that we were "the most valuable investment she could make." I will never forget the day she took me on a tour of the Sanford campus. Her VIP status got us many waves and entry into all the special stops as she illustrated the tour with fun stories of her college days back in the 40s, which to us was ancient history. I could see myself there. I began to understand what college life might be like, and for the first time, I felt confident that I might even fit in and succeed. I could picture myself all dressed in red attending psych classes and mentoring younger dorm students and maybe even trying out a frat party in the hopes of setting eyes on a tall, blue-eyed pilot like my Grandpa once was. After the tour, Grandma sat me down and told me that she had been saving for quite some time, and her money was in an account labeled, "Higher Education." She (in her utmost serious tone) looked at me and said, "Do not let money get in the way of your education. You can go anywhere and do anything you are willing to say yes to."

My journey led me a little more south than Stanford, and I accepted an admission offer to UCSD as a psychology major. I got a job as a hostess at a local restaurant to help pay my bills, and I will never forget the phone call to Nome Ct. to share the news. Grandma and Grandpa both got on the line, as they often did, and cheered as if I had been named the dean of the university. Grandpa had worked as a "head hasher" in his fraternity dining hall, so my burger delivering must have brought back all kinds of memories. I felt such pride at that moment. I was actually on my own, going to college, starting my life and my cheerleader grandparents were stroking my confidence exactly as I needed them to. I am so grateful to them for setting the example and giving me the message that I could achieve anything with a good education.

I could go on listing cookies in my life I attribute to Jean Coblentz, but the final one I will end with is the way she taught me that it is possible to be a loving wife and mom, uphold a rewarding career that sets your soul on fire, enjoy a thriving social life, AND all the while, change the world. For a long time, I believed that you had to choose between housewife or earth-shaking executive. My Grandma demonstrated that having it all just means saying yes to what you want, making your own rules and allowing seasons of life to give more energy and attention to different things. In one of my discussions with her I asked about this crossroads that many new moms face and how she decided to give up her career at Hewlett Packard when she got pregnant with her first daughter. Her answer was one that inspired me to dream big and never settle: "What sets you on fire?" What is the most important to you? Nothing in this world is a guarantee. You never know what little moments will lead to major opportunities." She was also such a devoted wife to my grandpa. She called him her "current lover," and until her final days, lit up when telling stories about the blue-eyed hunk who stole her heart. I have heard that there were certainly some bumpy times along the way (hence the tale of the missing roses on their anniversary,) but throughout my entire life, all I saw were two people who celebrated each other and loved hard. I strive to be the kind of woman, mentor, wife , mother, sister, daughter, friend, boss and confidant who takes her cookies, recreates the recipe and makes it her own, and then passes those new cookies to those around her. Thank you, Grandma, for your immeasurable impact, and for your twinkly-eyed smile that I know will shine on me forever."

—Kelly Crittenden, Granddaughter.

The Family of

Jean Galt Coblentz

Invites you to join in the celebration of her 90th birthday, featuring a reading from her upcoming memoir!

• • •

Sunday, December 27th
2-6pm Open House
1467 Nome Ct.

Please RSVP by 12/15 Kathy Coblentz Miana

90

Jean's 90th Birthday Invitation

Celebrating Jean's 90th birthday. Kathy (standing) (l-r)
Scott and wife Joleen, Milena, Jean, Kelly, Torren,
Marty and wife Laurie.

Kath's Afterword

"This is my mom's story, and although she was able to see most of it, I want the reader to get a sense of what Mom's later years looked like as well as the years she's talked about thus far. Those are the result as previously mentioned, of hours and hours of interviews with me and my best friend, Joan, over glasses of wine and dinner prep, with Jean's granddaughter Kelly, during a trip to Capistrano Beach, and with personal historian, Sue Knight, at our home in Sunnyvale.

It was always our family's intention that Mom and Dad could and should be able to enjoy their later years in the comfort and serenity of their own home, which they truly loved. They had their routines, and when I returned from Europe in 1998, I was lucky enough to live with them for three years while back in college full time. This gave me not only an intimate glimpse into their relationship, but also the opportunity to know them better as aging parents. It's an experience not everyone is lucky enough to have, nor might many people choose to have. Long before I returned to California, I remember chopping wood in the Dolomites where I spent my winters, thinking about what a blessing it would be to be able to assist my parents as they grew older, and take care of them, however their needs manifested. At the time I had no plans to leave Italy, so it was just a thought, the germ of an idea, perhaps.

My life trajectory after returning to California prepared me amazingly well for exactly what had touched my heart as only thoughts and ideas back in Italy. Even then, I was interested to read about death and dying, works by Elizabeth Kubler Ross in German, and stories of near-death experiences and reincarnation. I have respect for that last event of our lives and understood the beauty of being with a loved one through this transition period.

So fast forward to 2003, and I'm still living in Sunnyvale, not even a mile from my parents, able to visit often which I did, and able to share in the day-to-day activities of their lives. My best friend at the time, Kim Dines, is a Physical Therapist and adored my parents. She helped me to realize that, under almost any circumstances, Harry & Jean could stay in their home and not have to move to a retirement community, which they had thought about. They, as many aging parents, did not want to be a burden on their kids, so thought moving to an assisted living arrangement would solve that dilemma. Kim, in her 35-year career as a PT, had worked with many elderly patients and observed a myriad of living situations including those with and without caregivers. She laid out a plan, which pleased and impressed both of my parents (both being consummate planners), as to how they could live out the rest of their years in their home, with Kath nearby for oversight.

As a result of studying Kim's plan and coming up with their own pros and cons of living at home vs moving to a retirement community, they called a family meeting, where all the kids were required to attend. Kim was there too, but only answered questions, as my parents wanted to present it in their own words. It was clear that their desire was to stay at Nome Court, the home they'd created. They felt Kim's outline and details addressed and covered most, if not all, scenarios which would be feasible with both parents staying at home and with Kath nearby to manage and coordinate any core needs. And so, it was decided.

Dad continued to play golf, which was very convenient to Jean! She needed her freedom to move and continue with her many community and university involvements without feeling she was abandoning Dad. She loved his golf game stories and often teased him, as she's mentioned in her interviews. She often said she hoped and prayed he'd be able to play golf right up until he died. It was that important to his lifestyle – those were his friends and that's what they did outside of the family.

We had lovely family gatherings as often as was possible, and Dad, though he had congestive heart failure, had become the "poster boy" for the PAMF Cardiac Rehabilitation Program.

He took his doctor's recommendations to heart and religiously charted his BP and salt intake, attended cardiac rehab classes two to three days a week (depending on golf schedule) and charmed the nurses there!

Where Mom and Dad had previously travelled far and wide, sometimes with the Stanford travel study group, other times with her sister, Alice, (as already mentioned) on cruises & safaris, there came a time when they loved car travel and would rather visit places "closer to home."

Dad's heart finally was nearing its last beats, and one Saturday evening Kim and I came over to check in on him and saw how hard everything was for him and how much trouble Mom was having helping him get ready for bed. We had a feeling he'd need to go the hospital the next day, and sure enough we called 911 the next morning and although Mom requested he be taken to Stanford, the medic said "no, we have to get him care ASAP," so El Camino in Mt. View would be where he spent his last 11 days.

"Fortunately, this was just days after Mom's surprise 80th birthday party which we'd celebrated on Thanksgiving Day of 2005 and all the family members were still in town. My husband, Renato had come over from Italy to celebrate Mom's birthday (he adored and totally admired her) and I'll never forget how gracious Dad was to him both at home and in the hospital, wishing him safe travels back to Italy. We were all there every day and it wasn't long for Dad, as he was on dialysis and a respirator for most of the time, but he certainly was surrounded by his loving wife and family. He realized he would have poor quality of life if he ever made it home, and given *the decision to once again be intubated (therefore unable to talk) or not, he chose not to be and soon after passed away peacefully.*

My parents had already addressed these circumstances and had contracts with the Neptune Society, so we were able to leave the hospital after he passed, Dec 11, 2005, knowing he would "be taken care of" by professionals. Two weeks later Mom and I went to their offices in San Jose and picked up his ashes. Both my parents chose to be cremated."

—Kathy Miana

Milena and Jean.

Thanksgiving '94 Harry with his granddaughter Milena.

Mom wrote:

4/24/10

To My Beloved Children:

I write this to explain why my Health Care Advance Directive is very specific that I do NOT want to be resuscitated in case of heart attack or stroke or other things in that line of occurrences.

At this moment, I consider myself to be in very good health, mind reasonably sharp, hearing and eyesight on the decline and my "smeller" is "wandering." I love living independently in this wonderful house to which all are welcome to return (for brief periods!!!), I am involved in challenging, and mostly productive ventures and still feel I add value to many of them. I've had a great life with few regrets.

Should the things mentioned in the first paragraph occur, it is highly likely that many/most of paragraph two would cease. I can easily see weeks/months/years of painstaking rehab, probably in a nursing facility (compare that to my living in Nome Court), the brain might never come back (the greatest tragedy) and the person you "love and "adore" today would cease to exist, leaving behind someone who isn't me.

And, in addition to my quality of life having gone down the tubes, $$$$ will have gone down as well, and I would much rather you be left with both good memories and the $$$$.

Here is another fact: Emotions ebb and flow as the tides, which is the only way we can survive. In the midst of high emotions, things are said, and decisions made (with logic seeming appropriate for the moment) which, in the cold light of day, one wishes had not occurred. I would rather you have the sassy, loving Mom to remember (I describe myself that way now) instead of an invalid who was struggling, and you were having to worry about her, sometimes with thoughts that make you feel guilty for having them.

See, I have given you a gift. Understand where I am coming from and live to be grateful. Trust me on this: because I said so and because I love you.

Mom aka Jean Coblentz

Kathy Relates the Following:

"Back at home over dinner, after Dad's passing, Marty and I talked with Mom about how she saw things going forward. She wanted to stay in the house and didn't feel the need "for company" after Marty suggested I should move in with her! Knowing I was less than a mile away, I had things covered nevertheless! It turns out, just two years later, my daughter Milena (Mom's first grandchild) came to California to live. She and her Gramma Jean had an already close relationship, which just deepened during the three and a half years Milena lived with me in Sunnyvale. I was working at a PT Clinic, and Milena, who was just getting a feel for life in California (coming from Milan, very different!) had lots of time to spend with her Gramma Jean, so guess where they went? Yes, to Stanford, and Allied Arts, and Avenidas, and Book Club…everywhere Mom went, Milena went. She met all of Mom's friends and still today welcomed in their homes and held fondly in their hearts. The best part of the deal was that Milena got to know Gramma Jean in a very special way. They're really a lot alike and heaven knows what an advantage that was for Milena, to spend so much quality time with her grandmother. Milena's a great cook and for a long time (till Milena started working and travelling again for DKNY) we were over at Nome Court fixing dinner three or four nights per week and taking Gramma places on the weekends.

In early 2011, Milena received an offer from HR at DKNY to move back to the Milan office. She had already determined she wanted to move back to Italy for lots of good reasons which I understood and supported, so the timing couldn't have been better. I travelled back with her, but before we left, Mom made me an offer I couldn't refuse.

She'd come to the realization that going forward in life, at some point she would need help. I knew it was the right thing to do, and yes, the timing was perfect. I moved back into Mom's house exactly 62 years after I was born, on my birthday,

◀Margaritas at the beach.

▼Jean and Milena at the Stanford Stadium.

Kathy continues:

June 1st. Mom sweetly pointed that out to me and probably wrote a poem about it! At first, she didn't need any assistance, so it was just getting used to living together. Mom had her routines, and I had my work schedule, but it fortunately allowed her great flexibility during the week. And I was able to make sure things went smoothly for Mom as well.

Shortly after Milena moved back to Italy, in 2011, Mom and I planned a trip over to see Milena's new apartment and do some travelling in Tuscany. Milena's godmother, Dr. Jennifer Lendl, joined us on the trip. A Stanford alumnus (class of '73) and close friend, Jennifer wanted to revisit the Stanford Florence Campus where she'd also spent a year and arranged for us to have a dinner at one of her former professor's homes. We four travelled fabulously together and had a wonderful time touring the countryside and towns and villages and getting to know some of Milena's good friends in Milan. Mom got a real feel for Milena's lifestyle far away from California, and Milena was happy to show off her stylish American grandmother, who quickly made friends even without speaking a word of Italian. Mom's genuine charm and caring spirit was evident, and Italians too commented on the twinkle in her eyes.

The remarkable thing about this trip is that Mom realized that the Stanford Associates Board of Governors, (of which she was a member for life) was meeting for the annual homecoming weekend activities during the planned 2nd week of our October trip to Italy. Mom was 86 at the time and was not going to miss an opportunity to see her friends again. We decided she'd fly home alone after a week with us and arranged (changed ticket dates) for my sister-in-law, Alma, to pick her up from San Francisco Airport and take her to the event the following evening. Mom had a perfect attendance record at the Board meetings, and she didn't want to pass up an opportunity to see members from all over the US. Her dedication and love for the group was so strong that it easily took first place against any other activities. We were confident she'd make it home ok, with wheelchairs and attendants doing their parts. That again was 2011, and Mom's eyes were just starting to worsen, but she never complained and always adopted an attitude of "do your best". She's often been called a "trooper", was a wonderful travel companion, and here too, a role model for how to travel gracefully in a three generational adventure.

Speaking of three generational adventures brings to mind our East Caribbean cruise which we took in 2014; Mom describes in her writing. It truly was heartwarming to see the constant response of fellow travelers to these three women, clearly with loving bonds between them. We chose our activities thoughtfully with regard to

Mom's more limited abilities. I think she'd had knee revision surgery not long before the trip.

My bucket list included a helicopter ride, so when it was offered as an excursion, I signed the three of us up for it. My brothers were less enthusiastic about the idea, thinking she was too frail, but ultimately, I was in charge and knew Mom's mobility levels better than they did. She loved the ride, sat next to the pilot, and flirted the whole time. Same on the catamaran, flirting with the handsome young crew while everyone else had jumped overboard to swim and have drinks on the shore. We took a walker with us for any longer walks and Mom managed marvelously.

Mom's positive attitude never wavered all throughout her remaining years. We were well matched in our even temperaments and got along fabulously. All of you who knew her, know what a delight she was to be around, and how considerate and kind as well as insightful she was, eager to make you feel special because that's what she truly felt. Those characteristics remained, as well as her organizational genius. She was always looking for ways to contribute to her associations, wanting to encourage the younger generation, to the best of their ability. Mom was the oldest, so her accumulated life's wisdom was the treasure she shared.

Great grandsons Zack and Torren

Jean and Harry's grandchildren and great grandchildren.

Granddaughter Trina

"These treasures she shared, of course, with her grandchildren and great grandchildren. Mom slowly started to show signs of dementia and it annoyed her at times, but mostly she made light of it. She had admitted for years that her biggest fear was that she would develop Alzheimer's. To her good fortune (and ours), she did not. In fact, I identified Mom's dementia as "delightful dementia." She was a delight with and without her memory! Her core goodness and humor; so essential to her nature, never left her. Wherever she went, whoever she met, she was good humored.

During the last few years of her life, she took several falls, and each one proved a trauma to the brain. A noticeable decline in cognition was the result. This is very common in older adults with dementia. Any trauma—physical, mental, emotional—will stress an already struggling brain. Fortunately, she got her wish to die in her sleep, peacefully, no pain or suffering.

Once it was no longer safe for Mom to be at home alone (while I was still working at the PT clinic), plan B was put into action. Long before it became necessary, we had visited an Adult Day Care in Menlo Park, California and one in Mt. View, but neither proved to be a good fit for Mom. I had heard about a wonderful caring gentleman, a real music aficionado, named John Lehman, who'd developed the "Vintage Music Therapy" program and was providing sessions at various elder and rehab facilities throughout the south bay. He now works full time a the exceptional, highly rated Adult Day Care program Sarah Care in Campbell, California. They provide full daycare services six days per week, a godsend for working family caregivers, for adults and seniors with dementia, Alzheimer's, Parkinson's, and other disabilities. I contacted him and, because Mom was still at home, he came to the house and presented his program to Mom and me and my sister-in-law, Karen, who frequently helped me with Mom's care and supervision (such as when I travelled to Italy to visit my daughter).

John had long ago recognized the major role that music plays for the brain, and in this case, for the aging brain and even the brains of Alzheimer's and Dementia patients, helping to reawaken positive memories and emotions through association. He has a huge recorded library of music from the 40's, 50's, and 60's and has it on iPod mini's, separate one for each decade) and on it, he announces the song and the artist, the music plays and then, like the radio used to do, signs off with, for example, "and that was Patsy Cline singing "Walking After Midnight." He rightly reasoned that people with dementia might not remember the artists name or the title, after hearing the song, so are reminded at the end.

Mom's morning routine was coffee first, then buttermilk, while riding her recumbent bike listening to all those oldies which made it easy for her to keep peddling, and peddling. She'd tell people she was watching the "squirrel Olympics" out the back, as the critters darted along the fence tops.

Mom's health was otherwise excellent, as many of you may know. She was taking no meds at the time of her death. She took lots of supplements and, although we can't prove one way or another their efficacy, I suspect they helped her stay as healthy and strong as she was. She had a special relationship with her primary care doctor, Dr. Peter H. Cheng, lead geriatrician at PAMF Palo Alto, as they also served on the Avenidas Board together.

When her last major fall occurred, she broke her elbow and needed surgery which meant anesthesia. This we had noted with previous surgeries, hip revision and knee revision, were the toughest part of the whole process for her. She had a high tolerance for pain, so didn't take pain meds so to speak, and rehab always went well, but the insult to the brain from the anesthesia cocktails left their mark, and she could tell. So that's what concerned me most about the last fall, which occurred just three months before she passed away. On the bright side, she adored her orthopedic surgeon and didn't hesitate to flirt with him either as we went for post op visits. She said, "I still know how to pick good looking men". Again, here, her focus was on what she could do rather than what she couldn't do. And #1 on her list of likes was always MEN! She absolutely charmed her exceptional Chiropractor, Dr. Thomas E. Bloink of Los Gatos, to whom she was introduced through our close friend, Dr. Jennifer Lendl. Mom would watch the Stanford football games with Jennifer, who was the first woman statistician for the Stanford Football team in the early 70's. It *was always fun to watch the game with her, as she'd often call the plays before the referees! I got all my football culture from those afternoons and learned a lot. It was fun to see the two alums cheering for their team.*

I kept Mom out and about as much as I could, finding venues she'd enjoy and keeping her in touch with Book Tasters and Allied Arts as long as the events were still meaningful for her. She was active with Stanford Associates until we all agreed it was time to quietly retire from even that Emeritus position, just as she'd requested be written into the minutes, when she'd been given that honor.

Just as important as her social and academia connections, were the family gatherings, larger or smaller, depending on people's schedules. Milena came over twice a year from Italy in her gramma's later years, wanting to spend as much time with her as she could, and her sons of course would visit whenever they could, Marty living near Medford, OR and Scott then still in Sacramento, now in Gardenerville, NV."

—Kathy Miana

It's In Your Contract

Scott's daughter, Kelly, solicited stories, comments, and tributes, from Mom's extensive list of friends and associates, about the impact Jean had had on their lives. She weaves some of her gramma's essence into one of Jean's favorite responses, "It's in your contract."

"Now we all know that Jean has undergone quite a few medical procedures over her lifetime. She is famous at the Stanford Hospital, not just for her fundraising efforts and ties to the university, but for her kindness and unbreakable spirit. Without fail, time after time we hear stories of the nurses all fighting to be on Jean's case for their shift because of her rock-solid positive attitude. While being poked, prodded, and questioned, Jean remained kind and respectful to her medical staff... and almost always made them laugh, even when she is in pain herself. This is what I call the cookie contract.

So, when I say words like "I feel so lucky to be in your family Gramma", I already know how she is going to respond. Jean, in her sweet wise way simply smiles and says, "It's in your contract".

It wasn't until fairly recently that I realized what she meant by those words. This "contract" is taken seriously, and its terms are simple: ....in this family, we cheer for each other. Without judgement. Without conditions. Upon entering the Coblentz clan, whether by marriage or blood or friendship...and heck, even the mail man probably feels this sense of acceptance and love from Jean. She navigates this world viewing all human interactions as a sacred contract. A common theme among responses from people for this book were, "Jean never spoke badly about anyone." I know this to be truer than true, and it was clearly an art form she has been practicing her whole life, stemming from her parent's example. Meeting Jean, people get the sense that they are safe in her presence. She silently establishes this "contract" with her smiling eyes, focused attention, and energetic heartfelt connection regardless of status, relationship, or difference of opinion."

—Kelly Crittenden, Granddaughter.

"Just Do It: I used this now famous Nike slogan a lot in the 50s. It is how I got so much done. These served as great words of encouragement to others. My son reminded me that I used that phrase with them when they were small, and I needed their cooperation. I was not a fan of procrastination."

—A Favorite Saying.

Appendix

"*Moderation in all things: I'm sure these words came from my parent's midwestern roots. A practical guideline that I proudly used in successfully raising my four children who are strong believers in this phrase and have used it in raising their children.*"

— A *Favorite Saying.*

Appendix 1: A Few Original Notes from Jean

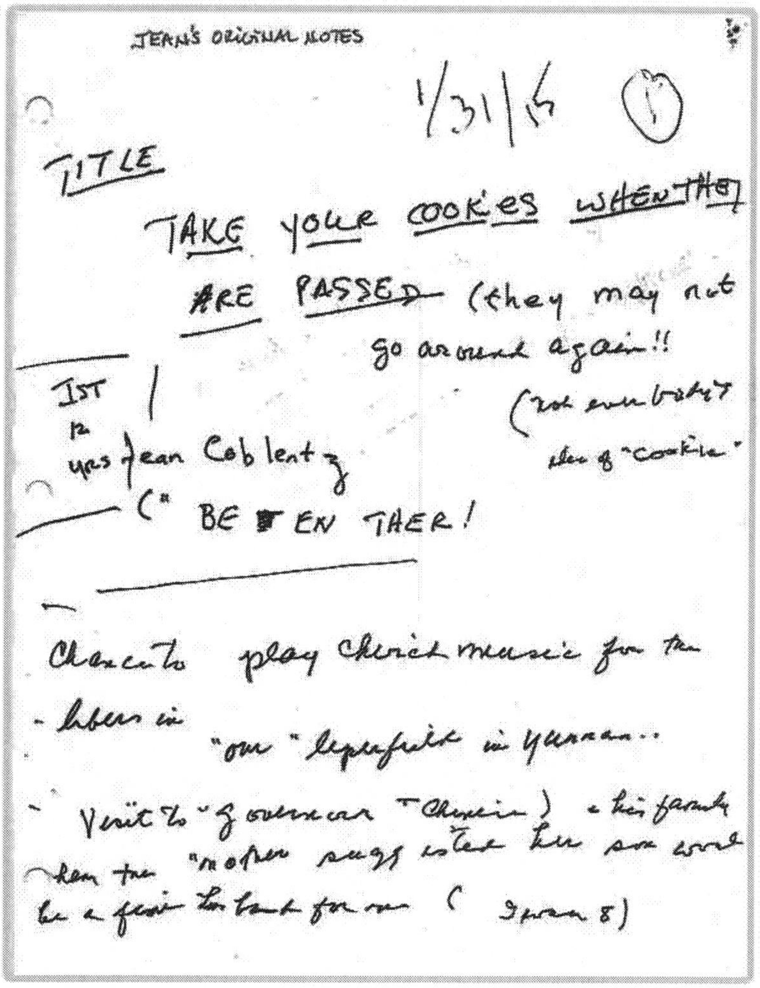
JEAN'S ORIGINAL NOTES

1/31/15

TITLE

TAKE YOUR COOKIES WHEN THEY ARE PASSED (they may not go around again!!

1ST
yrs Jean Coblentz
(" BEEN THER!

Chance to play church music for the

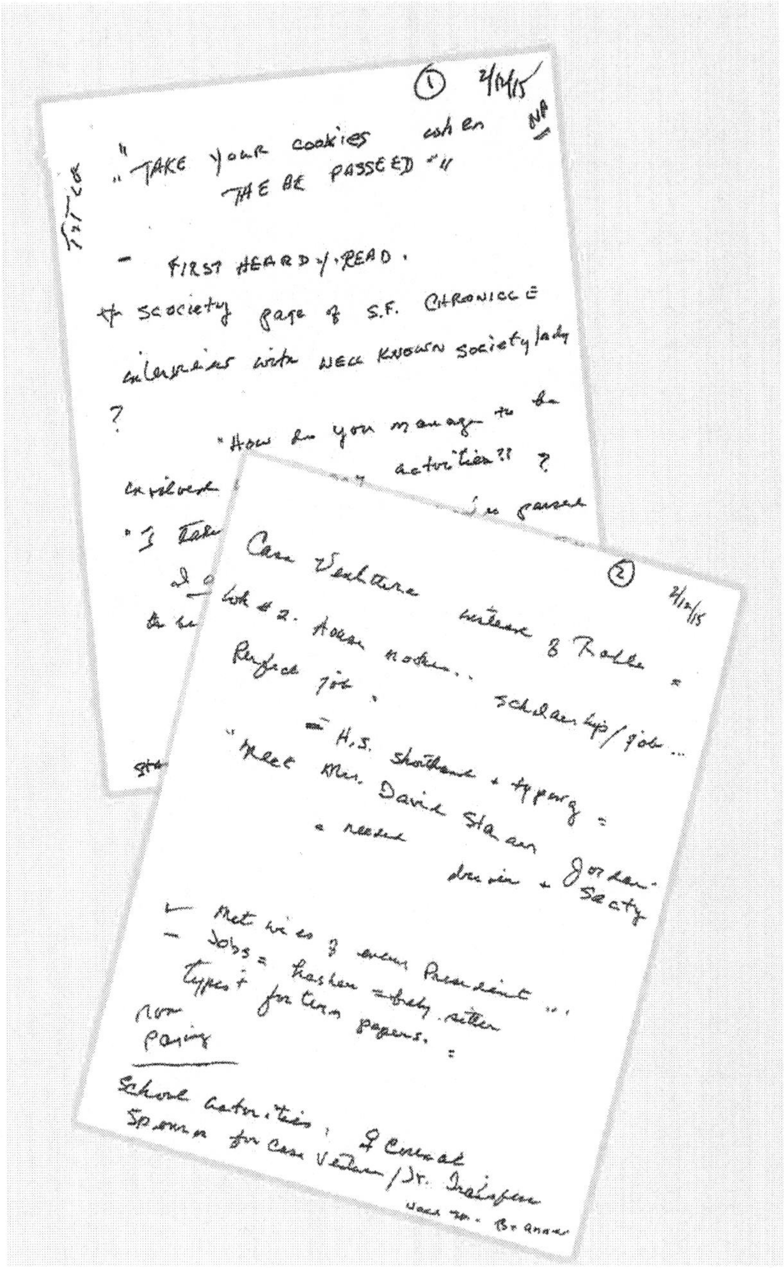

③ 2/12/15

Talk @ Stanford - I going back
to work . - Do something to
follow up ... - - Val - Want to hear
You ! H. maker Sur. 8 I
*1. to . Chair . " Ever thought of
working for me

- Stffee Stanford Assoc. (Histories)
" Great Parents group.
Book club
* 1462 Home Ct. = Inet. no. snow !!

Harry . march re - 50th anniv. -
- S.F. (Parnevue)

Grade majors ; first grade ?
(Si don'tevial Psychology . - Saturday
visit Trans Career -
Hewlett - Lucile Packard

P.G. - Kate
Stay home - Scouts - school
board
(Blood Saline = pressure on
School teams . Little League .
- W-3 A Cuf fee - Parents ch. Arf ;

401

Growing of, daughter of molecular researcher
in Yerevan Province, these gave me a very
different introduction to money since there
was no where to go and nothing to buy for
children. I was not quite 12 when we
were back in the states and I got my first
allowance. I was given weekly fee only if
we had turned in our balance sheet and
it had to balance to the penny
be stern
keeping

upper
hands

---

promptness, balancing the "books" at the
end of the day, and making certain one
was clear about duties & expectations.
   Just after graduating from H.S. I
had a job at the Kaiser - Permanente plant
near the Stockton Depot. I was only 16 but
had great skills in typing and shorthand
(these I had gotten from an "extra" class
taught by one of my H.S. profs — I worked my
way partially through Stanford — much of the
money coming from these skills., so I will
always be grateful to this teacher
   I had graduated, valedictorian,
and had been admitted to Stanford due to the
"Sales job" Austin H.S. teacher had, who felt I
must go to Stanford and managed the paper
work for my admittance and a scholarship.
   So I have 2 HS teachers to thank after my
                                         parents.

Appendix 2: Jean's Notes from 2000

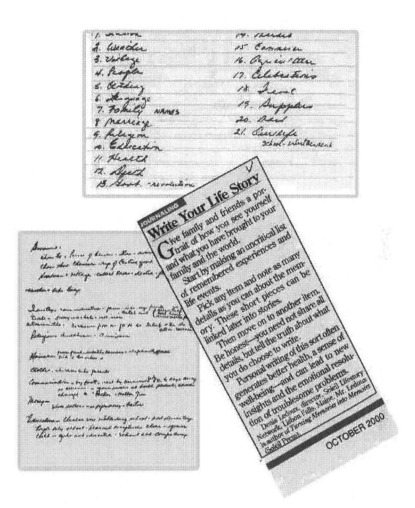

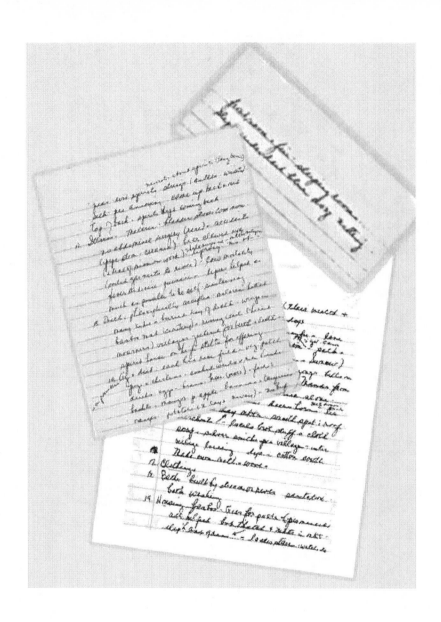

Appendix 3: Baby Book

Baby Arrives

Jean Galt - 5:15 A.M. - December 27- 1925 *Sunday*

Alan Moore Galt - 6:35 A m. - May 4. 1927 *Wednesday*

Alice Galt - 11:45 A.M. Aug. 8. 1931 *Monday*

Cornelia Galt - 5:45 A.M. Dec. 1. 1935. *Sunday*

Baby's Birthplace

Kiulungkiang - Yunnan, China.

Kiulungkiang - Yunnan, China.

Appendix 4: Jean's Baby Book

Baby's First Visitors

John Goodenberger, really her
first visitor, since his mother
and dad assisted at her arrival.
  Mary Low and Teddy Beebe.
  Mr & Mrs Beebe.
    Sang Kao, Sang Kang, Ai La & Ai Li.

Gifts

            Sweater, booties and blanket
          from Mrs. Beebe.
            Jacket from Aunt Hilda
          Blankets from Aunt Maude.
Dresses, rattle, booties, etc from Grandma
Moore and aunties.
  Kimono and dress mitt from Grandma Gait
Kimono, soap, brush & comb set, ribbons,
lace, wool jacket, rubber sheet, etc from
Aunt Marguerite.
Dresses, lace, embroidery patterns from Births
Socks & stockings from Bowens & Brownes.
Silver mug from Dr & Mrs Cedric Nelson.
Rattle from Mr & Mrs G. M. Felton
Embroidered coat from Miss Madelaine.
Silver spoon from the Jacques.

Baby's Christening

Baptized at regular Communion Service - Jan. 17 - Rev. Goodenberger officiating. She wore her hemstitched and embroidered dress, with her pink and white sweater and hood wrapped in her blue bunny blanket.

Alan was baptized when he was about 3 mo. old. He was very naughty and cried during most of the ceremony. He wore an embroidered dress.

Baby's Weight and Height

	Jean		Alan	
	weight	height	wt.	ht.
Birth	6½#	21"	7# 5℥	21"
1 week			7# 6℥ 8# 5℥	
2 weeks			8# 15℥	
3 weeks			7# 14½℥	
1 month	7# 6½℥			
2 months	9# 6℥			
3 months	10# 11℥	24½"		
4 months	11# 8℥			
5 months	12# 9℥			
6 months (Cow's milk for Jean)	13# 6℥			
7 months	14# 8℥			
8 months	16# 12℥		18½#	28"
9 months	17# 2℥	29"		
10 months				
11 months				
12 months	21# 11℥	29¼"	23#	30"
1 year	chest 19½"	head 18¼"	chest 19½"	head 19"
2 years	17" chest	35" head		
3 years				
4 years				

Baby's First Outing

Her first public appearance was on the day of her baptism. Soon afterward she began morning and evening jaunts in John's cart. Her first real trip was her journey to the vacation place on the mountain – April 16. She was carried in a "hauwii" with John and did nobly!

Marie's first journey was a trip to Siam at the age of 5½ mo. An overland journey of more than a wk. A visit in Chiengrai followed by a train ride to Bangkok (o+hr) where a week was spent. Returned north and visited Chiengmai, later returning to Chiengrai, and, eventually, reaching home again after having been on the road from Oct 24-27 – Dec 16. During the trip his conduct was remarkably good and any of the friends met on the way would have been glad to keep him. Jean also took the journey – and a fine time was had by all!

Jean + Alan both took another trip with their mother and daddy – on how back to the newly built leper village. in Feb. 1938 – to escape flying bullets from a local Chinese war. We remained for 5 days.

411

Baby's First Tooth

Her first lower tooth appeared when she was about 5½ mo. (June 21) Three more followed in quick succession.

Alan's first tooth - an upper one - came thru when he was about 9 mo. old. Before a month was past, however, he had six - 4 above and 2 below.

Lock of Baby's Hair

Her two grandmothers were presented with her first baby hair - which grew down in her neck.

First hair cutting!

Baby's First Words

Jean.
Begins to say "Da-Da" and form
an association between the words
and person at about 9½ mo
Waved "by-by" at 8 mo.
At 2 years she was chattering incessantly.

Alan- At one year he makes a sound which
(by interpretation) means Jean!

Baby's First Steps

Creeps rather haltingly (on one elbow) Oct. 7 -'26.
Doesn't walk alone well until 16 months of age
then she makes good progress.

Alan learned to creep and pull himself up to
a standing position, while we were visiting
in Chiengmai Siam. He was not quite 7 mo old.
Walks alone shortly before his 1st birthday

Baby's First Fall

Jean –

Fell from big wicker chair Sunday PM. Oct. 24. '26. A bump on her forehead and some skin from her nose seemed to sum up damage.

On May 10. '27 she fell from the second story porch while visiting at John's house. She was quite shaken up and her tongue bitten enough to require 2 stitches. In a day or two she was quite recovered.

On Jan 10. '28 she fell from second story door way. She skinned her nose and bruised her hip - but after a day or two of lameness she was quite all right.

When about two Alan, playing at Jacques in Alem - fell from a chicken house roof. Bitting his tongue in exactly the same place as Jean. Each wears the scar.

Baby's First Birthday

Jean's birthday celebrations are indivisibly blended with Christmas, save that she has her special candle cakes.

Alan celebrated his first birthday with the whole station - Goodenbergers. Parks and Callenders- in attendance at an afternoon tea. His cake delighted him and he smeared his face generously. He was thotfully remember by toys - suits etc.

Jean's First Months

Jean's First Year

Alan, Jean's Brother

Galt Children Growing Up

On the banks
of the Mekong River

Jean and Alice

▲ Mabel and her
3 children

▲ Jean and sister Alice

Alan and sister Alice

▲Yokohama, Japan
1928

Appendix 5: Jean's Birth in China

AMERICAN CONSULAR SERVICE

Yunnanfu, China, March 17, 1926.

Dr. Curtis M. Galt,

    American Presbyterian Mission,

        Kiulungkiang.

  Sir:

    I have to enclose herewith a copy of the Report of Birth of your daughter Jean which has been recorded in this office and filed in the Department of State, Washington.

        Yours very truly,

          M. S. Myers,
          American Consul.

Enclosure: As stated.

131.

M/H.

REPORT OF BIRTH

OF CHILDREN BORN TO AMERICAN PARENTS.

AMERICAN CONSULAR SERVICE.

Kiulungkiang, Yunnan, Feb. 10, 1930

Name of child in full   Jean Galt   Sex female

Date of birth   December   22   1929   6:10 A.M.

Place of birth   Name   Kiulungkiang   China

Father.

Full name   Curtis H. Galt   (H.Martin)   Age 32

Occupation   Medical Missionary

Present residence   Kiulungkiang, Yunnan, China.

Birthplace   Douglas, Otoe Co. Nebraska, U.S.A.

Naturalized (if foreign born)

Registered as American citizen   Yunanfu, China,   February 27, 1924.

Passport   7718   April 20, 1928   Porto Rico.

Mother.

Full name   Florence Mabel Galt   Age 27

Name before marriage   Mabel Sears

Present residence   Kiulungkiang Yunnan, China.

Birthplace   Alexandria, Nebraska, U.S.A.

Naturalized (if foreign born)

Registered as American citizen   (Included in husband's registration)

Passport   (Included in husband's passport)

Number of previous children   none   Number now living   one

Physician or nurse   Curtis H. Galt   Kiulungkiang

Subscribed and sworn to before me at

this   day of

Appendix 6: Book Clippings About Curtis Galt

MINUTES

OF THE

General Assembly

OF THE

Presbyterian Church in the U. S. A.

Third Series—Volume III—1924
including
Part I. Journal and Statistics.   Part II. Board Reports

Part II

The Reports of the Boards
TO THE
One Hundred and Thirty-sixth General Assembly

Grand Rapids, Michigan, May 22-28, 1924

PHILADELPHIA, PENNSYLVANIA

Office of the General Assembly, Witherspoon Building

JULY, 1924

very satisfactorily by the Tai workers. Owing to the fact that there was no doctor in the Station, the medical work had to be closed.

STATIONS AND WORK

Kiulungkiang (Chiengrung): 180 miles southwest of Yunnanfu, capital of the province of Yunnan, China. Occupied as a mission station 1917. Missionaries—Curtis M. Galt, M.D. and Mrs. Galt, Rev. Ernest C. Goodenberger and Mrs. Goodenberger, Claude W. Mason, M.D. and Mrs. Mason.

Work of the Station—
Station Chapel, 1 Sunday school, Evangelistic work in dispensary, Bible Class. Day school for boys, day school for girls. 1 primary and intermediate school. Hospital and dispensary.

Yuankiang: 110 miles southwest of Yunnanfu. Occupied as a mission station in 1922. Missionaries—Mrs. W. Clifton Dodd, Rev. Charles R. Callender and Mrs. Callender, Rev. Lyle J. Beebe and Mrs. Beebe, Charles E. Park, M.D., and Mrs. Park, Rev. Edward W. Perry and Mrs. Perry, Miss Frances Brewer, M.D., Rev. Kenneth Campbell and Mrs. Campbell.

Work of the Station—
Station Chapel, 81 groups of believers, 18 Sunday schools, Woman's Bible Class, Men's Bible Class, 3 primary and intermediate schools, night classes for men, women and children. Dispensary work.

TRANSFERS.—Dr. and Mrs. Claude W. Mason from Yuankiang to Kiulung-kiang.

ABSENT FROM THE FIELD DURING THE YEAR.—Mrs. C. W. Mason, Rev. and Mrs. C. R. Callender, Dr. and Mrs. Charles E. Parks.

HISTORY.—In 1917 the Siam Mission with the approval of the Board, opened a station in Chiengrung in the Yunnan Province of Southern China, which had been explored by the late Rev. W. Clifton Dodd, D.D., and who, with Mrs. Dodd became its first resident missionaries. The long distance from the stations in Siam, the intervening mountain ranges, preventing easy access, the great extent of the field, and its high promise, led the Board with the concurrence of the Siam Mission and the China Council, to constitute Kiulung-kiang (Chiengrung) and a new Station at Yuankiang as a separate Mission, to be included in the China Missions of the Board, under the field jurisdiction of the China Council. This was done in January, 1923.

Kiulungkiang (Chiengrung) is the capital of a district called by the Tai people, *Sipsaungpanna* (12,000 rice fields). The population is about 400,000 scattered over a territory larger than the states of New Jersey and Delaware. *Yuankiang* is an important city in the large and populous district of Muang Chung, fifteen days' travel further north. The total field of the new Mission embracing an extensive area in the great Province of Yunnan and parts of adjacent regions, is probably the vastest unoccupied mission field in the world. The evangelistic development has already been remarkable.

Mention of Curtis Galt in the book: The Minutes of the General
Assembly of the Presbyterian Church, Third Series, Volume III-
1924 by Presbyterian Church in the U.S.A. General Assembly.

Division of Schools and Hospitals

Presbyterian Hospital, San Juan. It is hard to realize that the
wonderful new hospital building of which Presbyterian women have
so justly been proud should after only six years be proving totally inadequate to meet the demands made upon it. Every one of its seventy
beds has a waiting list; its school of nursing is crowded in dormitory
space and in classroom quarters; its clinic of over forty-two thousand
patients has taxed the waiting room, the dressing room

school. Of the seventy-five active members of the newly organized
association of Registered Nurses of Porto Rico, forty-seven are
graduates of the School of Nursing of the Presbyterian Hospital.

Dr. Curtis Galt completed his year of interneship in June, 1923,
and is now in Yumasfu, China, under the Presbyterian Foreign
Board. Dr. Douglas Collier of Denver, Colorado, interne for the
present year, plans to go to India in 1925.

One of the doctors writes: "In most cases a study of the economic
status of the patient is as necessary as that of their physical ailment.
A woman came to the dispensary suffering from a tropical disease the
only cure being a milk diet. She was told to drink two liters of milk

THE CONTINENT

Combining THE INTERIOR (Established 1870) and THE WESTMINSTER (Established 1904)
PUBLISHED WEEKLY

THE McCORMICK PUBLISHING COMPANY, Proprietors

OLIVER R. WILLIAMSON, Publisher

EDITORIAL, ADVERTISING AND SUBSCRIPTION OFFICES

CHICAGO
509 South Wabash Avenue

NEW YORK CITY
Presbyterian Building, 156 5th Avenue

Entered as second-class matter October 5, 1910, at the post office at Chicago, Illinois, under the act of March 3, 1879. Acceptance for mailing at special rate of postage provided for in section 1103, Act of October 3, 1917, authorized on July 15, 1918. Copyright, 1923, by the McCormick Publishing Company.

Subscription Terms—The subscription price of THE CONTINENT is $3.00 per year payable in advance. Single copy 10 cents.

Postage is prepaid on all subscriptions in the United States, Hawaiian Islands, Philippine Islands, Guam, Porto Rico, Canal Zone, Cuba and Mexico.

Foreign Postage—For Canada 50 cents and for all other countries in the Postal Union $1.50 should be added for postage.

Remittances should be sent by draft on Chicago or New York, Express or P. O. money orders payable to THE CONTINENT. If personal check is sent, 5 cents must be added for collection fee charged on it by the banks. Discounts on foreign exchange must be charged to the subscriber.

Acknowledgments—Within two weeks the date following name on "address label" will show to the first of what month subscription has been paid. No other receipt is given unless stamp is sent.

Change of Address—Kindly send us both old and new addresses two weeks previous to the date of the desired change.

Continuation of Subscriptions—Your annual remittance, or instructions for the continuation of subscription, should reach us before the 1st of the month shown on address slip.

Manuscripts—THE CONTINENT does not accept responsibility for damage or loss of manuscripts sent to it for consideration.

Advertising rates on application.

Around the Shop

IT IS STRANGE how easily one imagines that what the other fellow pays for must be cheaper, while what we buy costs just as much as ever.

There have been reductions in some important items of living cost, mainly those which lead back to the farmer. But on the whole the average family is not able to discover much of a shift to its benefit.

Few products have had so little favorable change as those coming from periodical and publishing houses. The paper on which these words are printed costs at this time 109.7 per cent more than it did in 1915—more than twice as much. Instead of steadily decreasing, the price of paper has gone up only recently; it has never been below double what it was in the first year of the war.

As paper is the most important cost item in the manufacture of a periodical, the effect of this continued high cost is obvious.

Volume 54. Number 1   Whole Number 2743

IN THIS ISSUE

January 4, 1923

Inspiration 5
Editorials—
  The Revelation of Prayer............... 8
  Should Not Come Back a Hero.......... 8
  Cannot All Agree on This Much?....... 8
  Don't Get Off the Main Track.......... 9
  Its Very Form Makes It Bad........... 9
The World 6
If Money Could Buy Them....J. H. Jowett 10
Moving On at Metlakatla..Calvin C. Hays 11
American Women on Trial I—
  ....Hilda Richmond 13
Have Laymen the Grit to Do It?......
  ....Jonathan Jones 13
Helping a Man You Don't Like..........
  ....John Timothy Stone 14
Young America—Breaking Old Mr. T.
  Board's Heart....Frances Margaret Fox 15
Sunday School Page—
  Take Stock of Your School. Gerrit Verkuyl 16
  International Lesson (Jan. 18)..........
  ....Andrew C. Zenos 16
With the Young Folks (Endeavor Topic
  Jan. 18)................................ 17
Bible Day by Day (Devotional Topic Jan.
  18)......................Robert Freeman 17
In the Field of Missions.................. 18

Printing — composition and presswork—folding, binding, mailing and postage stand today at the highest rate attained in the history of modern American publishing. Salaries and wages add to the total of continued high costs, though we imagine that in no periodical office they are—as with paper and printing—doubled along with the cost of living.

Only a few periodicals have dared to reduce subscription rates. In every case we know of it was done to hold a dwindling circulation, with the hope that increased advertising would make up the loss.

Of course if only one-fifth of the families in the Presbyterian Church subscribed to The Continent we could sell the paper still farther below cost, and advertising would probably meet the loss. But they don't, and—well, we don't like to say they won't, because they really haven't had it put up to them. They don't know what they're missing.

Reviews

"Jean Galt Coblentz was an amazing woman, and I was so fortunate to know her during the last few years of her life. This book gives you a broad view of the woman she was and the life experiences that made her that way. From her birth and early years in China, moving to a small farming town in Central California, attending Stanford and meeting the love of her life, Handsome Harry, Jean had experiences in first two decades of her long life, beyond anything we could imagine for ourselves. From this book, you will learn how all the people she met and the opportunities she was presented, the cookies, formed the character and the spirit of this lovely lady.

People she mentored (mostly young women) were effusive in the praise for her place in their lives. Associates in her various jobs, both volunteer and paid, were enriched by working with her. And you get the idea from their praise that it was 'working with" not "working for." She loved keeping in touch with folks as shown in her Christmas Letters, sent to over 200 people each year (whether it was December or June).

She had a sharp wit to go with her sharp mind. She loved a good book, a nice glass of wine and a good movie. But mostly, she loved people - - helping them along their paths in life. Just a brief warning: when you start this book, make yourself comfortable, because it is truly unputdownable! (a word Jean would love!)

—Michael Wright, Phtographer

"Take Your Cookies When They're Passed is a remarkable book by an even more amazing woman. From her early life in China to all her work at Stanford University, Jean has led an exemplary life of service and leads by example when it comes to overcoming challenges."

—Kimberly Burnham, PhD (Integrative Medicine).

"An inspiring history of an extraordinary woman, Jean (Galt) Coblentz shares her life's lessons of seizing opportunities ('taking your cookies') for success and happiness. Her journey endows wisdom of love, laughter, friendships, family and community."

— Dr. Joan K. Vrtis, an honored recipient of
Jean's valuable guidance and friendship